PRAISE

BOOK TW

SEARCHING *for* FAMILY *and* TRADITIONS
at the FRENCH TABLE

"For those of us who love France and also who have a deep respect and interest in the tales of the older generations, this book is a real gem. Carole and Josiane are invited into many households on their travels, and they provide wonderful snapshots of the families, their history, and that of the regions. The book is overflowing with descriptions of the wonderful regional produce and tales of times gone by. . . . The author has generously ended the book with a collection of some of the wonderful recipes for us to enjoy making in our kitchens, whilst embracing the flavors and traditions of French family life. . . . I would highly recommend this excellent book, and I am sure it will be enjoyed by anyone loving France, cooking, traditions, and history. A French culinary extravaganza!"
—TheColumbiaReview.com

PRAISE FOR

BOOK ONE *of*
SEARCHING *for* FAMILY *and* TRADITIONS
at the FRENCH TABLE

". . . engaging. . . . Bumpus's writing is perspicuous and economical. . . . The recipes, too, are enticing and detailed, and the book as a whole should appeal to Francophiles and ambitious cooks. A culinary adventure that's enhanced by familial and regional histories."
—*Kirkus Reviews*

"Mouth-wateringly delicious, evocative, and utterly charming."
—*French Book Worm*, on Good Life France.com

"If you love all things French or just a good travelogue with a culinary angle, *Searching for Family and Traditions at the French Table, Book One* is for you. This wonderfully written culinary and travel memoir, the first in a planned series, combines a love for French culture and food with the personal reflections and stories of families the author meets during a road trip through Paris and three other regions. . . . Bumpus gives us a very personal glimpse into the people, places, and food of four regions of France. The narrative is engaging, highly descriptive, entertaining, warmhearted, sometimes funny, and often touching. Her curiosity about what holds European families together reveals levels of the human experience that may focus on the culinary connections but goes far beyond a family's kitchen table. Highly recommended."

—Kimberlee J Benart, Readers' Favorite

"This gorgeous book—part travel memoir, part collection of regional French recipes—connects food to families and families to their ancestral lands. An intimate, enlightening, and satisfying read . . . From family stories of the French Resistance to dishing on President Chirac's favorite meal, this enjoyably intimate travel memoir will appeal to Francophiles and foodies everywhere."

—Martha Conway, author of *The Underground River: A Novel*

SEARCHING *for*
FAMILY *and* TRADITIONS
at the FRENCH TABLE

SEARCHING *for* FAMILY *and* TRADITIONS *at the* FRENCH TABLE

ᘓ BOOK TWO ᘔ

Nord-Pas-de-Calais, Normandy, Brittany, Loire Valley, and Auvergne

by

CAROLE BUMPUS

SHE WRITES PRESS

Published 2020
Printed in the United States of America
Print ISBN: 978-1-63152-896-5
E-ISBN: 978-1-63152-897-2
Library of Congress Control Number: 2020904539

For information, address:
She Writes Press
1569 Solano Ave #546
Berkeley, CA 94707

Book design by Stacey Aaronson

She Writes Press is a division of SparkPoint Studio, LLC.

SEARCHING *for* FAMILY *and* TRADITIONS *at the* FRENCH TABLE

Book Two

I dedicate this book to my husband, Winston Bumpus, who has supported my love of culinary travels, my lust for discovering a good story, and my desire to share these stories with the world. My Book Sherpa, Extraordinaire! And to my son, Andrew Smith, who, along with my husband, has listened to me, helped me with recipe testing, and encouraged me at every turn. Both have their own stories waiting to be revealed, but in the meantime, they have supported my dream.

And, to my dear friend, Josiane Selvage, who took me by the hand and continued to lead me on this most incredible edible journey! As she says, "We need to take more trips soon, so I don't have to rely on my own diaries." My life, and the lives of my family since Josiane, have never been the same. And we are all better people because of it.

"I am more modest now, but I still think that one of the pleasantest of all emotions is to know that I, I with my brain and my hands, have nourished my beloved few, that I have concocted a stew or a story, a rarity or a plain dish, to sustain them truly against the hungers of the world."

—M.F.K. Fisher

CONTENTS

Map of Brittany

Brittany

෴

Map of Loire Valley

The Loire Valley

❧

Map of Auverne

> Auverne

❧

Recipes from the Chapters

PROLOGUE

Have you ever strolled down a cobblestone street in a foreign village, passed an open window, and heard laughter flowing out to greet you? Have you ever stopped to listen to the banter and wondered what it would be like to live there? In that house? That village? And oooooh—what was that wonderful aroma? What could they possibly be having for dinner?

My book series, *Savoring the Olde Ways*, is a compilation of stories and recipes I had the good fortune to gather during interviews and conversations with families as I traveled throughout France and Italy. Part culinary memoir and part travelogue, these books present the personal experiences of three generations of families, as told to me inside their homes, along those very streets.

The title of the first book in this series is *Searching for Family and Traditions at the French Table, Book One.* It describes the first half of the culinary adventure I took with Josiane and my husband, Winston, from Paris, in the Île-de-France, through the Champagne, Alsatian, and Lorraine Regions and back to Paris. This second book, invites you to embark on the completion of our adventures—beginning in Paris, where we leave my husband off for work, and head north for two to three weeks more into the regions of Nord-Pas-de-Calais, Normandy, Brittany, Loire, and ending the tour in the Auvergne.

I am, indeed, grateful to Josiane Selvage, my great French friend and interpreter, who accompanied me on more than one culinary treasure hunt of a lifetime. I am forever in her debt. It was Josiane who opened my eyes and my heart to all the French men and women you will meet within these pages during our travels. *Merci! Merci!*

And, my thanks also go to all those who readily opened their doors to us to share their home, favorite recipes, and treasured cultural traditions.

Now, welcome to the second part of a most extraordinary adventure!

"It seems to me that our three basic needs, for food and security and love, are so mixed and mingled and entwined that we cannot straightly think of one without the others."

—M.F.K. Fisher

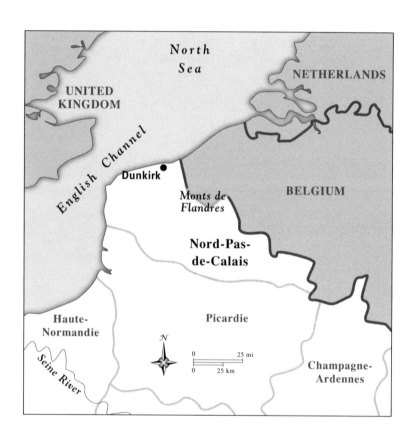

United Kingdom, Netherlands, Belgium, North Sea, English Channel, Dunkirk, Monts de Flandres, Nord-Pas-de-Calais, Haute-Normandie, Seine River, Picardie, Champagne-Ardennes.

N

| 0 | | 25 mi |
| 0 | 25 km | |

CHAPTER ONE

Paris and Ever Northward

*T*he cold, gray mist lifted slightly off the Seine as we passed over the Quai d'Orsay near the Tuileries in Paris. Josiane Selvage, my good friend and travel guide extraordinaire, and I were comfortably settled into her Citroën station wagon, beginning the second leg of our illustrious culinary tour. The evening before, we had driven from Josiane's brother's home in the Lorraine to the City of Light to bring my husband, Winston, back to Paris. The three of us had just completed three weeks of an incredible gastronomic journey. We had been collecting traditional French recipes and family stories throughout the regions of the Champagne, Loire, and Alsace. But business was calling Win's name, so we spent one night at a Parisian hotel before continuing our journey north. We were en route to the regions of Pas-de-Calais, Haute Normandy, Bas-Normandy, Brittany, the Loire Valley, then ending in the Auvergne, the "heart of the nation," where our journey would be complete.

Only a couple of years earlier, I had retired as a family therapist and had begun traveling through France and Italy with my friend Sharon Shipley, a culinary teacher and chef in Sunnyvale, California. We both were on a search. She was searching for traditional recipes, and I followed suit by interviewing the families she found who still used these recipes in their cooking. (Actually, I was more interested in their stories than the recipes.) It was during that trip that I decided to compile the interviews into a book about European families, their traditions, and their favorite foods.

It was purely a fluke that after I returned from a trip with Sharon, a mutual acquaintance introduced me to French expat, Josiane Selvage, in my hometown in California. But it was not until Josiane and her mother, Marcelle, who was visiting from France, offered to "enlighten" me about their French family's traditional recipes that I was truly hooked. From the day the two women arrived in my kitchen for the first of several interviews, my life was never the same. Over cups of coffee and wedges of lemon-curd tart or cookies, we stumbled through our language barriers to form a most incredible bond while sharing our cultural stories. One of our first conversations replayed in my mind:

"So, you are interested in learning how to prepare our French cuisine, *n'est-ce pas?*" Marcelle peered over the top of her coffee cup at me as she spoke.

"Yes, Madame," I said. "I would love to learn what makes your cuisine world famous. Your *haute cuisine.*"

"Our *haute cuisine?*" Marcelle took a bite of the lemon-curd tart I had so painstakingly baked, hoping it would meet my guests' approval. A twinkle flitted through her dark eyes.

"Yes," I said again, "but more than *haute cuisine*, I would prefer learning the fine art of traditional French cooking."

Marcelle carefully dabbed her lips with her napkin. "Well, Madame, our traditional cooking is rarely considered fine, but we certainly keep a respectable *cuisine pauvre.*"

I was brought up short at this French term and turned toward Josiane for an explanation.

"Carole, *'cuisine pauvre'* means 'poor kitchen' and refers to traditional peasant cooking. These are the recipes that have been handed down through many, many generations in our own family and are the types of cooking Maman taught me."

Following many delightful conversations, with a few cooking classes tossed in for good measure, plus stories of how Marcelle had put food on the table during World War II, Josiane offered to continue my education by guiding me through France—on a culinary tour with her mother. *What could be more enjoyable?* The idea of traveling with these two delightful women, searching for traditional family recipes and learning more about their family history, sounded like a dream. I couldn't wait.

But we were forced to wait. When the catastrophic events of 9/11 happened in New York City, our tour was cancelled, and a month later dear Marcelle passed away. The news was devastating on all fronts. I pushed my disappointment aside, as our trip to France was not a priority. But when Josiane returned from Marcelle's funeral in France, she called and insisted she escort me on our previously planned tour. "It would be our tribute to my *maman*," she said. I couldn't refuse.

Six months later, Josiane, Winston, and I were traveling through France on the first leg of our culinary journey.

Moments before we had climbed into her car, Josiane pulled a colorful scarf from her handbag, wrapped it around her neck, and tied it deftly. "So, Carole, should we be off?"

Yes, I was ready. But once we'd waved goodbye to Winston, who looked forlornly after us from the entrance of our

Paris hotel, I felt a bit guilty. He had been an easy traveling partner, as he adored Josiane as much as I did. But I had to admit I was looking forward to some "girl" time. I sighed.

Josiane headed down the Champs Elysées, past the Arc de Triomphe and onto the Periferique, the auto route that would sweep north to bring us closer to Rouen, where we would visit one of Josiane's oldest high school friends, Louisette. Promises of extraordinary stories and recipes wafted about the car.

The morning fog lifted as we drove, and the sun turned the day into a wonderland of springtime frost-etched fields. The pearlescent sky transformed from gray into a bright blue dome, with the sun's reflection almost blinding us as the car continued north. Peggy, Josiane's French-speaking GPS, accompanied us, with intermittent protests in the language that still eluded me. Yes, I did need to try harder to pick up French. My mastery had been meager at best during the first three weeks of our tour.

Barely minutes after leaving the outskirts of Paris, Josiane's cellphone rang and she chatted animatedly, nodding all the while, as if the caller could see her response. She ended the call and began thrumming her fingers on the steering wheel.

"So, when are we to arrive at Louisette's?" I asked nonchalantly, loving the freedom of not having to coordinate the details of this trip. Josiane had taken her role as tour guide seriously and had arranged for all our stays with her friends and family members.

"Actually," she said, "that was Louisette who called. We were to meet her at four o'clock this afternoon, but an important meeting came up for her. She called to put us off until tomorrow. I guess . . ." she continued tapping her fingers, "we could venture through some areas of the World War I and II battlegrounds—along the Somme River. You were interested in some of the World War points of interest, weren't you? That was part of my mother's story, as we believe her father died at the end of World War I. She was born on the last day of that war, so she never knew her father."

I nodded. That was one of many sad circumstances that had befallen Marcelle, and part of why I was so intrigued with her story. *What had happened?*

"I remember we talked about following the war trails near here," Josiane continued. "And perhaps we could stay in the coastal village of Honfleur."

When Josiane and I had first set our sights on this cross-country trip, it was eighty-four-year-old Marcelle who had convinced me that if I truly wanted to know about the French and their traditional cooking, I should travel with her and her daughter. Checking out this area of the Somme had been part of Marcelle's plan. Maybe we should have a look.

We followed the A16 through the open countryside. The morning sunlight danced across kilometers of bright yellow fields of colza and filtered down on us as we passed through dense forests, followed along rivers, and crossed over streams.

"What did you say colza was used for?" I asked.

"Cooking oil. We use it instead of canola oil in the northern parts of France.

"Ah, makes sense! Say, where are we right now, Josiane?" We had been driving for about an hour, and the cityscape of Paris had long disappeared.

"About 100 kilometers north of Paris, not far from the city of Amiens." She clicked on the turn indicator to exit the highway and drove down a side road.

"I just saw a sign indicating a war site," she said, as she pulled over to a small off-road parking lot, "and I need to stretch my legs." A granite obelisk rose high above the bushes overlooking the Somme River. We climbed out of the car and walked over to the obelisk, where Josiane swept tall weeds and debris aside with her hand.

"Carole, this is what I was hoping for. This monument marks the site of not one, but two World War I battles. The first Battle of the Somme, this says, was in July 1916. It was one of the bloodiest battles of the war." Josiane continued reading out loud. "The second battle was in 1918."

"1918? Josiane, I wonder if this is near where your grandfather—Marcelle's father—may have died."

"Of course, that is pure speculation on our part," Josiane said, running her fingers along the side of the obelisk. "But my nephew Christian is going to do some internet research, as he thinks it is a real possibility. Not long before she died, Maman asked him to search for her identity, as she was unclear about her real last name. You see, just because my grandfather didn't come home from the war, doesn't mean he died. I'll give Christian a call later today to spur him on."

My head snapped back as I contemplated this tidbit of possible history. "That's odd, but possible. So, his research would be a great help, wouldn't it? Eighty-four years, it would be."

We stood on the embankment looking down to the river valley far below. "*Somme*" is a Celtic word that means tranquility, which seems at odds with such an inharmonious history. Josiane explained that thousands of men on both sides—the Germans and the French, plus the Brits—died along these valleys in both world wars. *Is it possible this place also holds tight to its secrets?*

I stepped back. "I guess we'll have to wait for more information confirming your grandfather's identity. Right?"

Josiane nodded and swiped at a tear. It had been barely six months since her mother died. Too soon to press.

"Are we headed in the direction of Nord-Pas-de-Calais?" I asked.

"That is part of the Flemish Region of Belgium or Flanders on the northern border of France—along La Manche."

"La Manche? Where is that?"

"That's the French name for the English Channel. It's where Dunkirk is. Maman mentioned Dunkirk to us when she was speaking of World War II. Why do you ask?"

"I have a good friend, Veronique, who was raised in Dunkirk, as were all the generations in her family. I contacted her just before this trip, and she suggested I get in touch if I was ever in the area. She and her husband and two small daughters are preparing to move to Singapore for her husband's work. But she should still be in France. Should we call and see if she's available to meet?"

"It certainly can't hurt." Josiane pulled her cell phone out of her purse and handed it to me. I stared at the phone, willing my hand to reach for it but knowing if I got a French operator, I would have to ask for a number in French. Then be told the number, and the misunderstanding would be rife with angst—a whole hullabaloo. Believe me, I've tried. Instead, I dug into my purse and pulled out Veronique's mother's full name and handed it to Josiane. Within moments we were on our way toward Dunkirk, with an offer from Veronique to spend the night at her family home. What a gem.

"How do you know Veronique?" Josiane asked after we had been on the road for a while. We had stopped in Albert for lunch en route. Ironically, World War I and II battleground brochures were everywhere, with a special museum for battle enthusiasts. I wondered if we should check out a museum or two in search of Marcelle's father, but because his last name remained a mystery, I kept silent. This may have been too uncomfortable for Josiane.

"I met her sailing. Her husband used to race on our boat when we lived in Austin, Texas. We spent time with several French couples on Lake Travis, and I remember how animated Veronique became when she talked about her childhood. She told us a lot about her family's traditions, the history around Dunkirk and, of course, World War II. I think you will find her delightful. Plus, she has promised to share some regional recipes and family stories from World War II."

As it turned out, Veronique's family home was not in Dunkirk, but outside the city limits, in the countryside to the east—within the Monts de Flandres (Flanders Mountains). As we drove, we passed hops fields, streams with traditional windmills, and *bocages,* which Josiane explained were hedged farmlands.

"What are 'hedged farmlands'?" I asked.

"Farms that are bordered by hedges instead of rock walls. Say, it looks like we are almost back to the Belgian border," she said as she took note of road signs in Flemish. Three weeks earlier, we had passed from France into Belgium as we headed to the Alsace for a visit, taking a roundabout route to avoid the heavy snows in the mountains between the Lorraine and Alsace.

Josiane checked again with Peggy, who was confused because Josiane had not followed Peggy's designated route. It was late afternoon, and we were getting antsy. But after wending our way along a small brook through a wooded area, we drove around a curve to find ourselves in a knell at Veronique's family farm. The modest and cozy-looking farmhouse sat back off the roadway. Typical of Flemish construction, the house was brick with a steeply pitched roof and stepped gables. The front of the house was painted white, but the sides and the back revealed a bright red-brick construction. Powder blue shutters were attached to the many windows, the front door on the lower level, and the dormer windows that protruded from the weathered tile roof. Window boxes were filled with bright red geraniums. Veronique bounded out the front door as the car pulled into the farmyard.

This young woman, in her mid-forties with light blonde hair, deep blue eyes, and classic "Dutch-girl" good looks, swept me into her arms. Her warmth immediately extended to Josiane, and I realized those two were cut from the same cloth. Both had buoyant personalities and embraced life with full force. Raucous laughter tumbled out of each as if they had known one another forever.

Veronique led us into the house and introduced us to her mother, Madame Pund. Through the thin lines of Mme. Pund's eighty-year-old face, I detected a finer bone structure than that of her daughter, but equally lovely. She, too, had deep blue eyes, but parchment-white skin and silver-gray hair pulled back into a bun. She moved through the room with some discomfort yet carried herself in a regal manner. She quietly welcomed us into her home, asked Veronique to take us to a room upstairs, then disappeared into the kitchen to finish the evening's meal. It was at her table that the family's stories would be told.

Once Josiane and I had washed up, we headed back downstairs to the kitchen where Veronique was helping her mother prepare the *hors d'oeuvres*. As she cut slices of a chilled *terrine*, and her mother placed gherkins and pearl onions onto a plate, Veronique told us it would be only the four of us that night. Veronique's husband had taken the children for a visit to his parents in Switzerland, and her father, M. Pund, had passed away several years before.

"So," she said, "you will just have to settle for us. Ah, but it will be a ladies' night."

"I'm so sorry to miss your husband and the girls, Veronique," I said, "but I'm so pleased to see you. Thank you for having us on such short notice. May we help? Veronique? Madame Pund?"

"Sure. You can grab that hanging basket and fill it with the toasted rye bread," Veronique said. "And, Josiane, you can finish setting the table."

I looked around. On the far wall of the kitchen was an enormous brick walk-in fireplace. The crackling fire in the hearth lent warmth and charm to the low-ceilinged, but otherwise darkened room. Herbs hung in strings from the blackened beams, along with a sundry collection of copper pots and sauté pans. Beyond the pots, and hanging from a peg, were the hand-woven baskets. After Josiane finished setting the table, she bustled over to look at the baskets.

"Carole, did I tell you that my father taught me to weave baskets just like this?" she asked, with an air of excitement.

"Is that right?" Veronique asked. "My grandfather taught me to weave these, too."

"They look like a similar weave. Oh, it does bring back such wonderful memories for me," Josiane said. "I'll have to tell you about it. Ah, but another time. Looks like we are ready to eat."

"Tonight," Veronique said, as she led us to the table and had us sit, "I am going to introduce you to my mother's most traditional dish. I know that is part of what you have been writing about. It is her famous *Potjevlesh*, and it is always served with a good, strong fermented beer. You do like beer, don't you Carole? Josiane?"

"Absolutely," Josiane said. I nodded.

"As much as I enjoy wine—and I do," Josiane said, "I really love beer best—especially these wonderful local beers you have here in the Nord-Pas-de-Calais." She repeated what she had said in French, so that Mme. Pund, who did not speak a word of English, was included in the conversation.

Mme. Pund nodded vigorously and lifted her glass of beer in a connecting cheer. "*Tchin-Tchin,*" we all saluted.

"Now, to begin with, Carole, this Flemish specialty, called *Potche-Vletche* or *Potjevlesh* in Flemish," Veronique said, "means 'meat pot.' As you can see, my mother has prepared it as a *terrine* of three meats that have been roasted together with the bones. In years past, this usually was leftover meat from other meals put all together—it could be rabbit, chicken, and pork; or veal and bacon—all roasted with a lot of herbs like parsley, lovage, onions, shallots, garlic, a splash of white wine . . . What, Maman?"

"Never with beer. We cook a great many things with beer, but not this recipe," Mme. Pund said emphatically.

"Yes, this never contains beer, but then it is cooked all together, and the bones create a kind of jelly. So, the rabbit gives its flavor to the chicken, and the pork gives its flavor to the beef—not big pieces of meat, mind you, just small pieces. And after everything has cooked you take out the bones and place everything into a mold like a *pâte* mold and press it down, then put it into the refrigerator. So, when we eat it, it is sliced, and the nice part is—you will see, Carole—you will find a scrumptious piece of rabbit, a piece of beef . . . *Voilà!*"

She picked up a slice of bread, smoothed a knob of *terrine* on her bread, took a bite, then bit into the pickle, the onion, and then took a sip of her beer. She continued in this order until her plate was clean.

"Ah, this is quite delectable," I said. "Every mouthful a succulent surprise!"

"And, despite no beer in the dish," Josiane said, as she smiled at Mme. Pund, "a glass of beer is a perfect accompaniment."

"Often this dish was served," Veronique began again, "if you had guests for a few days, then this would be prepared of all the leftover meats. My mom would always prepare it, and because I don't like a lot of jelly, she would press it overnight in the refrigerator and remove some of the jelly. You don't see any jelly, right? For some reason I don't like the texture of the jelly, so she always makes this special for me. Some people think the jelly tastes better and indicates better cuts of meat. Therefore, some hostesses might want to prove they are wealthier by serving their meat covered in jelly. To me, it doesn't matter. I still don't like the texture of the jelly," she concluded, and popped another morsel into her mouth.

Because the first course had been so filling, it was followed with a simple but refreshing salad. I was relieved not to have more courses to follow. Too many nights of waddling out of the kitchen meant too many nights of restless sleep, indigestion, and an expanding waistline. I stood at the counter along with Josiane and Veronique, all of us helping Mme. Pund with the dishes.

As each woman took her turn either washing or drying the dishes, Veronique began to tell some of the stories that I had hoped to hear.

"*If time, so fleeting, must like humans die, let it be filled with good food and good talk, and then embalmed in the perfumes of conviviality.*"

—M.F.K. Fisher

CHAPTER TWO

A Band de Pêcheurs or
Carnaval de Dunkerque

This is all of our stories, we French!"

"My father and his father's side of the family all came from Dunkirk," Veronique said. "They were all sailors, and some were officers in the French navy. My grandfather worked in the mechanical part of the ship, and my great-grandfather was an officer. My great-grandfather's time was spent between sailing vessels and motorized ships, and he sailed all over the world . . . to Asia, to America. This was before World War I, and when he returned, he brought gifts, like kimonos from Japan and porcelain from China. Things like that."

"So, all three generations were Navy?" I asked to clarify. I was carefully wiping a tureen dry. I placed it on the counter near Mme. Pund, who picked it up and placed it on a shelf in her china cupboard.

"Yes, but my father was in the Navy for only five years. In fact, it was my father who broke the chain of generations by not continuing in the Navy. Right, Maman?"

After the questions were put to her in French, Mme. Pund smiled wryly and nodded.

"So, your grandfather was the mechanic on the naval ships, is that right?" I asked Veronique. "Was that during World War II?"

"Yes."

"And your *maman?* Was she also raised by the sea?" I asked.

Veronique turned to her mother and translated my question. Mme. Pund's dark eyes lit up as she waited for her daughter to answer. Veronique continued. "Maman also came from the Dunkirk area, but in the countryside. She grew up not far from where we are now, between the Belgian border and Dunkirk. Josiane, do you know the village of Bergues?"

"Oh," puffed Josiane, "but, of course. Carole, it is only a few kilometers from here. We almost made a wrong turn in that direction this afternoon." She flipped her hand in the air in mock exasperation.

"Yes, it is not far," Veronique said. "Because of the proximity to Belgium, my mother was more influenced by the Flemish people than my father was, who grew up in Dunkirk."

Again, Veronique translated to include her mother in the conversation. Mme. Pund nodded as she placed a wooden platter of cheeses on the table.

"Carole," Veronique said, interrupting herself, "I have to tell you that these cheeses include a soft, red-mold cheese known as *Livarot* and one known as *Pont-l'Évêque.* Both are from northeast Normandy—not far from here. She pointed to the center of the tray. "This square cheese is a strong flavored local cheese called *Maroilles.*"

"You will hear of these cheeses often, Carole," Josiane said, "especially if you stay in this area. All are pungent but extremely tasty! *Oui,* Veronique?" The biting aroma of each cheese emanated into the room and, for the uninitiated, the scent of moldy socks came to mind, as my eyes began to water.

Veronique started to sit back down, then popped back up from the table to take the basket of sliced baguettes from her mother. She handed the pitcher of dark beer and glasses to Josiane to put on the table, then helped her mother back to her seat.

"Oh, but of course!" Veronique boomed. "We French love our stinky cheeses!" She added a "poof" and a flourish. The Gallic "puff" or French gesture I had come to love was a part of this region we were visiting as well. During our earlier travels in the past few weeks, I had been introduced to this mostly indescribable puff of air emitted from the mouth. It seemed to be accompanied by a toss of the hand whenever words failed. I was thinking of adopting the gesture, as words were constantly eluding me.

Taking up a slice of bread, she cut a smear of cheese off the corner of the *Maroilles,* poured beer into the empty glasses, then continued her story.

"All Maman's side of the family were farmers and raised horses. These were plow horses used to work the fields."

"If she lived far from Dunkirk, how did your mother meet your father?" I asked. As Veronique turned to ask her mother, I watched a glimmer of a smile cross Mme. Pund's lovely face.

"They met through mutual friends after the war. I think they are eight years apart in age," Veronique said, almost in a whisper. "I don't want to embarrass my mother, but she is older. My father was in the Navy for five years, and while he was there, he learned some securities skills. After the war, there were no laws that would help protect homes, factories, or boats from fire, so he decided to start his own business to implement fire security. I think that is why he chose an older woman." She arched one eyebrow. "He wanted someone strong, like my mother, to help him begin a new business."

"So, your father opened a security business?" Josiane asked. She helped herself to the *Maroilles* and then the *Livarot*.

"Not exactly. After the bombings of World War II, most of Dunkirk had to be rebuilt, and most of the houses, businesses, and factories were rebuilt of brick and stone. People were eager to prevent a great loss of any type again. So, my father set up a company to provide fire alarm systems and all manner of equipment for firemen. He also helped to prevent fires on boats and naval vessels, on the fireboats."

"What an ingenious endeavor," I said.

"Oh my, yes."

"Would your mother be comfortable with me asking her about the war?" I asked softly.

Again, Veronique turned to her mother, who indicated that her daughter should tell her father's story first. Mme. Pund was a strong woman, but shy. She leaned forward to pick up a baguette slice, cut a wedge of the *Maroilles* and slathered it onto her bread. She sipped a new glass of dark beer and listened with great attention to her daughter's English version of the story.

"My father often told us about the time when they were forced to leave Dunkirk. Because of the bombing and all. He was only a little boy at the time, but his father, my grandfather, was in the Navy and out to sea, and all the other men of the family were away at war. My grandma decided they had to flee from Dunkirk—she, my father, age nine, and her sister, who was about seven months pregnant. They left with the only car in the family. The funny part is no one knew how to drive the car." She leaned over to her mother and in French explained which part of the story she was telling. They both burst out laughing. Mme. Pund waved her to continue.

"Usually it was the men who drove the car," she began again, "except in an emergency. My father used to tell me," and here Veronique switched to a deeper voice as she repeated the words she'd heard from her father when he told the story— 'I will never forget the long narrow road on that fateful trip. It was my aunt who ended up driving, even though she was very pregnant. She could barely reach the pedals. And she didn't know how to use the brake. *Mon Dieu!* When she had to stop the car, it became my job to quickly jump out and put a block of wood in front of the wheels to get the car to stop. You can imagine all the hollering. And yelling. I was so scared, but it was kind of funny at the time, too! I suppose that was a lot to think about at that young age! Anyway, the horns would honk wildly because the drivers ahead of us were waving their hands and complaining because my aunt kept bumping into them. I almost got squeezed to death between the two bumpers. Did they think of that? And, of course, she would stall the car each time she stopped or started, and the people behind us were frantically yelling. For my mother and aunt, I suppose there was a lot of stress because the three of us were all alone, leaving behind everyone and everything we had ever known. But I must admit, at that age it was a little bit like a lark!

"'And while we were driving, there was a lot of bombing of the line of cars, a strafing from the German planes. My aunt would pull off to the side of the road and we would all jump into the ditch. I swear my mother saved my life—again and again and again—because she kept jumping on top of me. She said it was to protect me. But she was almost killing me at the same time.'"

"It must have been like in a movie," Veronique continued excitedly, "my grandmother jumping on him to protect him from the bombs." She smiled at the memory her father had created for her and had repeated many times. She then took a bite of cheese and washed it down with a swig of beer.

"And, of course, my grandmother and her sister were always thinking of his future . . . just in case they were killed. My grandmother's fortune was a huge brick of gold." Veronique held up her hands, about two feet across to indicate the dimensions. "Probably not that big, but my father had to carry this gold brick, which was tied around his neck and hidden under his shirt—it was pretty uncomfortable for him.

"Whenever he had to leap out of the car, he would have that gold brick with him and it was heavy and painful, as you can imagine."

"Especially with his mother jumping on top of him," laughed Josiane.

"Exactly." Veronique roared with laughter.

"So, where did they go?" I asked.

"My father said they really didn't know where to go, so they decided to head toward Brittany. They ended up spending a few months in Brittany, and they rented a room with a beaten earth floor."

"Like a dirt floor?" Josiane asked.

"*Oui!* It was dirt. And he was the only boy wearing shoes."

"Ah," interrupted Josiane, "I'll bet that was because the other children were wearing *sabots*—clogs. Right?"

"Right. How did you know?"

"Veronique, that is part of *my* family's story. My great-grandfather was a shoemaker in Brittany before and after World War I, and my mother was proud of the fact that she was one of the few children who had regular leather shoes. Not those humble clogs for her. But back to your father's story . . ."

"While his family lived in Brittany, they resided in a small village, and he was considered a city boy—even though he was just from Dunkirk. But what seemed strange to him was they kept calling him 'the Parisian,' and he had never been to Paris. I guess that was the only city they knew of."

"How was your father able to communicate with the other children in Brittany?" I asked. "I imagine the dialect was different from his. Flemish is more Dutch, isn't it?"

"Yes, it is! Hmmm . . .let me think. I believe at the time they spoke French in the schools. But apart from the schools, if they spoke to him at all, it might have been in Gallo."

"Gallo? Not Breton?" Maybe because I was struggling with the language barrier myself, I wanted to know how people were able to communicate. Especially under such strained circumstances.

"I believe Gallo was spoken on the Eastern edges of Brittany," Josiane said, "while Breton was spoken more in the Western regions. I'm not certain, but I think it's true. My mother grew up speaking Breton, which is more Celtic or Welsh than anything else. I'm not certain where the lines of language began and ended. But it led to great confusion."

"They may not have said anything about it to my father, thinking he was Parisian. What *did* he say?" she pondered, her forefinger rubbing her chin. "It was something about having to wear a strange cloak to school so he would fit in . . . because that was traditional for them . . . But anyway, he went to school with those boys for three or four months, and then it seemed not a good place to remain, so they decided to join another sister of my grandma's who lived in Reims in the Champagne region."

"We were just there a few weeks ago," I said, sitting up straighter.

"Veronique, that is where my favorite cousin and his family live—near Reims," Josiane said. "And not far from where I grew up in the Lorraine."

"Then you may be familiar with some of this history. My great-aunt and uncle who lived there used to run a soap factory. But he was part of the Resistance and was captured by the S.S., so my great-aunt continued running the factory by herself. It was not easy, because she had been a housewife with two small children, and then suddenly lost her husband and had to become a businesswoman during the war."

"*Mais oui*," Josiane said, "my father was also in the Resistance—actually, he was a *Maquis* in the Auvergne region during the war. That's where I was born."

"Your family certainly moved around a lot, too," Veronique said.

"Yes, and it had to do with the same war." She smiled kindly. "Continue your story. I'm sorry I keep interrupting."

"No problem, Josiane. This is all our stories, we French. While the war continued, all the family tried to stay together— my grandma, I think, had six sisters and two brothers, and at least three of the sisters stayed together during that time in Reims."

"During that time, Veronique," I interrupted, "where was your grandfather? Did they even know if he was alive or dead?"

"During that time my grandfather was no longer working in the Navy, but he was still working in the harbor of Dunkirk on the tugboats. His job on the boats was to help ships navigate through the harbor, which at that time was filled with mines left by the Germans. It was a dangerous mission. I remember my dad telling me that the only time he saw his father cry was when he talked about the day, he was on a tugboat that helped lead a British ship very carefully, very slowly through the mines. Once they reached the other side of the mines, all the sailors on both boats jumped with joy. They were successful! Whew! They were throwing *bisous* . . . kisses of love . . . from one boat to another . . . such happiness. But as the British ship continued, apparently, they had not cleared all the mines, and suddenly the ship blew up. It must have been utterly horrible for my grandfather to be watching the sailors' joyful faces—and then to see those same faces—well, they were gone, and everything was covered in blood." Veronique shuddered. "It might not have been the worst memory for him, but to experience such joy and then such loss within a split second was . . ." she hesitated and swallowed hard, "extremely devastating."

Veronique paused a moment more before taking a sip of beer. This incident had happened not to her or her father, but to her grandfather, forty years before her birth. Yet, familial love is strong. She spread another baguette slice with cheese. Sadness filled her voice as she turned to explain to her mother what she had been talking about. Her mother looked down at the tabletop. This was a memory the family had known only through the pain of retelling. Like Veronique said, the story belonged to all of them.

Veronique started speaking again. "When my grandfather had nothing more to do on the tugboats in the winter months, he tried to find his family. He had received a note from his wife, my grandmother, saying they were in Brittany, so he rode his bike to Brittany. Arriving in Brittany, he found they had gone to Reims, so he pedaled to Reims. There he found my grandmother and, of course, my father."

"How did he stay out of the clutches of the Germans?" I asked.

"Poof!" Veronique said, throwing her hands in the air and emitting another Gallic puff. "I'm not certain how he managed." She scratched her head and looked puzzled.

"Good question," she added. "I'm sorry I didn't think to ask him when he was alive. But I believe at that time the family had a small *café* in Reims, and Reims is where my father went to school, I think, for about two more years. I imagine my grandfather was not far away from them, albeit in hiding.

"My father," she continued, "also remembered when they came back home to Dunkirk and found their old home still standing. Their house was next to the priest's house and opposite the church, so they said the house had been protected by God. Next to their house and in the middle of the road, great craters were left from all the bombing, but their house was intact. When all the family arrived, they found that their houses and the church were safe, but the rest of their city was blown to bits. They were extremely grateful yet quite surprised. But why not? They were protected by God!"

A joyful laugh rolled from deep within her, and in no time at all, we were joining in. It is never what Veronique says that is so humorous, but how she expresses it. Clearly this was the nuanced and unique version her grandfather had told her, and like all good granddaughters, she had gulped it all down as the holy truth.

"If your mother is all right with this topic," I said, "what was her family's experience of the war?"

Veronique asked her mother. "She says she is honored you should ask. Her family had a farm right on the edge of the area that was evacuated—where the Germans came across the border. Dunkirk is in the farthest northeast corner of

France, along the Belgium border. All the other farmers and their families had fled, but my mother's family, whose farm was the closest to the war zone, chose to remain and hold their ground."

Veronique translated as Mme. Pund spoke. "I remember hearing all the shooting and grenades going off around us, but for some reason we were never frightened. I guess because we had a root cellar to go down into when it got extremely bad. Parts of our out-buildings were bombed, but we felt we were lucky. Our house, fortunately, was not damaged, but we sustained damage to the corrals and the barns, where the horses were kept. Because we were not far from the small city of Bruges, across the border, there were many, many people who fled across that same border to gain safety at our farm. During all the war we shared our house with others and kept only one room in the house for ourselves.

"There were two families who came and stayed during the entire war and many others who were fleeing would stay for a night or two—or part of a week—before continuing on." Again, Veronique stopped translating and turned to her mother.

"Maman, did you know these people? Did they pay for anything?"

"No, no, no!" Mme. Pund replied. "You see, when I was eight my mother died, so I was raised by my stepmother, who always said, 'We are not allowed to take advantage of the drama of other people.' She believed that if we survived, it was because we were good; and if we were bad, we would not survive. We were lucky because we had the farm and the animals. We gave a breakfast of bread with *saindoux* for everyone, and we tried to treat everyone equally."

"Oh! Oh!" Josiane interrupted. "You remember my mother telling you, Carole, about *saindoux, mais oui?*"

"Yes," I replied. "You described it as pork-flavored rendered lard, or pork belly. Your mother called it strictly *cuisine pauvre* or peasant food. I remember her recounting with such eloquence, 'Imagine a jellied substance the flavor of bacon glistening on the only piece of bread left for the family and then you, too, can imagine the powerful draw to each savory morsel which slipped across our tongues.'"

"When you have nothing else to eat, it becomes a feast!" Veronique said. She nodded for her mother to continue.

"My stepmother told me, we can't eat butter because not everyone has that, so we will all eat *saindoux* with our bread. She was a good and fair woman."

"That's what my great-grandmother used to say to my mother," Josiane said. "Plus, my mother grew up loving *saindoux* spread on dark bread." Mme. Pund smiled and nodded in agreement.

"Well, that certainly spells it out," Veronique said. "I remember, too, my mother telling me they had one little boy who remained with them throughout the entire war. He was the son of a seamstress and was malnourished because his mother did not have enough food. So, he lived with my grandparents in order to survive."

Veronique mentioned this to her mother. "Ah, petite Pierre," Mme. Pund said, "he was like my little brother. When he first arrived, he was almost dying, but then he became healthy, or healthier, because he was living and eating with us."

Mme. Pund continued. "My father was the man the Germans would call on to negotiate for horses or cows. They would come to him and say, 'Tomorrow, we will need ten horses.' My father, who was well trusted and respected, would go to the other farmers and say, 'Tomorrow, we need fifteen cows or fifteen horses.' And, of course, the Germans never paid for any of these. So, the farmers would give maybe one, if they could give up one. But I was proud of my father because, even though the Germans didn't care who gave them the cows or horses, my father would always give at least two of his, so the rest of the farmers would know he had been fair with them. They would have to bring one or maybe two, and then they would have thirty, and they knew that the Germans would choose ten of the best. The farmers sometimes would bring their worst animals, but to negotiate with the Germans—so there were no reprisals—they all had to work together, and some would have to give up their better horses or cows."

"You have a fine memory, Madame Pund. How old were you during that time?" I asked.

"I was a teenager, and sometimes when I was milking the goats . . ." She began to giggle like the girl she used to be. "I would pee into the milk before giving it to the Germans." She laughed out loud. "It was one way of expressing my resistance to the German invasion."

We laughed with her. Her dark eyes flashed with mirth as she recalled her memories.

"Tell them about the Canadian soldiers, Maman," Veronique said, then realized I was still needing a translation. She tittered at her error and explained.

Mme. Pund continued. "When the Canadian soldiers came to liberate the village at the end of the war, I was about sixteen years old."

"I'll show you a picture of her at that age." Veronique jumped up from the table and disappeared. She reappeared with a photograph of her mother as a young lady with raven-black, rolled hair.

"Oh là, là," Josiane exclaimed, "you were quite the beauty!"

"Yes, she was," Veronique beamed. "She used to tell me how impressed she was by the Canadian soldiers. Right, Maman?" Her mother grinned and nodded.

"*Mais oui*," Mme. Pund continued. "The Canadian soldiers were our liberators, and we were beholden to them. Plus, they were quite handsome, too!" She blushed.

"I used to ask my mother," Josiane interjected, 'How was it during the war?' And now I ask you the same question. Were people honest? Was there a black market? How did people manage?"

"I was fairly young during most of the war," Madame Pund said, "but I do remember a lot of people selling butter at a high price. At least half the people were taking advantage of others during the war. If there was a black market, I wasn't aware of it."

"My father told me that when he lived in Reims, his aunt made soap to sell," Veronique said. "His mother often offered to help. She would load her bicycle with soaps and took them for miles and miles, trying to sell them. Finally, she was able to trade all her soap for a ham, but when she got home, she found the ham was rancid. Oh, pooh! Occasionally people took advantage of others. It's human nature, I think." Veronique jumped up and raced out of the room, returning with another photo. It showed a young boy wearing a beret and a cocky smile.

"This is my father before the war. He told me that because he was the only kid in the family, he always had to go with his mother. He went on many of her trips to sell soap. He sat on the back of the bicycle and the soap was piled in a basket in the front. He remembered the bad ham and how disappointed he felt because he had been looking forward to that ham all the way home. That winter, which was one of the longest and coldest in history, they had eaten very little meat, and the ham would have made a pleasurable feast."

Madame Pund spoke briefly to her daughter. "Ah, *oui*, Maman," Veronique replied.

"My mother just reminded me about a World War II memory of hers. It was just before the Liberation—around the time when the Canadians came. The Germans knew the war was over for them, and they left our area. When the word went out that the Germans were gone, everyone who had evacuated the area of the Dunkerque Pouche happily returned home. My mom wants me to tell you about Bergues, the village we talked about earlier this evening. It was a charming little town near their farm, built with beautiful fortifications or city walls surrounding it, created by Vauban, the architect for Louis XIV. The fortifications were constructed in a star shape and built near the water to help defend the city." She paused to think, as she seemed to have gotten sidetracked. We nodded for her to continue.

"Anyway, the Germans had taken over the village during the whole of the war, but when they left, the population came back. But this was a big mistake, because the Germans had booby trapped every one of their houses. Once the people arrived home, they were joyful to see their homes still standing. But when they opened the front door . . . KA-BOOM . . . everyone was killed, the house demolished. Of course, the families did not all arrive at the same time, so when new arrivals came, they saw the demolished houses and believed the bombing had happened some time before. They had no idea it had just occurred. The same thing happened over and over, and many people were killed. My mom witnessed these happenings because she had gone to the farmers' market with her father and her sister to sell butter, cheeses, and some horses. They would be standing in the marketplace in the center of town and . . ." Veronique gulped and looked over at her mother.

Madame Pund had remained stoic up until this point, but now one feeble hand dabbed her eyes with a lace handkerchief, as her head bent low.

"Veronique, this must be devastating for your mother to talk about," I said, inwardly berating myself for having brought up this subject.

"And yet this is one of the stories she insisted I convey to you. She is brave, my *maman*," she said, as she patted her mother's hand and spoke softly to her in French. Her mother nodded but kept her head down.

"She says that when she and her family witnessed the devastation taking place around them, they at first hadn't realized what was happening. But then they felt guilty because they hadn't warned other people before it was too late. And these were people they had known all their lives.

"So, there they were, arriving with all this hope, for they had survived the war, and after four long years they opened their door to say, 'I'm so glad to be home' . . . and boom! My mother has talked about this many times over the years. I know it deeply affected her. Fortunately, the village included many people who survived and were strong in character, because the entire village has been rebuilt.

"If you have time to see it, maybe tomorrow, you can go to this beautiful little village, still with the star-shaped fortifications and all the streets circling inside the star, with an operating drawbridge. Yes, this is a sad story, but also a beautiful one . . . one that reveals the strength of the French people." She cradled her chin in her hands.

At this point, Mme. Pund seemed to be slipping deeper into her chair. I hoped this discussion of war had not been too overwhelming. I decided to shift the topic.

"Tell me about some of your favorite traditions or the holidays you celebrated when you were young," I said.

"Whoo boy!" Veronique said, rocking back in her chair as she began thinking. Once she translated the question, her mother sat up with interest.

Veronique began. "I remember the fishermen would go to Iceland each year to fish for herring. They would leave Dunkirk for almost six months. Before they headed out, which was in February we would have a *Carnaval.* They would call themselves *La Bande de Pêcheurs*—the Gang of the Fishermen. They would lead the *Carnaval de Dunkerque,* and it was not like in Nice, France or in New Orleans where they have great floats, but they—the fishermen—would lead a parade. And everybody would be singing sailors' songs."

Veronique got up from the table and began to sing in a rough, low tone replicating the voices of the fishermen. She hunched down and moved like a husky sailor, swinging her arms wildly and singing, marching around the table as Josiane, Mme. Pund, and I laughed with delight.

"Do you remember any of the words?" I asked.

Veronique shrugged. "The words, of course, were all in French . . ." she hesitated, then blew out another Gallic puff. I waved her off.

"They would play the drums and be most lively. All the *bande* were dressed like fishermen, so all those who joined the group dressed either as fishermen or as Negroes. I don't know why. That's just who used to be on their boats, I imagine. The *pêcheurs* were considered the leaders of all of *Carnaval.* They led us in the old working and fishing songs," she said as she continued circling around the room, "and people from all over the city joined them in this festival. The city streets were filled with people dressed in costumes, dancing and singing—but always these same rough songs! Right, Maman?" Her mother's smile broadened with the telling. She was enjoying this subject.

"Like pirate songs, you say? Or sea shanties?" I turned toward Josiane. "We used to sing pirate songs when we were all sailing together—Veronique and her family were with us on our boat. Those tunes you taught us, Veronique—were some of them the old pirate songs?"

"*Oui!* But, of course. They were pirate songs. *Carnaval* was most amazing. I guess you had to be there to understand all that was happening. It wasn't rough, exactly. Yet it was rough. In fact, each year someone gets hurt, but you just must be prepared for it. We still do this whenever we come back to visit in February." She turned to see her mother beaming and ready to take up with her in song.

"Remember, Maman? It could be absolutely wild. Everyone would get caught up in the pushing and shoving movements of the *pêcheurs*. Sometimes it could be a bit raucous."

She had mentioned more than once how raucous it got. I wondered if she was tamping it down a tad. It probably had a lot to do with the amount of beer we'd consumed. Or, perhaps, the beer the *pêcheurs* had consumed. Ah, but Veronique was not finished.

"There is always an official tour of the city—a parade route of sorts—with the *bande*. It winds down past the *mairie* (city hall), and the mayor stands on the steps throwing herring out to the crowd. This is a symbol of the rich fishing season. He can only do this if the fishermen had a good haul. It is fun! Then there is a ball or dance, but everything is the same . . . the same *bande* and the same costumes." She took a deep breath.

"You become like a caricature, like a *corsair*, a pirate. You don't dress like a princess or someone well dressed. Even the older people wear masks, like a French politician, a Le Pen mask or a President Jacques Chirac mask, or you go like somebody else. And the fun continues into private homes. Those at home wait for guests to arrive. And when someone rings the doorbell, the host answers but doesn't recognize the guest. As the visitor begins to talk, like the character of their mask, the host tries to guess who they are. Usually the 'pirate' goes to the house of someone he knows and tries to trick them. For instance, the guest might bring up something about the host's personal life in the voice of Chirac or Le Pen, and the host doesn't know for sure who they are, but the host's role is to give them wine and food until they discover the friend's identity.

"Sometimes people have an open house, but they call it '*chapelle*,' which means chapel. I don't know why they use that term. Do you, Maman?"

"I'm not sure either, Veronique. Maybe because it's similar to the wine mass?" Mme. Pund shrugged.

Veronique continued as she circled the table once again. We were getting dizzy. "Some people like participating in *Carnaval* because they like doing *chapelle* or having an open house. You go from one house to another to trick your friends, enjoying their food and wine and they don't even have to recognize you to have a good time.

"But the thing I like most about *Carnaval* is that every-body—I mean everybody—is eyeball-to-eyeball, meaning they are equal in status, if only for that one night a year. I remember one time when my math teacher was standing next to me.

Or it could be a cleaning lady, or the director of a factory, or the banker. And everyone is going 'ho-ho-ho' like a pirate. No more proper neckties, no more 'how do you dos.' It's just fun. You are part of this party, and you do not have to be from the same social group. You will behave, obviously, but it's just pure fun!"

"Your parents participated in this *Carnaval?*" I asked, looking at Mme. Pund.

Veronique nodded her head. Mme. Pund said, "*Oui*, we used to do that, but not in our own house. We could not hold *chapelle* because we did not live on that square in Dunkirk where the *Carnaval* took place. But we would spend the whole day all dressed up, going from one friend's house to another. We were having such fun."

"My mom is eighty-three, and she still enjoys herself. Right, Maman? Last time, she wore a pilgrim bonnet I gave her as part of her costume." Veronique smiled at her mother.

"Well, I have to ask this. It's my job," I said. "Did they eat special foods on that day?" I was, if nothing else, diligent about getting the food details.

"My, yes. Onion soup is served all day long and, of course, French fries and mussels."

"Oooh, my husband would love that. We had that last night in Paris," I said.

"I'm so sorry Winston is not with you. It would have been great to see him again. I remember he loves mussels, too. Mmm. *Moules et frites*," Veronique swooned.

"I loooovvee mussels too," echoed Josiane. "Just a simple meal of mussels simmered in a little white wine, garlic. Mm-mmmm! Just delicious!"

"Was fish a big part of your diet, Veronique?" I asked.

"No. Every Friday we would eat fish because we are

Catholic. But only a few other times. I remember my paternal grandma coming to our house with fresh mussels and she would crack open the mussels and cook them for us. From time to time, she would bring gray shrimps, which she would peel. They are quite small, and even though they are pink they are called gray shrimps. No matter that they are very tiny—they are quite tasty. Not sweet. They were not like little *homard* (lobster), but like *langoustine* (scampi), and wonderful. My grandmother came often to help us, because she felt it was difficult for little kids with tiny fingers to peel the shrimps by themselves. She would spend the whole afternoon peeling the shrimps for us. She was so good to us."

I love how she says "shrimps" in the plural. Charming!

"Remember, Maman? And there was only my older brother and me. And Grandmama would pile the shrimps onto brown bread, with plenty of butter—a thousand of them piled high—and we would . . ." She opened her mouth wide, then chomped down making a loud sound like she was devouring them, smacking her lips together when she was through. What an entertaining method actor we were privileged to watch.

"How were the shrimp prepared?" I asked, thinking they couldn't be raw. Or could they?

"You just boil them in water, without anything else in it, and they are wonderful. At a restaurant, you might find them fixed two ways. They might use mayonnaise with sliced tomatoes all covered with shrimps, or they might prepare it like a croquette—a *beignet*. It is prepared with a sauce base of flour, eggs, cheese, and water, then mixed with the shrimps and deep-fat fried."

"We call those fritters in the States. They are wonderful." I said. I was thinking of our wonderful East Coast clam or corn fritters.

"But there is not just one shrimp in the sauce. There are many, many boiled shrimps inside and the batter is thick, like mashed potatoes. Then it is fried in oil, but it is not greasy at all. It is my favorite dish when I am back home here in France. It is called *Croquette de l'Crevette.*

"Carole, these are wonderful," Josiane chimed in. "I don't recall anything like them in the States. Just good bread, some butter, no lemon—nothing to interfere with the taste of the little gray shrimps."

Despite being full to the gills and having swilled down more glasses of beer than I usually consume, the thought of food once again piqued my appetite.

At that point Mme. Pund shook her head sadly and stood up to head off to bed. I jumped up to thank her and took her by the hands. "Veronique, please tell her for me, how much I appreciate her kindness, her hospitality, her marvelous dinner—and especially her stories. I shall be certain to preserve her memories. *Merci beaucoup.*" Mme. Pund smiled, kissed me on both cheeks, and headed to her bedroom.

With the closing of the bedroom door, there was a lull in the conversation as the three of us sat mulling over the stories that had just been revealed. But the night was yet in its embryo, and we carried on into the wee hours of the morning, laughing, sharing, and telling each other even more stories.

Normandy

CHAPTER THREE

Karyn's Kitchen

Le Havre

*T*he following morning, we women arose with the sun, which in that early springtime sky meant well after the cock had crowed. I left Josiane emailing her nephew Christian as I padded downstairs toward the sumptuous aromas coming from the kitchen. I found Veronique and her mother at the breakfast table, leisurely sipping their morning bowls of *café*. Veronique pulled out a chair for me, as her mother stood and moved slowly to the massive wrought iron stove. An intoxicating scent of apples and cinnamon filled the air as she peeked into the oven to check on some invisible breakfast treat.

"Oh, my! What is she baking, Veronique?"

"A local apple specialty called *douillons aux pommes.*" Seeing the confused look on my face, she threw her head back and erupted in laughter. As I've mentioned, with Veronique there is rarely a dull moment.

"It means Apples in a Nightdress, so you are appropriately attired for this *petite déjeuner* (breakfast)," she said, eyeing my nightgown. "It's an apple, peeled and cored, then wrapped in puff pastry, slathered in plenty of sugar, butter, and cinnamon, then baked. Smells gooood, doesn't it?"

"Heavenly," I said, drooling at her description.

"How did you sleep last night?" Mme. Pund asked as she placed a steaming bowl of *café au lait* on the table before me.

"Marvelously! Thank you." I smiled up at her. "Josiane is completing some necessary emails, then she'll be down."

"What are your plans from here?" Veronique asked.

"I'm not the driver, but I believe we are heading to Normandy, then on to Brittany. We are trying to time our arrivals to meet up with some friends and family of Josiane's— to interview them and, of course, gather recipes and cultural information. After Josiane's mother, Marcelle, died six months back, Josiane decided to make a major effort to connect with her family—while there was still time. Plus, we had originally planned to take this trip with Marcelle. It would have been her mother's final visit back to her beloved Brittany. So, we are traveling in her memory."

Later that morning, sunlight streamed in through the back window of the station wagon as Josiane and I headed out from Veronique's family home. The short visit had been enjoyable, but Josiane was determined to keep to her schedule. We were expected late that afternoon in Rouen at her friend Louisette's home. Louisette would be home from work to greet us around 5 p.m. But that would be in six or seven hours.

As we headed northwest through Dunkirk, then began to follow the coast westward past Calais, I asked Josiane, "How far are we from Le Havre?" I had spotted a road sign with the city name and thoughts of a dear friend of mine, Karyn Foucher, popped into my mind. She and her husband, Laurent, had been sailing friends of ours, too, in the U.S., but after a work contract in the U.S. had ended, they had moved back to Karyn's hometown of Le Havre with their two small daughters.

Josiane replied, "Le Havre is right along this same coast, La Manche—or as I told you before, is called the English Channel—but, it is a bit farther west than Rouen. Did you want to go there? We have time, I believe."

"I'd like to try," I said. "She was such a dear friend."

Josiane looked again at her watch and calculated the time it would take to get to Rouen. "Why not?" she said. "Give her a call and see if she is available."

I pulled out my cell phone and called the number Karyn had given me "just in case I found myself in her part of France." And I was shocked when she answered and exuberantly invited us to her home. I explained my mission: that I had missed the opportunity to interview her when we lived in Austin, and now, if she had time, I would like to follow up on that promise. She sounded pleased.

We easily found her neighborhood and house and entered through an open gate that led up the driveway. The two-story stucco house was taupe in color; tucked into the roofline were two dormer windows that winked at us as we stepped out of the car. The front porch was elegantly wrapped in a black wrought-iron handrail. The front door, a French door at that, opened before we could knock.

After a big embrace, I introduced Josiane. Karyn, overjoyed to have us visit, whisked us inside. Her dark eyes sparkled as we moved from room to room. Her neatly coiffed hair embraced her pixie-like face and her laugh was easy and relaxed. I was glad to see her. I knew moving back to France from Austin, where we had met, had not been her choice. But I was relieved to see she had made the adjustment. I tried to remember her age and imagined she was in her thirties. I was probably her mother's age, if I thought about it. But we had always had an easy and comfortable friendship in which age never entered the conversation.

Looking around her home, I saw that she may have left her heart in Texas to move back to her hometown of Le Havre, but with Texas stars and paintings of bluebonnets from the Texas hill country splashed across her walls, her toes were still deep in that southern state. She settled us in the kitchen where she had prepared coffee and a plate of cookies, while her two-year-old daughter, Cassiopée, played with pans on the tile floor.

After catching up on her family news and sharing the gossip from the U.S., I said, "You promised me that one day I could interview you. I wish we had more time right now, but would you be interested in sharing some of your family recipes and stories? Maybe you could begin by telling me about growing up in Le Havre?"

She scooted her two-year-old up on her lap. She took a sip from her coffee before flipping her mahogany-colored hair behind one ear and away from her child, then began matter-of-factly: "Le Havre is a city of about 250,000 people. It's always been a seaport, but for the past one hundred years or more, it has been an industrial city. We have a lot of chemical factories. I don't find it a pretty city, because of the damage from World War II. Le Havre was totally devastated and bombed. After the war, the city hired an architect named Auguste Perret to beautify it. He must have tried hard, but it still resembles an eastern European town, like Stalingrad.

Lots of concrete, wide streets, but still on the water. In the wintertime, the wind blows hard, and here in Normandy the weather is always cold and rainy. Sometimes, like in the summer, it's pleasant because you have the sea, and there are some nice places to visit not far away, like the coastal resort towns of Honfleur and Deauville, which are about fourteen and fifty miles away respectively. But as a place to grow up, Le Havre was really horrible. Simply dreary, gray, and horrible."

"Okay then, instead of Le Havre, could you tell me about your family when you were growing up?"

Karyn stood up and put her daughter into the highchair. She handed her a cookie, passed them to us, and began again.

"I grew up as an only child. Every Thursday night, my cousins and I would go to my grandparents because they were not working that day. We would arrive at their house after school, first take our bath, then watch a little TV, and my grandmother always made *crêpes* for us. I guess we did that until I was eight or so. It was a routine I could count on.

"When I was nine, my parents split up, and I began living with my grandparents full-time. During my elementary school years, my great-grandfather would pick me up each day after school, since my grandparents were working. They worked in a theater."

Karyn popped another cookie onto the tray of her daughter's highchair. "My grandfather worked in the ticket booth, and my grandmother worked as an usher. She was the lady who took you from the entrance to your seat. I don't know if they did this in America, but in France you were supposed to give her a tip. The first part of the show was a documentary, and then in between the movies, and during the intermission, ladies sold ice cream, cookies, candies, and chocolate from big baskets. It was my grandmother's job to handle that, too. My grandfather would run the mechanical part of the film."

"Oh, he was a projectionist," Josiane chimed in. Josiane had learned English in the U.S. in her thirties, so she was eager to help Karyn, who was struggling with her English. *I am beholden.*

"At the beginning of many shows—not only the movies—they used to have chanteuse—or singers. Sometimes they had big names like Charles Aznavour, Josephine Baker—a lot of big stars."

Josiane's eyes widened. She recognized both stars; I recognized Baker.

"During World War II?" I asked. *I'm always seeking the war connection.*

"Yes, my grandparents were born in 1923. They would have been eighteen in 1941. My mom was born in 1945, right after the war." *Yes, her mother is my age.*

"Did your grandfather go into the war?"

"No, I'm not sure why. But I know they had a rough time, though, because they stayed in Le Havre while the bombardment continued. There were also many food restrictions. Because of that experience, when I grew up in my grandparents' house, they always had a lot of food—like a small supermarket set up in their basement. They made certain I had everything, and I knew they were compensating for the time when they had had so little. They overstocked the cupboards with cans of food—just for the pure pleasure of knowing they could have something if they simply wanted it."

"I can understand that," I said. "I'm told that my family, too, struggled to have enough food during the war, but especially during the Great Depression. But we never experienced life with war on our doorsteps. The aftermath of war must

have made a huge impression on all the following generations of your family."

"Yes, I think that I am a lot like my grandparents, because
they taught me how important it is to make certain we do
not have to do without. They were nice people, mind you.
But my grandmother was also extremely strict and severe.
Quite straight. My grandfather seemed to be more of a sensi-
ble guy . . . fragile, though, and I think the war left more
'stretch marks' on him than on her. I am speaking of him in
the past because he died just two and a half years ago. I considered him to be my 'Daddy'; in fact, he gave me away at my
wedding . . . and I think this is the part that I have not dealt
with yet. I stayed close to him and I learned of his sickness
not long before he died."

"I remember when that happened, Karyn," I said. "I knew
you were close, and now I understand even more of your
connection."

"Fortunately, I was able to come back from the U.S. to
see him in April of that year, and he died the following
month. My family had not told me how ill he was before-
hand, until I forced them to tell me the truth . . . and by then
it was almost too late. They said they didn't want to worry
me." Tears welled up in her eyes; her head dropped down.

"At least you were able to see him before he passed
away," I said softly.

"Yes," she said, "but I found it painful because I wanted to
have spent more time with him than I had been allowed. He
died at age seventy-nine."

Josiane nodded soulfully. "I understand. I barely had time
to say goodbye to my mother before she passed away last
fall."

A silence filled the room; the only sounds were coming

from the baby, who found pleasure in mashing her cookie against the tray.

"When my own mother died," I said, "I thought I had been well prepared, as she had been ill for a long time. But I realized no matter how much time I'd had to prepare, I still was not ready. It is never easy to lose a parent."

Karyn wiped away her tears. "It is odd that my grandfather died first. He was the one who always worried about my grandmother, because she had had a heart attack. She had difficulty walking around, and he worried about her falling. He thought he would be the last to go, but my Mom and I always thought that it would be best if he was first. He was such an old-fashioned guy, and not able to prepare a meal on his own, much less take care of himself in other ways. As it turns out, my grandmother is still living, but in a nursing home."

"So, who taught you how to cook?" I asked, changing the subject. "Your great-grandmother? Your grandmother or your mother?"

"Oh, not my great-grandmother," she laughed, tossing her hair back again. "She was not a good cook."

"Even with her running the *café* in Le Havre?"

"No, because a *café* in France does not serve food like you might think. It is mostly drinks, like alcohol, sodas, coffee, or tea, like in a bar. In France the word *café* simply means coffee."

"I didn't realize that," I said. "So, did you help your grandmother in the kitchen?"

"I helped her, but mostly with the cleanup afterwards. She didn't like a speck of dust on anything. No flour on the counters. No crumbs left on the table. When I helped, it was just to clean up the mess."

Our eyes went to the cookie mess happening beside us on

Cassiopée's tray. Cookie crumbs were all over her ringlet-circled face. An angelic smile smeared with chocolate residue beamed across at us. We couldn't help but laugh.

"I'm not like my grandmother at all when it comes to raising my daughters. I remember my grandmother would ask me to help her cook at home, but truthfully, she never had the patience to teach me. Neither did my mom. I didn't learn to cook until I met my husband, Laurent."

"Does he cook?"

"Very well. Better than me! But now I'm starting to cook everything, because I want to do that."

"You must enjoy cooking now, don't you? In Texas you were quite good at it."

"Thank you, but I'm always fearful of the results!"

"Aren't we all. I still marvel at the tasty sea scallops you prepared for me and my husband in Austin. How did you do that? I have searched through all my French cookbooks, and I haven't seen anything that tells me how you managed that. They were fabulous. Where did you learn that?"

"From my mother and grandmother. My grandmother taught me a trick. When you cook sea scallops they usually shrink. She learned during the war if you put scallops in a bit of boiling milk for just a minute or two, they will absorb the milk, puff up, and not shrink. You then take them out of the milk, place them on a paper towel to absorb the milk, then sauté them in a plenty of butter, garlic, parsley . . ."

"Let me tell you, it made the difference," I said.

"Another way I learned to cook scallops is an extremely old way," Karyn continued. "You put the sea scallop back into its shell and add a Béchamel sauce, a little Swiss cheese, and pop it into the oven or under the broiler. This is usually an appetizer, but I think it is too rich. I suppose the new way to cook them would be to eliminate the cream sauces and cook with fewer calories."

"You were in the States too long!" I laughed. "What kind of foods do you remember enjoying when you were growing up?"

"The *crêpe*. That brings back such wonderful memories."

"Oh, you too," Josiane squealed. "That's exactly what I would say." She leaned forward in her chair and scooped up another cookie.

"Were your grandmother's *crêpes* sweet or savory?"

"We had both. In the beginning, she placed a piece of ham, Swiss cheese, a mirror egg, or a flat egg..."

"A mirror egg?" I echoed.

"That is the same as your sunny-side-up egg. The *crêpe* would be folded over like a quesadilla. You know how that is shaped?" I nodded. We had both lived in Texas.

She continued. "Sometimes it is simply flapped over. That's what my grandmother did for us kids. After that, we would eat *crêpes* with a bit of sugar or chocolate or delicious chestnut purée. Of course, that's not good for weight watchers, but we loved them. It was particularly good for the stomach," she said, patting her belly. "And the spirit."

She paused for a moment. "I also remembering having veal liver, which I love."

"That's interesting," I said. "My mother used to plague us kids with beef liver, but once I discovered that Campbell's Cream of Mushroom soup could mask the musky flavor, I learned to enjoy it as an adult."

"But, Carole," Josiane said, "veal liver is much tastier than beef liver."

"But, of course. Veal would be more tender. How was the veal liver prepared?"

"Sauté the veal liver lightly in butter, and for the adults

you add a bit of onions. At the end you sprinkle on a bit of raspberry vinegar. That's for the grown-ups, not the little ones. Do not overcook."

"My *maman* usually used *mel four*, also a type of vinegar," Josiane said.

"*Oui!* That too. I had almost forgotten," Karyn said.

"That makes sense," I chimed in. "The vinegar would cut the wild or strong flavors, right?"

"Definitely," Karyn said, nodding. "And my grandmother also would cook round rice in milk with sugar, vanilla, and raisins, in a dish called *teurgoule*. And she prepared *semoule*, which is semolina, a tiny grain, much smaller than couscous.

"On holidays or birthdays, my favorite meal was always the *crêpe* or veal liver. My birthday cake would be homemade or purchased from the *patisserie*. A birthday celebration in France is becoming more American, where you have a lot of friends over. But when I was a child, we usually just had family. When we reached our teen years, we might invite some friends over, play records or music, lower the lights, and dance a little."

"What were your favorite holidays?" I asked.

"I remember going on holiday with my grandparents and my cousins in the summertime."

"Oh, you're talking about vacations. Tell me about them."

"As a teen, we went twice to Brittany, to a small village, not to the beach. I believe it was Mür de Bretagne. Absolutely in the middle of nowhere. We stayed in a hotel. Another time we went to a vacation camp and rented a small cabin in Chantonnay, which is in the Pays de Loire (Loire Country). Funny, I don't remember ever going to the beach."

I can imagine this is every teen's experience of vacation with family. It can be loathsome. Nothing positive to report.

Karyn continued. "Oh, but the most wonderful vacation we ever had was in the Balearic Islands south of Spain. We went to a resort with a swimming pool. Of course, there was a beach all around, but we never went to the beach. We stayed at the club enjoying the pool, the activities, and the hotel excursions. That was the nicest time. Of course, we did not go every year.

"You know, the person I am today is because of my grandparents. They showed me how to respect people. How to be nice. Sometimes, I think, too nice." She laughed.

"They did a lovely job, Karyn," I said. She blushed and tipped her head.

Suddenly she popped up from her chair and pulled a platter of *charcuterie* and a bottle of white wine from the refrigerator and brought them to the table. She took a fresh baguette from the pantry and handed it to me with a cutting board and knife. I began to slice the bread into chunks; Karyn opened the wine and filled three glasses. We were set. With our mouths filled intermittently with salamis, cheeses, cornichon pickles, little onions, and wine, our conversation rambled on. It was a delectable repast.

"Sharing food with another human being is an intimate act that should not be indulged in lightly."

—M.F.K. Fisher

Normandy

CHAPTER FOUR

An Algerian Influence in France

Rouen

A couple of hours later, we were whirring through the countryside as Josiane raced to reach the city of Rouen just after Louisette had arrived home from work. She knew we had only that evening to chat, and she wanted to make sure I received another unique French point of view.

"Who is Louisette?" I asked. "And how does she fit into your family's story?" I was looking forward to meeting another family from Normandy.

"Good questions, Carole. She was a friend of my best friend, Gigi, in high school. That's how I met her. She grew up in Bouligny, in the Lorraine near my hometown of Piennes, and her father worked in the iron mines with my father. She has remained a friend even though her family moved from France to Algeria and stayed there for over thirty years."

"Why Algeria?"

"Louisette's father was Algerian, and when the Algerian War with France ended, he took his French wife and their daughter, Louisette, and moved back to Oran in Western Algeria, near Morocco. So Louisette has recipes to share as a Frenchwoman from a foreign land—Algeria."

"Marvelous! I'm sure there will be more than a few couscous recipes. Say, didn't two of your brothers serve in Algeria during the war? What time frame was that?"

"The Algerian War was waged from 1954 to 1962. My brother Martial spent a year in Algeria when he was in the Army. He used to talk about working on a farm there, which is what he does here. He seemed to enjoy that experience. And my brother Gérard was in the Navy over there. They both had stories to tell. *Oh, là, là.*"

Josiane rolled through the downtown section of Rouen, crossing the Seine once, then twice, weaving her way to her friend's home. In an offhand way, she pointed out the Old Market Square where Jeanne d'Arc had been burned at the stake, then proceeded north into the hills above the city. No further explanation followed. I remembered a conversation in Reims with Martine, Josiane's sister-in-law—at the start of our culinary tour through the Champagne country—who'd told us that Jeanne d'Arc had led the French Dauphin to Reims and the cathedral there to be crowned King of France after the Hundred Years' War. Knowing how she had met her end made my head swim.

We wound our way up the streets to a row of apartment buildings perched at the top of a hill, pulled into a parking lot, and prepared to unload our suitcases. I looked around. The cream-colored, modern-looking apartment buildings appeared to be about ten years old yet looked like they had been through their own war. Window screens hung askew, paint was peeling off the doors, debris lay about the front entrance, and broken auto glass lay at our feet in the parking lot.

"Louisette's apartment is on the seventh floor, Carole, and there are no elevators. Sorry, but I don't think we should leave anything in the car," Josiane said, focusing on the debris at our feet.

I stared hard at my suitcases, urging them to carry themselves—hauling luggage was never my best moment.

"I know there is a lot to carry, but as you can see, this is not a safe neighborhood," Josiane prompted again. "This is a place for refugees of all sorts."

"Refugees? Is Louisette a refugee?" I pulled my large black bag out of the station wagon.

"I would say so. Louisette and her husband were forced to flee from their home in 1994. The Algerians were beginning to take back their land and had become more threatening to the French who lived there. It was the beginning of terrorist attacks in Algeria. When Louisette and her husband left, they were allowed to take only the suitcases they could carry. Nothing more. I'm certain she will tell you about it."

I looked down at my large bags and realized I had never been forced into such devastating circumstances. I needed to buck up! Dragging our suitcases across the parking lot, we turned into a stairwell and up, up, up we went toward Louisette's apartment. What made the struggle so memorable was not the seven-story slog, but the deep abiding aromas that filled the stairwell. What were those wonderful fragrances? Was that cumin, saffron, or perhaps cinnamon? My appetite was whetted with every inhalation and every step. Was it coming from more than one kitchen? Each floor seemed to add to this ethereal aromatic cloud.

I don't know if she heard us banging our roller bags up the stairway, but Louisette opened the door immediately upon our arrival and hugged Josiane to her. Louisette was tall with angular features, short curly brown hair, and a precise way of speaking. The quiet warmth she showed me—a veritable stranger—helped me feel comfortable as soon as I entered her home. And the fact that those aromas were emanating from that very apartment was gift enough to add to our welcome.

Louisette apologized for her husband's absence. "Majid is in Heidelberg, Germany where our son, his wife, and our two granddaughters are preparing to move back to Paris. We're excited to have them much closer to us, and Majid is helping them."

"Carole, you would enjoy Majid," Josiane said. "He is a most gracious and entertaining host. Please give him my love when you talk to him next, Louisette. And mmmmh, it smells so goooood in here."

After using all our energy to drag our bags up the stairs, and having staved off our now urgent hunger, we took the flutes of champagne Louisette handed us, as she motioned us to step outside.

"The sun is setting over the city," she said, "so let's take our glasses onto the balcony."

We were just in time to catch the golden sunlight flicker off the tops of the Rouen Cathedral and the buildings far down the hill below.

"*Tchin-tchin!*" we said in unison. Within minutes, a palette of heavenly hues turned a rosy peach as it glanced off the Seine in the distance, dimmed, and was gone. The air immediately chilled and Louisette ushered our little party back inside.

I had moved through the apartment so quickly when we arrived, I had barely noticed Louisette's home. The rooms were not spacious, but large enough to embrace her whole family. Throughout the home, bits and pieces of Algeria hung on the walls, rested on the floors, and graced her living space. For someone who had not been permitted to take any of her belongings when she fled Algeria, she had managed to collect or re-collect some treasures from her former life.

Louisette disappeared into the kitchen and returned with a platter of mini-blini with duck *pâté* and a *tzatziki* sauce that she placed on a copper coffee table before us. Josiane and Louisette chatted for a few minutes to catch up, in French, of course. Then Josiane turned to me. *"Question, s'il vous plaît?"*

Maybe I wasn't prepared—as I never really seemed to be for the impromptu and even the choreographed interviews—but I found myself quickly shifting the mini-blini to my opposite hand so I could get to business. I grabbed pen and paper. "So, Louisette, where were your parents from?" Flipping on the tape recorder, I took a breath and a sip of my aperitif.

"During World War II, my father fled Algeria to France. Once the war was over, my parents, who had met and lived in Paris, where I was born, moved with me to Bouligny, near Piennes. That is where my father took a job in the iron mines. After the war, the mines were the only places hiring . . ."

"Exactly as I told you, Carole," Josiane chimed in. She smiled broadly. She had brought me to yet another person who shared a similar perspective on her beloved France.

"Oui! Lorraine is where I was raised. I don't remember living in Paris. *La* Lorraine is my country! I went to school there, and my best friend was Ghislaine, and that is how I met Josiane. I still have a number of friends there and even continue to vacation there."

"Gigi was the connection between Louisette and me," Josiane said. "I told you about her, didn't I, Carole? She was my brother Gérard's first love." Her eyebrows arched high.

I nodded. Her brother had fallen madly in love with Gigi in high school. And when she would have nothing to do with him, he joined the Navy and sailed away—to Algeria, it turned out.

Josiane turned back to Louisette. "I remember your mother very well. I can still see her with the car keys jingling, jingling in her hand. You had a little Renault and, extraordinarily for a woman of that time, she was able to drive. Your mother had class! But I can't remember why you ended up living in Algeria?"

"My father was Algerian, and he always said that when he retired, he would go back to his home country. Sure enough, he did, and I had no choice but to go along with his decision. For me, it was a real shock. I had friends in Bouligny and Piennes. I was going to college and doing well. It was terribly difficult to move away from all that I knew and loved. But, my mother supported his decision fully."

"It was also heartbreaking for Gigi and me," Josiane said.

"Moving to Algeria was disastrous, but also a little exciting. I was young—seventeen, eighteen. Everything was different. I was discovering not just a new country, but a new language, a new way of life, another climate. Of course, it was overwhelming at first."

"Wasn't it shortly after you arrived in Algeria that your mother developed cancer?" Josiane asked.

"Yes—and peace be with her—she died exactly a year after we arrived in Oran. I was nineteen then and wound up alone with my father. But in the meantime, I had met Majid. My mother had met him, too. Josiane, I remember you came to meet me in Paris when I came from Algeria to visit my mother at the Villejuif Hôpital, the hospital. Then I returned to Oran. Shortly after that my mother passed away, and it was not clear what my father's intentions were. But when I realized he planned to arrange a marriage for me, and of course not with Majid, things became strained. So, I married Majid!" Her voice rose in triumph.

"You married and lived happily ever after," Josiane laughed.

"Yes, we got married, we were happy, and we had children. The end."

"Wow! Was that a difficult transition? Were you readily accepted into Majid's family?" I asked.

"I can't say I ever really integrated into Algeria. I did have contact with his family, and they were good people. In fact, my in-laws thought our marriage was acceptable and were very supportive. We would all get together, including the children and grandchildren, so it was a happy time."

"What was it like to get together as a family?"

"To socialize, we would sit on thick pads, like mattresses, covered with beautiful fabrics and resting on low wooden frames. Food and drinks were served on low copper tables, like this one, and quite common in most houses," she said pointing to the table before us. "But the table was much lower to the floor.

"Their tradition was to sit low to the ground for conversation among family members. But for me it was uncomfortable. They realized I had difficulties sitting like them, so they gave me a little table to sit at. There they all were, sitting on the floor chatting and laughing, and there I was, higher than anybody else, feeling I wasn't part of them. And I wasn't. The family sat close together, and they all would eat out of the same bowl with their fingers. That, too, made me uncomfortable, but my in-laws kindly gave me a plate and a napkin. In fact, it was quite an honor, but I felt like I didn't belong. And it was my own doing. Finally, at one of those family gatherings, when they brought me the little table, I said 'No' and sat near the ground and ate like them.

"Unfortunately," she said, laughing, "I wasn't wearing a long dress like the Algerian women, but a short skirt. It was not practical or even decent. I tried to pull on the hem of my skirt to hide my knees, and my mother-in-law came to my rescue with a piece of fabric to cover myself. I think that was the only concession I made," she said matter-of-factly.

I looked up from my notes to see if she was joking, but to my surprise she clearly was not.

"I didn't have problems with my in-laws, like many others in that situation. I really liked them. When I visited, I would always bring them something. And my mother-in-law regularly came to our home, because of my children, and stayed for a few days. I enjoyed her company, but I didn't encourage her to stay more than a couple of days, because I could see she was not at ease in our French household, with my French furniture. I never did adopt their lifestyle or customs. But I no longer had a problem visiting their home."

"Did you prepare French food, or did you cook Algerian food for your husband?" I asked.

"I knew how to cook some Algerian foods, because my father was Algerian, but I mainly cooked French food. Even though Majid didn't know about all the sauces, like *béchamel* or *béarnaise* sauce, he was willing to learn, and he learned fast. I also worked outside the house at a French school, so a woman came every day to our home to take care of the children. As it turned out, I didn't have to cook, because Khadra did it all for me. And because she prepared Algerian food, I didn't have to learn."

"She was quite a cook! I remember her *gambas. Oh, là, là,*" said Josiane. "That's shrimp, by the way."

Louisette continued. "We have many delicious Algerian specialties. Of course, there is couscous, but also vegetable soups like *shorba,* and pastries with honey and almonds. And because Algerian families are large, they eat lots of bread.

They never eat big pieces of meat, except on *l'Aïd El Kebir*. This holiday or holy day is known as the Lamb's Feast, an important Muslim religious celebration, where each person receives a big portion of meat. That in itself is special."

"Could you describe some foods you ate at this celebration?"

She crossed her legs and took a sip of her aperitif. "First, the couscous was presented in a salad bowl, or similar deep dish. Four to five persons share that dish, each one eating with his fingers, making his own hole into the couscous and eating from that hole. The use of silverware is limited. There is meat in the couscous, usually lamb or chicken. Chicken is the cheapest meat and most readily available. Muslims never eat pork.

"In the old days there were many butchers in Algeria, and they carried all kinds of meat, but the meat was overpriced. The *merguez* sausage that we grew to love is an Algerian specialty with leftover beef or mutton. It is spicy and filled with fat, but delicious!"

"Oh, I love *merguez*, too!" Josiane said. "I cook with it whenever I can get it in the States."

"Speaking of food, may we adjourn to the dining room? I believe the chicken *tagine* is ready," Louisette said, getting to her feet.

The three of us migrated into the dining room, which was formally set on our behalf. A crystal bowl of fresh flowers sat in the middle of the table, with silver and china gracing all three places.

"This is lovely, Louisette. Thank you for going to all this trouble," I said.

"Yes, this is lovely. Are these some of your things from Algeria?" Josiane asked. "I thought you were unable to bring anything back."

"After several years we collected some of our old things, and added some new, but mostly these are antiques from my French grandmother. Unfortunately, we have very little from our old way of life." She sighed. We took our seats.

"You said when you lived in Algeria you didn't live in an Algerian manner. What did you mean?" I asked.

Louisette served us from the steaming hot terrine of chicken, couscous, and vegetables. The fragrance of cayenne, cinnamon, cumin, and saffron filled the air. The heady aroma almost distracted me from listening, as Louisette replied.

"In Algeria I had a quality of life that I would not have had in France—not with my educational level. But I lived in a French area of the city, so I was surrounded by my own language and my own culture. Of course, I was working. My husband was working. But I had Khadra, my cook, maid, and full-time nanny. When I came home in the evening, I had a ready-made meal. It was quite wonderful, and I was terribly spoiled." A sad grin caressed her otherwise sharp features.

"When her children, Nour-Eddine and Nadia, came to visit me in California during their vacation, Khadra came with them. I loved it, too," Josiane said.

"She was such a wonderful help and was not very expensive. When I see young people here struggling—both parents working and they still must take care of their children, the house, shopping, cooking, cleaning—I realize how privileged I was. Where I work now in Rouen, I regularly have calls from employees forced to stay home because of sick children. At home in Algeria, if the children were sick, I still could go to work."

The first morsels of the chicken tagine were almost too hot to taste, but once the spices inched across my tongue with delayed delight, my mouth was ecstatic. "This is delicious!" I murmured through another mouthful of food. "Simply delicious!" Again, a shy smile glimpsed Louisette's lips as Josiane echoed my sentiments.

"Thank you. I hoped you would like it," she said. For not having had to cook for years in Algeria, she had certainly learned to make up for it.

"You mentioned earlier that you were working at a French school in Algeria. Were you teaching?" I asked.

"I was working in Administration. I always worked in an office. I still do."

"How did people react to women working in Algeria?"

"Many women worked as teachers, M.D.s, nurses, and lawyers. Education was free. The only thing a young woman needed was parental authorization to study."

"Is it still the case in Algeria?" Josiane asked. She scooped another spoonful of couscous and chicken and ladled it onto my plate, then her own.

"When I left a few years ago, women still could work and study. But they had to wear the chador, a face veil, to go to the university. We didn't have harsh times like the women in Afghanistan. But during the past few years the living conditions have worsened."

"Are women doctors still able to practice, and can they treat men?" I asked.

"I believe so, but no matter what, an MD is an MD whether the doctor is a man or a woman."

"That's amazing. I read that many Muslim countries no longer allow women to function as doctors, even if they need doctors."

"When our French soldiers left Algeria, following the Algerian War in 1962," Josiane said, "customs, traditions, and religions were evolving in a rather European way, meaning they were more relaxed and accepting. Algeria had been a

French colony from 1830 to 1962. Now, it has gone back to stricter rules, and is still getting more and more restrictive for women. The *integrists* are gaining ground."

My eyebrows must have shot up, because Josiane immediately explained that *integrists* are a fundamentalist sect of Muslim that is more radical in nature and more conservative in their view of women.

"But the Algerian women fight it," Louisette said.

"Did they have any clout?" I asked.

"In the government, there used to be women as Ministers. But now? I don't know. Women still work freely in Algeria. Their situation is not comparable to the life of women in the Middle East, like Afghanistan."

"It sounds like you kept your French identity in Algeria. Is that right?" I asked.

"*Mais oui!* I guess I am like my mother—very, very French."

"Very independent, too!" Josiane laughed.

"She was something, wasn't she?" said Louisette. "And, yes, it is true I made little effort to be part of Algerian society, but I certainly tried with my husband, and now I recognize how understanding he was. He is a very good and generous man."

"Carole," Josiane said softly, "Majid is a man who will make you forget about racism. You cannot help but respect and love him."

"What was your relationship like with your father, Louisette? After your marriage?"

"I had always had a good relationship with my father before my marriage, but when he refused to allow me to marry Majid, I never saw him again."

"Oh, no!" I hadn't expected her response and found myself floundering for words. "How sad for you—and your children," I stammered.

"Yes, it was sad. Later, I learned that he remarried." She stood up to pour more wine, while Josiane carried empty plates to the kitchen and returned with a platter of cheeses. They both settled back down at the table.

"Louisette, did you raise your children according to the Algerian traditions, or the French, or both?"

"I tried to give my children a French education. Regarding their religious beliefs, I had only one small conflict with my husband. It didn't last very long. Majid is so nice, he understood. It happened at the time of Ramadan."

"Is Ramadan when Muslims fast and repent?" I asked.

"Yes, Ramadan is an important pillar of Muslim religion. It is a happy and joyous period, especially at the end of the day when fasting is over. Fasting is from sunrise to sunset, so people can eat during the night and go to bed very late. Working hours are different, too. It is best not to have an important business to tend to at that time of year. They fast so they can experience how people who do not have enough to eat might feel. That is one of the reasons. There must be others, but I don't know what they are. Too bad that Majid is not here. You will have to come back.

"But to answer your questions, when our children were small, I didn't want my husband to impose his religion on them. I believe that when children are young, we can tell them the stories related to any religion. Those stories are very interesting, and I learned a lot about religion myself that way. But one year, when my son was fourteen, we asked the children to decide if they wanted to follow the traditions of Ramadan. My daughter said yes; my son said no. But his father continued to pressure him, and my son complained to me. I would tell him it was all right not to fast, but then if you went into hiding to eat, it didn't work so well. You smelled like food, and people noticed. I knew some people whose children said, 'Yes, Dad, we do fast and observe Ramadan,' but it wasn't true. I didn't want that for our children. So, I told my husband, 'You cannot force him to do the Ramadan.' And I told my son, 'Take responsibility, and tell your father what you want.' Then my husband said, 'I do not want to know anything, and the neighbors and my family should not know anything about it either.'"

"I was not obligated to do the Ramadan. Majid's family knew that I had a different religion, and it was accepted. But according to the Muslim religion, the children had to obey their father. Algerian society is very patriarchal, and the father must be obeyed. It finally went smoothly. I told my son to have his lunch as usual, but at the end of the day, he had to do like the whole family, come to the table with everybody else, and have the evening dinner. It was like a feast. We had wonderful dishes, we ate late, and after dinner we would go out and meet our friends, and we would walk and talk. The streets were safe. It was quite fun."

"How long does Ramadan last?"

"Thirty days. It takes place at the time of the new moon. Every year the dates change, and it starts earlier than the previous year."

"Do you remember some of the foods prepared for the feast?"

"Before I answer that, I would like to add that since we have been living in France, my husband continues to observe this religious period of fasting, and for him, I do as if we still were in Algeria. He sometimes tells me, 'Do not worry about preparing the soup! Just take a 'fast soup,' which is the *chorba*. The meal is usually a very fancy meal which begins with one dish eaten by all those observing Ramadan—the *chorba*—and each family follows in its own traditional way."

"Please tell me about the *chorba*. What is it, and why is it so special?"

"Like I was saying, at the end of the daily fasting time, there is one specialty soup, called *chorba* or *harira*. The *harira* is made in Oran, on the far western edge of Algeria, near the Moroccan border. In fact, the best *harira* that you can possibly eat is made in Morocco. This is the soup to break the fasting of the day. Then there are many dishes, all prepared in small quantities, for example, like what I prepared tonight with chicken, tomatoes, and bell peppers."

"Plus, those wonderful spices we smelled all the way up the stairway," Josiane said. "There was cumin, cinnamon, and what else?"

"I thought I tasted saffron. Is that right?" I asked.

"It is! I make this dish so often I compose it by rote."

"Well, it's a delicious 'by rote,' that's for sure," I laughed. "But continue telling us about the dishes of the feast."

"They also prepare *matouda*, which is mashed potatoes with a little bit of spices—often cumin, garlic, and parsley. We make little cakes with it, roll them in flour, and fry them. They are very good.

"I forgot to tell you about the *shorba* and *harira* soups. They are made just about the same way, with the same ingredients. The difference is at the end. In the *shorba* we add vermicelli, and in the *harira* we add a very special spice, which I have. And we add a little bit of flour mixed with water to thicken the soup. When Majid visits his family in Algeria, he always brings back some of that spice." Louisette jumped up and disappeared into the kitchen and returned with a small jar that she opened. It emitted a pungent aroma.

"This spice blend is called *la tête du magasin* or 'the head of the shop' because it is composed of many different spices. I believe it contains a little bit of black pepper, red pepper, cumin, coriander, cinnamon, saffron, and cayenne pepper."

Josiane and I passed the jar back and forth, sniffing and enjoying the fragrant concoction.

"Do you want to take some home, Carole?" Josiane asked.

My expression must have given me away. "Yes, along with this recipe. This has been absolutely delectable."

"I'll make sure you have some soup recipes when you leave in the morning," Louisette said. "You must understand that depending on the region where the recipe is prepared, the results are different. The woman preparing the soup will add her own spice or mix her own blend of spices. There are many family traditions that influence the cooking. I believe," she said, tapping her forefinger against her chin, "there is another spice mix called *Ras al-Hanut*, which is a Moroccan mixture composed of pungent spices such as cinnamon, cardamom, cloves, nutmeg, turmeric, and black pepper. That may be easier to find. The ten spices most important to Moroccan cuisine are cayenne, cinnamon, turmeric, ginger, black pepper, aniseed, sesame seeds, cumin, paprika, and saffron."

"This is so delightful!" I clapped my hands with joy. "I so appreciate you sharing your recipes. It sounds like your mixed marriage has been quite successful." I imagined that if you could share two religions and two cultures in one household, it must be a success.

"*Oui!* Very! Marrying a good man and creating my own family with two beautiful children has given me great happiness. I was raised as an only child, and Majid was raised in a large family, so we were fortunate not to encounter major difficulties. We were financially sound, our health was good, our children did well, and, yes, you could say our marriage was and still is very successful.

"I recognize that I had a good life. I know of many French women who were married to an Algerian husband, and the women had to raise their children in the Algerian tradition. They couldn't express themselves. Even some of the working French women were treated poorly."

"That's what I would have expected," Josiane said sadly.

"Yes, there were many sad situations, and lots of poor people."

I, too, expected it would have been the norm. I shifted the subject and asked Louisette, "Since you worked and lived in a French environment, did you learn to speak Algerian?"

"Sadly, I never made the effort, but I can understand a lot. My father would speak to me in Algerian. If I really wanted too, I suppose I could speak it. But it does not come naturally."

"How is Majid adjusting here in France?" Josiane asked.

"He's doing just fine. If it weren't the case, we would return to Algeria."

"Did he learn French because Algeria was a French colony?"

"Yes, Algeria was a French colony for 132 years. It has been celebrating its independence since 1962. So many Algerians have only regrets! The only income source for Algeria is from their own oil fields, but these have been developed by foreign companies, such as France, when it was a colony, and Russia and other foreign companies after its independence. None of it was developed because of Algerian technology."

"It really is too bad, because Algeria is such a beautiful country. Tourism could bring them so much more," Josiane said dreamily.

"Yes, they have the most beautiful beaches," Louisette said, as she picked up our cheese plates and headed into the kitchen. She returned carrying a plate of *Sablés de Caen*, small delicate cakes with cups of hot tea.

We sat for another hour talking, and after helping with the dishes I retired to the guest room, while the two old friends caught up. I lay across the bed and wrote down some of my thoughts from the evening. I had been invited into not only a French home, but a French-Algerian home. That gave me a totally new perspective and appreciation of Algeria and the wonderfully rich influences that country has given to France.

One thing I enjoy most about traveling through France—or any country—is experiencing the diversity of cultures found in a single country. Josiane taught me to appreciate not only the foods and customs of today, but also those of the past and of the immigrants who enriched the culture by adding their own flavors, recipes, and traditions. I'm one lucky gal!

Normandy

CHAPTER FIVE

Stepping into Norman History

Josiane and I left Louisette's apartment the following morning, as she headed off to work. I was holding a sheaf of recipes, which were all in French, but Louisette had certainly delivered.

"The time together was much too short," I said. "Thank you for bringing me here to meet Louisette. Her French experience in Algeria has given me a whole new appreciation of Algerian culture, and certainly their food and history. I must say, I found Louisette unusually direct."

"You're welcome. Yes, she was forthcoming. And that is what I like about her. You never have to guess what she's thinking or feeling. But we need to get a move on because I planned a busy day for us. I'm taking you through parts of Normandy you've never seen." Josiane put the car in gear and headed out of the parking lot.

"That would cover most of Normandy, as I've only been to a couple of coastal cities—Le Havre, Honfleur, and Deauville. And now Rouen."

"*Bon*! You've seen some of the best. And today we are on our way to Mont St. Michel. On the way I will take you to

Bayeux to see a unique tapestry that was completed shortly after William of Normandy conquered England in 1066. *Trés incroyable!* The entire story of William the Conqueror is woven into the cloth. It's not just about the war—it is so much more."

"Sounds fascinating! Where was it made?"

"It was made in England and later housed in the Bayeux Cathedral. If you can imagine, this cloth swept from the back of the cathedral, along the interior walls, past the nave, behind the altar at the front, and back down the other side. It is well over two hundred feet long. It is an amazing work of art, plus a hand-woven history lesson. These side trips I'm taking you on will show you more of the traditional methods used over the centuries, especially here in Normandy. We'll start in Bayeux."

We had reached the A13 thoroughfare at the westernmost part of the city and continued northwest at a lively clip.

"Beautiful! So, what we'll see in Bayeux is just one tapestry?"

"Not in the literal sense. It's a very long embroidered sequence of panels designed to tell the story of men, war, and how they faced the direst of consequences."

"It certainly fits at least one of the themes we are following. War."

"Do you wonder why you keep coming back to this subject, Carole?"

"Yes and no. It was your mother who taught me to bring up the subject. I'll never forget when I first asked about her life as a young wife, and she matter-of-factly described the devastating impact of raising children during wartime. From that point on, I brought up the subject myself. I want to understand French families, so I need to know what went on in their lives." I took a deep breath.

"But truthfully," Josiane said, "I don't know how possible that is. Once, when Albert Camus was asked to comment on his experiences in Paris during World War II, he said, 'To judge an event is impossible and immoral from the outside. It is in the midst of this absurd calamity that one retains the right to despise it.'"

"Wow! That sums it up, doesn't it?" I said. "I'll have to keep that in mind, since I'm writing from the 'outside.' And on that subject, I want to ask you about the Algerian War. I'm still trying to understand what Louisette told us. Did she move to Algeria during or after that war?"

"I think she went after my brother Gérard served in Algeria. I remember thinking I had lost two of my favorite people to Algeria. It must have been after 1962."

"I know nothing about this war, other than what you talked about last night. Can you tell me more?"

"All I remember was the war brought great divisiveness to our country. We heard about it every night on my father's radio. It began in 1954."

"Not so long after World War II."

She nodded. "France was just leaving Indochine, or Vietnam, where basically the Vietnamese had won. And the next thing our troops knew, they were being paraded through the streets of Algiers. As my brother Martial told us years later, 'There they were, marching along, resplendent in their red berets and green battle dress, as proof of France's resolve to keep Algeria French, but the Algerian people didn't even know we, the French, were coming.' In fact, when the settlers—the Algerian people under French colonial rule—saw our troops, they clapped wildly, thinking the troops were returning victorious from the Indochine War.

"I believe our men had been sent to reestablish French

rule in Algeria and immediately began chasing the 'nationalists' through the mountains and back again. It had something to do with a movement of Muslim puritans who wanted to restore the Islam religion back to its ancient rigors. Sound familiar?"

"Unfortunately, yes. The French were divided about this war, too?"

"Yes. I think the French had experienced too much war, and in too many places, both here and abroad. Too many mothers bemoaned the loss of their sons, and that time they became more vocal."

"If only women ruled the world," I muttered. "We were experiencing the same battle fatigue in the U.S. when World War II was followed by the Korean War, then Vietnam. Is there never an end?"

Josiane took a roundabout off the main highway onto a boulevard filled with brightly colored flowers. We followed the avenue into the ancient city of Bayeux, where she wheeled up to the famous Norman-Romanesque Cathedral of Our Lady in Bayeux.

We parked and I grabbed up a guidebook, as we headed up the walkway to the main doors.

"This cathedral was consecrated on 14 July 1077 in the presence of William, who was both Duke of Normandy and King of England," I read aloud from my trusty guidebook. "In fact, this book says this is the place where William (the Conqueror) forced Harold Godwinson (the last Anglo-Saxon King of England) to take an oath that led to the Norman conquest of England."

"That's what I recall, as well," chimed in Josiane. "The famous tapestry I told you about tells this very tale in meters of colorful threads and was designed to be used in this church. After lunch, I will take you to the museum that now safeguards the tapestry."

As we walked through the fine-looking church, I contemplated the millennia that had come before me—more than a thousand years of history, of people who had fought in dozens of wars, of the penitent, the stricken—all who had sought solace in this place. Despite being a Gothic cathedral, the building held an intimacy I didn't expect. The interior was well restored and there was a harmonic blend of Romanesque and Gothic elements. I marveled at the mix of architecture and the undiminished desire to continue the outreach of the church.

"I believe it's lunch time," Josiane said, interrupting the pall that was overtaking me. She always seemed to know when to divert my attention, and food most often did the trick. We made our way into a charming bistro, where we became "best friends" with Nicole, the waitress. As she served us a lunch of traditional Norman fare, including her recommended veal escalopes in butter, she returned again and again to answer our many questions about favorite holidays (hers was *Noël)* and traditional festivals—such as the annual Medieval Festival, a reenactment of William the Conqueror's days (or now, *Game of Thrones*).

"What specialty foods do they serve at the Festival?" I asked.

"Lentils! They serve lentils," she said.

"Lentils?" I asked, my face contorting in doubt. "Why lentils?"

"I believe it was a holdover from when the poor people had just lentils to eat, along with their bread. But most people come for the cider," she said and let out a giggle. "Nobody likes the lentils, but they are always available."

The doubt eased and I sat back and tucked into my *Tarte Tatin*, a delicate apple turnover, with all things butter, which made the apples sing in my mouth. Like Mme. Pund's—but without cinnamon. *Was that only yesterday?*

After lunch we headed down the street to the museum, where *La Tapisserie de Bayeux* was on permanent display. The linen tapestry is 231 feet long and 19.5 inches wide. Depicted in hand-embroidered scenes are the events leading up to and including the entire Battle of Hastings in 1066. The story is told from the Norman point of view, and the words are in Latin, or possibly Old English. Commissioned by William the Conqueror's half-brother, Bishop Odo, a bishop in Kent, England, the tapestry was created as pages of history to tell the story of William's crossing of the English Channel to successfully conquer England and become the first Norman or French king of England.

"What a daunting undertaking," I said.

"Yes, the meticulous detail could only have come from someone with personal knowledge of the events—sailing across the Channel with horses and soldiers aboard, the sailing vessels, the tools and weapons used in battle, the battles themselves, the chainmail uniforms of English and Norman soldiers—and so much more."

The afternoon was moving along, and Josiane directed me toward the door. "I have plenty of other things to show you," she said.

So, off we headed down the road to the copper and brass foundry in Villedieu-les-Poêles. That stop included another tour—about the manufacturing of traditional church bells. And madcap purchases of copper pots and pans for both of us, though we were not certain how we would get them home. Then, we hopped into the car and followed the late afternoon sun to our next destination, the Manoir de la Roche Torin.

Tucked along the southern banks of the Baie du Mont Saint-Michel, the setting sun flashed its last golden light across the windows of the stone-gray manor that loomed ahead of us—our destination for the night. Along the tree-lined entryway, we passed a small family chapel that appeared badly damaged. The stones and part of the roof lay in pieces on the ground.

"Is that damage from World War II?" I asked, wide-eyed. I'd already forgotten that this land had thousands of years of history.

"I don't think so, but we can find out." Josiane pulled up in front of the four-story manor house, which was made of irregular stones of granite and covered in a thick beard of ivy. An elegant staircase that swept down from the center of the house held a bevy of young men who rushed down the steps to assist us. I was relieved. Especially after hauling our luggage up seven flights of stairs the previous night and down again in the morning. Unfortunately for the young men, the luggage had to be hauled to our third-floor room. We were hustled into the main hall of the manor where we met our hosts, Guy Barreaux and his wife, before being escorted to our room.

After freshening up, we made our way to the main dining room on the lower level, where a large open-pit grill was set into the main wall. The heady aroma of the house specialty—spit-roasted *pré-salé d'agneau*, or roasted lamb—tantalized us both.

"What exactly is *pré-salé d'agneau?*" I asked Josiane. We were seated outdoors on a terrace, awaiting our table to be readied inside, and had ordered a bottle of local apple cider, another Normand specialty.

"You are in for a rare treat! The lovely lambs that graze

out there by the bay consume salt-encrusted marsh grasses."
She pointed just beyond the lawn of the manor, where sheep
were grazing along the waterline. "The salt seasons and flavors the meat—a rare delicacy from this area."

By the time we were led to our table in the glass-enclosed
dining room, only the lights high on top of Mont Saint-
Michel shone across the kilometer of water that separated us
from the island. A slight fog rising off the water eventually
obliterated the island and Mont St. Michel magically disappeared. We had arrived late enough in the day that I had not
realized how close the Mont was to where we were staying.

Josiane ordered *kir royales* for the two of us, which were
followed by a first course, *Poisson Soupe au Camembert.* The delectable soup was made with local fish and farm-fresh cream.
Tiny croutons bobbed across the surface like small boats and
anchored against lavish gratings of Camembert cheese.

"I've chosen a delightful Saumur wine, a Loire Valley vintage, to introduce you to that region before we arrive. That will
be after we leave Brittany. So much to see. So much to do . . ."

"And so many fine wines to sample," I added. "*Tchin-
tchin!*"

As you can imagine, my main course was the house specialty—the *pré-salé* lamb, while Josiane ordered *rouget,* a local
fish. Both fish and meat were moist and as succulent as the
rich aromas had promised.

"The lamb is only slightly salty," I remarked, "and tastes
surprisingly of a blend of fresh herbs." A savory mix of
aubergine (eggplant) and mushrooms lay under both the meat
and the fish, and *Potatoes Gratiné* made with fresh cream accompanied both dishes. Yes, the heart of the Normand diet
involves plenty of cream and cheese. And cider. *So how are the
French so slim?*

The cheese course followed, with an array of local cheeses such as *Livarot, Maroilles,* and *Gournay,* the likes of which we had sampled the past two nights. A lovely *Tarte au Pomme Flambé* with calvados was the final act, with flames literally shooting up but quickly extinguished before things got out of hand. Again, a new rendition on apple pie and the third time in three days we had eaten apple desserts. And, it wasn't even apple season. Or was it? We were in Normandy.

And with that, we trundled up the long stairway to our third-story room. It had been a long, full day. I doubt we remember hitting the bed.

In the morning, I awakened to peek out of our window and gaze across the waters of the bay to Mont Saint Michel. I had barely seen the infamous island the day before, and the morning sun revealed a distant golden crown rising above the tidal plain. I was giddy at the prospect that we would be spending part of the day there.

Josiane, on the other hand, seemed preoccupied with her computer and was making lists of contacts for another part of our tour. After breakfast she drove me to the base of Mont Saint Michel and bid me adieu. She had calls to make and had seen the Mont many times before, so I was on my own.

"No worries. It will be a challenge for you, Carole," she said as she shooed me out of the car.

I took the challenge and walked straight through the King's Gate and into a tourist office, where I took an English-led tour of the marvelous historic city.

Nestled on the Mont since the year 709, the village of Mont St. Michel was a swirl of cobbled medieval streets that marched up and up past one rustic half-timbered home and hostelry after another to bring the "pilgrims" over the past thirteen hundred years to their destination: the ultimate goal at the top, the Benedictine Abbey. I climbed up the Great Outer Staircase, past the well-preserved fortifications, which included medieval towers, corbelled turrets, bastions, ramparts, and parapets. All had been added over time and according to military need—giving the Mont the air of an impenetrable fortress.

Once the Holy Roman Empire declined, I was told, people turned to Christianity, and the Catholic Church became a steadying hand in a world without laws or direction. Monks from all over northern France and England sought a place to pray—to bring a semblance of peace to the soul if not the body. Over the many centuries, the protection of the Abbey meant the protection of all people. From William the Conqueror in 1066 to the soldiers in World War II, pilgrims have come to this holy place in the clouds to receive blessings and prayers for a safe return from war.

After a fascinating historical tour through the magnificent Abbey, I wandered back down the cobbled streets, contemplating how wars have caught people up in a whirlwind of choices—some easy, most extremely difficult. And religion became prominent in providing a safe haven. Yes, despite wars fought over religion, it also promised safety and calm. What a dilemma!

It was after one o'clock and I was famished. Putting aside thoughts of past wars, I decided to take time out for lunch at Mother Poulard's—or La Mère Poulard, where Josiane had promised I could find a traditional meal. It was there that I woofed down one of Mother's famous omelets. Prepared in large copper pans with extremely long handles, I watched the omelets being created over an open fire to bring these soufflé-like eggs to a delicate yet creamy texture. So light, so fluffy, and oh so delicious! Plus, a little tankard of cider. *Parfait!* (Perfect!)

When I finally met up with Josiane in the parking lot, she led me out to a point where we could look back across the tidal basin to the land. From there we could make out the manor where we were staying.

"I've heard back from my nephew, Christian," she said. "He is my brother Martial's oldest child, the one who was so close to Maman."

"Yes. He was going to do research on your mother's father—who might have died during World War I. Did he find out anything?"

"Yes. He had planned to meet up with us while we are in Brittany, as he lives only an hour or so south of here, near Rennes. But his business has called him out of the area."

"So, what did he say? Will we be able to meet with him on this trip?"

"I hope so. He has found information on the internet that he is excited to share with us!"

"Wonderful! What are the plans?"

"I'm working that out. If nothing more, we can visit his darling wife and daughters tomorrow, as that was what I had planned anyway."

As Josiane stood by the thick wall skirting the base of the Mont, the wind whipped up and blew her dark brown hair into spiky little points. I smiled at her and moved to her side to smooth down her newly formed horns.

"Oh, my goodness!" she said, whirling around. "*Vite! Vite!* Let's get back to the manor. I forgot that I scheduled an interview for you with the owner and chef, Monsieur Barreaux. Do you have your tape recorder and notepad with you?" She rushed me across the parking lot to the car.

CHAPTER SIX

An Interview with Guy Barreaux

Mont St. Michel

I snuggled deep into a down sofa in a quiet lounge adjacent to the dining room, arranged my papers around me, and flipped on my tape recorder. Josiane had once again sweet-talked someone into being interviewed by us. *She's such a gem!* I prepared myself for the unrolling of yet another story.

M. Barreaux, owner and head chef of the Manoir where we were staying, seated himself across from me. He and Josiane had been chatting amiably, and he seemed eager to hear our questions.

"How many cooks do you have working for you, Monsieur? And do you prepare just local foods?" Josiane asked, opening the interview.

"We have seven cooks from Normandy, and they typically prepare our local recipes. We do not represent all of Normandy in our recipes, as we use ingredients typical of just this area, such as fish and shellfish. I am happy to have you look at this menu," he said, handing the menu to me.

Although the menu was in French, it included historical photos of the manor and some family history.

"Josiane, ask him about the history of the manor," I said, pointing to the pictures.

"Did this manor come to you through your family?" she asked.

"No, it was acquired in two operations. First, my wife's uncle bought it. Later my wife and I bought it from him, with the intent to turn it into this hotel-restaurant."

"Were you already trained as a chef?"

"Yes, but when we purchased the house, I was working in other businesses. We bought the house solely because we wanted to return to our roots—to this region of Normandy. But the house required much restoration." He leaped up and disappeared from the room and returned with a photo album. He sat down between us on the sofa, which sagged with the weight of the three of us, as he began to explain.

"When this house was built in 1900, there was no electricity. So, we began our restoration in the room where we now have the large fireplace."

"Was the manor damaged in the war?" I asked, my voice rising. I was looking forward to more war stories.

"No, but when we bought it in 1966 it was in very poor condition, as you can see from these pictures. It was poorly maintained, particularly during the Occupation. Many of the walls took in too much humidity, so we had to take down walls and rebuild them entirely, but with the same stones."

"What an undertaking." I was staring at a photo with a jumble of stones on the ground next to one side of the manor.

"You were courageous to tackle such a big job," Josiane said. "Did you know at the start what you would have to do?"

"No, never," he laughed. "If we had known how much work was involved, I'm not sure we'd have taken on the project." He grinned and showed us two pictures of the manor with the sea reaching almost to the house during what he called the Great Tides.

"The Great Tides happen two times a year, on the spring and fall equinoxes."

"Have the high tides caused much damage?" I was thinking of the tides my husband and I contend with near the San Francisco Bay.

"No, not yet. But we have to keep an eye on them." He turned the page. "In this picture you can see snow on the ground, which is very rare."

"Really?" I peered more closely at the photos. "I thought because Normandy is so far north, snow would be common."

"Not really," he said. He settled in closer to me. "I showed you these pictures to let you know how we fell in love with this place. All our family comes back here to visit. My daughter, who lives in Paris, comes with her children for each vacation. Many friends also visit. When the hotel is closed for the holiday season, we have parties with friends and family, which is a special pleasure. We arranged the hotel as if it were a house, because it is truly our home."

"Yes, we noticed that, and it is very beautiful and comfortable," I said. "And thank you for sharing these pictures with us. Besides learning about regional recipes, I am also interested in how families share time together, and you have shown me exactly that."

"Monsieur Barreaux, Carole is writing a book about families and their traditional values—especially when it comes to food," Josiane said, steering us back to business. "When did you actually become a chef? You said it hasn't always been your profession."

"No, but I always liked the cuisine. I am an autodidact, or self-taught man. I never entered culinary school, but I prepare the cuisine with my heart and feelings. I have always prepared the food I enjoy."

Josiane turned to me. "Carole, when he uses the word '*cuisine*,' he is referring to cooking. He has always enjoyed cooking. '*Cuisine*' is also the word for kitchen, but in this case, he is talking about cooking and learning how to cook. Do you understand?"

Josiane must have a sixth sense when it comes to teaching me her language, because she always knew when I was baffled. Or maybe it was my facial expressions. I nodded.

"In your cuisine, are you most often using family recipes?" I asked, flipping to a new page in my notebook.

"I use some local recipes. You must have noticed lambs being raised on salted pastures—those covered twice a day by saltwater from the sea at high tide."

"Yes, I had lamb for dinner last night, and it was absolutely succulent."

"Ah, I'm so glad. The salt produces a special variety of grass, which the lambs eat, which produces a special flavor and tenderness. Thus, the succulence you mentioned. Each lamb is documented . . ." He must have noticed the perplexed look on our faces.

"Each lamb has a tag and is sold with a certificate of authenticity. It is a very specific type of farming. We buy lambs from a nearby farm that produces only this special lamb called *Grevin*. The name comes from the word '*grève*,' given to the strip of salt grass-covered land going from low tide to high tide and refers to the lambs raised there."

"We noticed many tags hung by the fireplace. Are they from the lambs you prepared?" Josiane asked.

"Yes, the tag is the guaranty of the product. As to the use of local ingredients, I have a friend and colleague whose passion is mushrooms, and he constantly works on developing ways to accommodate the variety of mushrooms of this area. He lives not far from here, in the forest of Bagnolles de l'Orme. That is his specialty, while mine is preparing *Lamb Grevin*. I am the only one preparing lamb in this way. We also prepare the pudding known as *Teurgoule*. Do you know *Teurgoule*?"

Josiane looked at me as if I might have the answer. I should have, but my blank stare led to laughter.

"It's a local dessert, and we use the recipe from one of our chefs. It comes from his mother, I believe, passed from one generation to the next. In fact, she still prepares it in the same manner, and I will have him give you this recipe." M. Barreaux disappeared into the kitchen and after a few moments returned with one of his chefs.

"This is Monsieur Patrick Foisnard, whose mother's recipes we use in our restaurant. He is the master chef in our kitchen."

M. Foisnard, a young man in his thirties, gave a slight bow of his head as he wiped his hands clean on his apron. He was timid, in fact a little embarrassed, but also eager to please his boss. He swept a lank curl back from his face and handed Josiane a folded slip of paper.

"Is this recipe from your mother?" she asked.

"*Oui*. It comes from my mother's grandmother, who received it from her mother. I wrote down the recipe for you. First, you need round rice. You let it soak in a saucepan with a little bit of water and let it swell, then drain it, but do not rinse, in order to keep the starch. Then bring one liter of whole milk to a boil, with brown sugar, vanilla-flavored sugar, and vanilla bean. Add the rice and cook for one hour at low heat. Then put the mixture in a terra cotta plate or terrine and bake at 145 degrees Celsius (300 °F) for two hours. Never stir when it is in the oven! You can stir a little bit when it's in the saucepan if you want, but not in the oven. During the baking process, the surface of the mixture will be covered by a film. The rice will remain at the bottom of the dish, and the cream will come to the top. *Voilà! Teurgoule!*" A shy smile flitted across his ruddy face.

"I believe the name of this specialty was mentioned to us the other day by your friend, Karyn," Josiane said, matter-of-factly.

I slapped my forehead as awareness finally seeped through. "I knew the word sounded familiar, but I couldn't place it."

Josiane continued, "And, the word is spelled several ways, Carole," Josiane explained. "If you research this, you will find that the word *teurgoule,* then *La Ceurgeoule* and *Turgoule* are each spelled and pronounced differently." She carefully spelled out the words, as I wrote them down. "All these names are for the same recipe that celebrates this very special age-old rice pudding."

"This is wonderful! Simply wonderful! So, if I calculated correctly, this recipe is from Patrick's great-great-grandmother. That's five generations! It is amazing! I would love to try it. Can you ask him, Josiane, if his recipe would work as well with two-percent milk? That is the type of milk we usually purchase in the States."

"I doubt that even our whole milk doesn't have as much cream as the milk from the wonderful cows here in Normandy," Josiane responded, then turned to ask Patrick.

"That may be so," Patrick said, scratching his head. "But it still may work."

"Of course, we *do* have the best cream in the world," M. Barreaux said, nodding proudly.

"*Oui,*" Patrick said, mirroring M. Barreaux's gesture. "We do have wonderfully rich cream."

"Then perhaps I should stick with the tried and true recipe by using the very best cream I can find. *Oui?*"

The three nodded emphatically.

"Here is another recipe," M. Barreaux added, "made with the *andouille de Vire.*" He handed the recipe to Josiane, who passed it to me, even though it was, of course, in French.

"Is this a recipe to make sausage?" I asked. "Or a recipe using premade sausage?"

"It is a recipe using our *andouille* sausage from Normandy only, not from Brittany. And it is prepared with mashed potatoes and an apple cider sauce."

"Yum," Josiane said, licking her lips. I wondered if she had taken time to have lunch.

Patrick began without hesitation. "You boil a couple kilos of potatoes with the skins on, and when cooked, you peel and mash, then add butter. No mixer. Then into the mashed potatoes, add chives and *cerfeuil.*"

A distressed look flooded my face. "I'm sorry. What is the translation for *cerfeuil?*"

"Like it sounds," Josiane said. "It is chervil."

Patrick continued. "While the potatoes are boiling, you use a half-liter of *cidre fermier,* or 'cider from the farm,' and pour it into a saucepan. Add two chopped apples to the cider, reduce over medium heat, and mix. Once it is mixed or stirred, add one-quarter cup of liquid cream or whipping cream, season to taste, and again reduce. We count about one-quarter pound of *andouille* per person, cut in thick slices, then reheat the *andouille* in the sauce, and serve warm with the mashed potatoes."

"Mmm. We will have to try that this evening," Josiane said.

"Absolutely!" I agreed, catching myself licking my lips. My eyes drifted toward the clock on the wall, and I calculated how long that would be. Only three more hours. I blinked and set back to work.

"What holidays do you celebrate here at the manor?" I asked, trying to keep on track. I knew we had only a short time left before the chef and his assistant would be called back to the kitchen.

"We have Easter, when we serve our lamb, then there's New Year's Eve . . . and now we have Halloween," M. Barreaux replied with triumph.

"And what do you prepare for Halloween?"

"We prepare a broth for the witches." He smiled. "More and more people have gotten involved with Halloween these past few years. It is the beginning of the end of the year, so Halloween gives a fun start to the holidays. And the people who celebrate Halloween come to our restaurant to have fun. It is not a family holiday, like Christmas. Here the restaurant is closed on Christmas."

"Monsieur Barreaux, how do you manage to keep your family together?" Josiane asked. Yes, she was sticking to the script.

"That's easy. It is our tradition. We celebrate holidays solely to be together. My chef, here, will go to his mother's." He turned toward Patrick.

"*Oui*, and my mother will cook for the holidays. Not me. It is a nice break."

"But you both seem to enjoy cooking, *n'est-ce pas?*" Josiane asked.

"*Oui, c'est vrai*," chimed both men.

"When I began to cook," M. Barreaux continued, "I was interested in the cuisine, but I like to cook by inspiration. I must like what I prepare. I came to this location for the salted pastures. Now, I see them every day—every morning, every night. It is reassuring to me. Sometimes when I travel, I bring back spices from foreign countries, which to me is more than recipes. In the past, Normandy cuisine used exclusively cream and butter. Now we use more spices. The Normandy people, when we mention spices, think the dish will be too spicy or hot."

"*Oui*," Patrick laughed. "But our menu has only two or three plates that are considered spicy."

"My husband grew up in New England," I said, "where he swears they boil all their food and pour off the flavor before serving. So, to us, spicy is good as well," I said. They nodded as if they understood me.

"Speaking of spicy, what is *badiane*?" Josiane asked, reading from their menu.

"I will show you," Patrick said as he dashed from the room.

M. Barreaux continued. "On our menu we do not write *épices* or spices. Instead we say *herbes aromatiques*. People seem to accept that description." He smiled at me. "We offer a *Saumon mariné aux épices de l'Ile de Zanzibar*. The very words make you dream of faraway places, *mais oui?*"

"That's salmon marinated in spices from the island of Zanzibar," Josiane said quietly to me.

"Sounds lyrical and delicious," I said.

Patrick rushed back into the room carrying a tray covered with samples of the many spices used in their kitchen.

"What is the recipe where you use the *badiane*?" Josiane asked again.

"Ah, it is a salad with duck gizzards. *La badiane* is the star anise used in the recipe." Patrick pointed to the dried brown stars on the tray.

"And this is *curcumin*, or turmeric." M. Barreaux pointed to a reddish-orange sprinkling of spices. "We make our own mix, using all you see here: mild pimiento, royal curry, and *baies de genévrier...*"

"That last is juniper berries," Josiane said. "By the way, are you using fresh coriander or cilantro?"

"No," Patrick said, "we do not have the fresh herbs, yet."

"We just use these spices," M. Barreaux said, "but maintain a very local taste, with the discreet introduction of subtle new flavors here and there. We don't want to frighten people off." His eyes smiled over the rim of his glasses.

Josiane turned to Patrick. "Did your mother teach you how to cook?"

"She started teaching me. And my aunt, her sister, was a chef by profession."

"You also have recipes from your aunt?" Josiane asked.

"*Oui.* My aunt taught me to prepare a lot of *charcuterie* such as *pâtés, terrines,* hams, sauces, etc."

"Does she also live in Normandy?"

"She lives nearby."

"What are the main reasons people come to your manor?" Josiane asked.

"Our local clientele come for the cuisine. And they will not choose the lamb, since they can eat it many times a year. But people coming from far away will have *l'Agneau Grévin.* We have people who come here for the quiet, because we are away from the main tourist crowds. They come from France, but we have many clients coming from the States, too. Like you," he said to me.

"Is it because of your ad on the internet?" I asked, which was how I had found his manor.

"No. It started with contacts we had with the American Embassy in Paris, with people who worked there. Through word of mouth, more and more Americans found us. We are always trying to adapt to the needs of our American clients. For example, we had a client from the States who wanted ice cubes in his glass. There was no one at the bar, so he went to the kitchen and was given ice cubes by the cooks. He was happy with that. Now we know that Americans want ice cubes in their water!"

"Yes, we are a strange bunch," I said.

He nodded. "We also have American clients who come back regularly, and from one generation to the next. I remember the comment of an unhappy French client: "Here, to be served rapidly, one must be American!"

I groaned. "I apologize for my countrymen. I'm sorry to say that some of us Americans can be quite insufferable. Impatient!"

"Ah, but this place is wonderfully comfortable," Josiane said, sliding down into the luxurious sofa.

"We want to keep it comfortable—and simple. When my American clients come here, they are warm and friendly. They come to shake my hand after dinner. They have eaten well, they are happy, and they want to thank me. As for the French clientele from the provinces, they are much friendlier than those from Paris. Parisians are horrible. And some of the people from New York are a bit like Parisians. You are not from New York, are you?"

"No. From the San Francisco Bay area. But I understand what you suggest," I said, as I patted the top of his hand. "Some fellow Americans are not good tourists."

At that point, Patrick, the master chef, bowed and left to go back to work.

"Are you always creating new recipes, using spices that are being rediscovered? Like using the *nouvelle cuisine* approach?" Josiane asked.

"We do not do much of that. For example, we have been preparing the *Saumon Mariné* for twenty years. We do not change the formula, since we have a clientele who come especially for that recipe. The formula is good, so . . ." poof. He breathed out as he tossed his hands in the air. *Ah, once again the Gallic puff.*

"Last evening's food was so beautiful," I effused. "And so delicious. The *aubergine-champignon* (eggplant-mushroom) mix you served with both the *rouget* (fish) and lamb was simply marvelous."

"Again, I thank you," M. Barreaux said. "It is not a *ratatouille*. The product is almost a *confit*. It is a mixture of bell peppers, onions, mushrooms, tomatoes, and we cook the ingredients at very low heat, for a very long time, until it almost caramelizes. Not too long ago, we had French clients who asked the waiter if we were buying that preparation in a grocery store! Too bad . . ." He shook his head.

"Oh, those spoiled French," Josiane exclaimed. "They do not know their good luck."

"Yes, spoiled and capricious French," he said. "And some Americans are spoiled, too, but warm. I remember one American who was coming back from the beach, his feet all muddy. He didn't want to come in with dirty feet and by hand signals he asked me what he should do. Well, I took a water hose and washed his feet. He just laughed and laughed. A Frenchman would not have laughed. They do not have that relaxed attitude. They do not have the same sense of humor."

"Do you sometimes come to the U.S.?" Josiane asked him.

"Yes. I have been a few times to Boston. When that terrible catastrophe of September 11 happened," he said, "I sent letters to my American friends and clients. They all sent us an answer. We here in France were also traumatized. We were thinking that it could have happened in any country. We felt that it had happened to us, too. It was a horror. We felt the emotions almost as much as people in the States did. That day we had a client who was an American pilot from one of the airlines involved in the disaster. He was beside himself. Absolutely fraught. We felt so sad for him. So helpless. But I think we realized that we are all from the same family—humanity."

"That is so lovely. Thank you for your kind thoughts," I said. "I would imagine your business also suffered from this trauma. I was supposed to come over to France at that time but had to cancel my trip—until now."

"*Oh, mon Dieu!* In the following week we had one-hundred-fifty cancellations, but we understood. And in that same period, we had unexpected American clients who could not fly back to the U.S. The ambiance was rather different. We Europeans have had wars; we have lost so many people." He shook his head sadly and shifted his glasses back up on his nose.

"I have known World War II, the bombings, and I have known the first American parachutists. In fact, we have an American cemetery here, nearby, and each time we go there, we still feel the same strong emotions. Even after all these years. We always think of all those young people who died at age nineteen and twenty.

"Of course, we were very touched by the war. The Germans executed my father's cousin. I was living in Valonnes at the time, near Sainte Mère l'Eglise, on the side of the landing beaches. We were fleeing under the bombs. There were dead people everywhere. When we see such scenes on television now, and we hear young people say, 'That is horrible,' we tell them, 'We have seen that. We were there. And it *was* horrible.'"

My mind once again overflowed with questions—about the war. How did they survive? Where did they go? How did they manage to live in the occupied zone? My head was spinning, just as it had a little more than a year earlier when I first interviewed Josiane's mother, Marcelle, about living in Paris during the war. I couldn't shake loose from the horrific images.

"Monsieur," I asked softly, "how old were you then? How did your family survive?"

"I was eight years old at the time of the war. We children adapted much easier than adults, but I know what fear is. The fear of bombings, of bombs . . ."

"Did you fear the Germans?" Josiane asked.

"Not especially. It was the war. They just took charge of us all. When we saw an airplane coming at us, we would dive flat on the ground. Oh, the noise! It was the hideous noise that caused such fear, as we knew they were strafing with real ammunition. Most of the planes near the end of the war were Allies. After that, when I went for military service, I couldn't bear the sight of a gun."

"Could you have been exempted?" Josiane asked.

"No, I didn't want to be. I had to do what I had to do. It is part of life. We were drafted and we didn't argue. We all had experienced much of the same thing. I wouldn't think to complain."

"Again," I said, shaking my head, "always the impact of war!"

"And we come back to that again," M. Barreaux said. "Sixty, seventy or more years later, there is so much of the same thing going on around the world."

"Because of the possibility of something coming up again," I said, "I imagine the old fears come flooding back. I spoke to a young French woman who told me of her French grandmother's reaction after 9/11. Because her grandmother had barely survived World War II in Paris, the grandmother decided she wouldn't take any chances that she might almost starve again. She immediately ordered over five hundred kilos of potatoes—just in case."

"Yes, but at the same time, in the whole world there is a surge of solidarity. It seems that people want to get closer. And with the news, if something happens here in France or anywhere in the world, the reaction is immediate. We are all one!"

"I do hope so," Josiane said. "I do hope so."

CHAPTER SEVEN

Sophie and Her Daughters

Rennes

We slowed as we made a U-turn in the cul-de-sac in front of a row of prim saltbox-shaped houses. All were similar in size but distinguished from one another by brightly colored paint. A look of "fresh and clean" seemed to radiate from each one. Breton lace curtains were blowing at the windows—it was a beautiful day, and the neighborhood seemed to be welcoming it by tossing open their windows.

We had driven out of Normandy and into Brittany for the day. Seeing Brittany was one of our major goals, yet I had missed the fanfare of crossing into this new region. I guess we'd had plenty of fanfare of our own, though. But I'm getting ahead of myself here . . .

At the house we pulled up to, a rosy-cheeked young woman peered over the heads of her three young daughters clustered in the doorway, awaiting our arrival. We were visiting Sophie, wife of Josiane's nephew Christian Pourrez, and their girls. Despite our hour-late arrival, she and her daughters welcomed us with open arms and many kisses. I loved the welcoming committees in France—the warmth was so genuine. Or was it Josiane? Or were they simply hungry?

It was Wednesday, and the girls had the day off from school, as did Sophie, who worked as a school counselor.

Sophie was a spry thirty-something. Blonde, with sparkling blue eyes, she reminded me of those hand-carved dolls whose high cheekbones look as if apples have been wedged permanently into place, but prettier. Her whole demeanor was vibrant, and her little Lucie, age five, was the spitting image of her mother. Her oldest daughter, Clemence, who had just turned thirteen, acted a bit more reserved. She was shy, but curious. I got the feeling she was taking as many mental notes as I was. The middle daughter, eleven-year-old Alice, was also a little shy but, as it turned out, she had so many friends coming to the front door during our visit that she didn't have much time for shyness.

All three girls were congenial hostesses. They scrambled to help their mother serve us champagne and crackers and nuts, while Josiane did some catching up. It had been a few years since she had seen them, and it was clear they adored her. She rummaged through a rumpled bag and pulled out presents for the girls, casually mentioning she hoped the presents were still intact. Yes, thank God, they were. She winked at me. We heaved a sigh of relief as the gifts were opened. Josiane was kissed affectionately once again and she nuzzled each girl in turn before settling down into a seat.

"I can't believe it!" Josiane said, catching her breath. She was still reeling from the drive we had made from Mont St. Michel through Rennes, an hour before. She began to laugh and confessed that we were grateful the girls' gifts hadn't broken in one of her suitcases. She explained that on our trip through Rennes, we had gotten a bit confused as to where we were (leaving out the fact that we were lost), and somehow Josiane had lightly—mind you, ever so lightly—rammed into the car in front of us at a stoplight.

"The owner of the car stormed back to my car," Josiane said, "and practically accosted me. In a shaken, high-pitched voice, the woman began to screech at me, as she informed me that she worked for the Rennes Police Department." Josiane took a deep breath.

"She informed me that in Rennes I couldn't get away with anything!"

In my defense, at the time of the incident, I hadn't understood the words she had hurled at Josiane, but her body language spoke volumes.

"And don't think of trying anything here, either!" the woman had spewed.

Josiane and I hadn't even felt the impact of the bump between our cars, so we were of course shaken by this vociferous woman who directed us around the corner to the Place des Lices in downtown Rennes, where she began to interrogate Josiane and demanded she fill out reams of forms for an accident report . . . right there on the spot.

As Josiane related all of this to Sophie and the girls in French, I was reliving the scene in my mind. It had been terribly unnerving, but I wasn't driving, and this was Josiane's home country and her brand-new car. I wondered how Josiane had remained so completely calm as she gathered her insurance papers from the suitcases in the back of the car. Had it been me, I might have been sitting on the curb bawling by then and was grateful I hadn't been driving. *Oh when, oh when am I going to learn to speak French?*

After almost an hour of dealing with this unhinged woman, she finally calmed down and drove off with only the demand that Josiane call her the following morning. She did have our license plate number, and who knows what else. Josiane had gotten back into the car and we continued on our way, despite both of us with shaky knees.

Josiane had rounded a corner and driven a few blocks up the street in hopes of finding the correct road (was there one to begin with?), when we heard considerable yelling and honking of horns. *What now?* Josiane pulled over again—and I think it hit us both at the same moment—we realized we had forgotten to close the tailgate of her car. Peering over our shoulders to see where the honkers were pointing, we sighted our suitcases strewn along the roadway behind us—including the special suitcase that held the girls' presents.

The story of how the suitcases took a detour was a hit with the girls, and we all laughed at the folly of it. But I could see it had taken its toll on Josiane, and we had been late for Sophie and the girls' lunch.

As they were all talking—in French—I was observing this delightful family. For a moment my mind swung back to our mad dash, Keystone Cops entrance into their home, and I felt happy to settle into my seat and do just that—observe.

At that point, Lucie fidgeted about, wiggled out of Sophie's arms, and zipped out the front door. It was a warm spring day, the sun was shining, and Lucie was not letting a moment pass without enjoying it. The squeak of tricycle wheels resounded from outside, along with the giggles of other children and a bit of French banter—then back inside she came, checking on us to see if she had missed anything—like lunch, perchance? She nuzzled back into her mother's lap, only to slide down between her knees and disappear out the door again almost immediately.

The midday dinner was finally served, with Clemence

working in tandem with her mother. She had helped to prepare this gourmet feast and had also baked the cake for dessert. The two of them worked together in the kitchen in a seamless and fluid manner. There was no screeching at the girls to get them to the table; no delay tactics from the girls. It was simply a family coming to *déjeuner* (lunch). We were served a tasty pork tenderloin (with apples and calvados, I believe), a plethora of side dishes, a prepared cheese platter, and of course the cake, which was remarkable.

As we began to talk about family and festivities, I remarked on how extremely competent Clemence was, and once the translation was made, she beamed. She had been taught a little English in school, she said, but was not comfortable using it.

I knew how she felt. I was struggling, too. I was playing the role of the somewhat competent *journaliste* from America—who didn't know the language and at that moment couldn't find her tape recorder or notepad. So much for competence.

Soon, though, after stopping, then starting the interview, we got underway and began discussing their favorite holidays.

"Halloween," they shrieked, "that is our favorite!" Sophie explained that Halloween was a relatively new idea to France. Her children had been celebrating it only for the past three years. But it was clearly a hit—very American, they thought.

"It's rather like Mardi Gras used to be," Sophie said. "The children now wear costumes and go from door to door to receive candy. At Mardi Gras, when I was a little girl, a parade would pass in front of our house and people from the parade were selling *crêpes*. Children could buy *crêpes* from street vendors, or we would go from door to door to receive *crêpes*. We love our *crêpes*! We had wonderful parades with floats and people in costumes. It was lots of fun. Today we do not have as many parades. Halloween has become a new occasion for people to have fun and celebrate."

"Do you still do the same thing for the carnival now?" I asked.

"No," she said. "There are no more carnivals like we used to have. But at school the teachers organize something for small children, where they wear costumes and throw confetti during a walk through the town. There is still a joyous ambiance among the students at that time. They do things that are rather foolish, like spraying their friends with funny spray foam or flour, and it sometimes degenerates into egg-throwing. So, people avoid going to town on that day."

"Good reason," I laughed.

"In Brittany, people are very traditional and there are many *fest noz*. (This is also referred to as *Breton Ceilidh*). This festival is held at night and involves consuming large amounts of food (*crêpes*, of course) and drink (cider), and above all music and dancing. All kinds of Breton and other Celtic music are performed by traditional singers and instrumentalists using the *biniou, bombarde*, and the *cornemuse,* which are the traditional bagpipes, oboes, and clarinet-type instruments. Folk groups each have their own dances, music, and costumes, and the dances are always done in a circle, or multiple circles. They usually continue late into the night and sometimes into the following morning, with some dancers claiming to be under the spell of the *korrigans*."

"*Korrigans*? What are *korrigans*?"

Sophie and the girls tittered. "They are our elves. Don't you have those in the U.S.?" They broke into fits of giggles but offered no explanation.

Sophie continued. "The townspeople do not always wear

costumes except when there are special events in town. So, during the weekends, people gather for the village feast, and there are collective dances, and everybody dances. It is not exactly ballroom dancing, but everyone dances their traditional folk dances. In the summer months and for the benefit of tourists, the locals wear their costumes and give a free show, and they encourage the tourists to join in and learn the dances. It is a very Breton thing to do. This," she said proudly, "is the patrimony of Brittany."

"This is marvelous!" I said. "How do you each participate in the festivals?"

Clemence, the thirteen-year-old, said, "Participate? Not necessarily." The very thought seemed to make her self-conscious.

"The group that participates is usually twenty to thirty years old, and the very young reject the tradition," Sophie said. "However, the schools organize at least one folk event two or three times per year. Parents are invited, they pay an entrance fee, and the money collected is used for a student field trip at the end of the school year."

"Is this considered a traditional event?" I asked. "Teaching the children about their cultural heritage?"

"Yes. The children are trained to dance the traditional dances for these special occasions. The tourism office of Rennes can give you the agenda for the year. There are *fest noz* everywhere throughout Brittany. Plus, there are fairs, like the Scallop Fair in one town and the Oyster Fair in another. And the Book Fair, too."

"It would be so nice, Carole, if while we are in Brittany, we could see at least one *fest noz*," Josiane said dreamily.

"Brittany is very festive," Sophie said. "We also celebrate All_Saints_Day on the first of November, when we still go to church as a family. And on *Les Jour des Morts* or All Soul's

Day, which is on the second of November, we place chrysan-themums on all the family graves and travel to towns where our families have graves and tombs. We also celebrate St. Cecile, the Patroness of All Musicians, which is in November or December, and the bands all parade through the streets toward the churches.

"Another favorite saint's day is St. Catharine, the Pa-troness of old Maids," Sophie said, as she smiled and slid for-ward in her seat. Clemence began to giggle.

"This has become a fun day for unmarried women who are twenty-five years or older and are considered old maids. They wear funny hats and draw attention to themselves. They even wear those crazy hats to work. And now it's for men, too, who haven't gotten married. They carry on in the same funny way, but without the hats. It is more of a joke than anything else. Just a time to have fun."

I began to ask Sophie about her childhood. "Were you raised in Brittany?"

"No. I am from Niort, which is north of Bordeaux in the western part of France. My grandparents were from the northwest part of Brittany but lived a long time in Brest. My grandfather graduated from Polytechnique, which was an Army school in Brest. They lived nearby in Lorient, Brittany, where my father was born.

"During World War II, under the government of Vichy and Marshal Pétain, my grandfather was one of the directors of the arsenal, which included the shipyard and the building of naval vessels. When he was asked to work for the Ger-mans in manufacturing weapons, he refused. My grandmother was terrified he would be shot or sent away, but instead he was only fired, and later granted a retirement from the Army, which he enjoyed for forty years."

Josiane murmured, "I was just thinking of Maman, who worked as a young single mother in a Citroën factory in Paris in 1944. Once the Germans took over, she was forced to work for them. She did not have the luxury of taking retirement, as she had a young son to care for—your father-in-law —your children's *grand-père*. So, your own *grand-père* was most fortunate."

"Yes, I'm sure he was," Sophie said. "When my grandfather was fired, he went to live in the *Zone Libre*—the Free Zone—of France in Niort. In the Bordeaux Region."

This bit of information surprised me, as I remembered Marcelle telling us that when the Germans marched into Paris, all of Paris fled. It was called *L'Exode*—the Exodus. And Marcelle and all her fellow Citroën employees made their way to Bordeaux. She ended up walking over 360 miles. "But weren't the Germans there, too?" I asked Sophie.

"Yes, but in the beginning of the war, the French people were free to work where they wanted and do what they wanted. The commerce and the economy were free. But in the occupied zone, the Germans requisitioned factories and businesses, and some people were forced to work for the Germans. The ones who refused to do so went into hiding. And my grandfather never went back to work."

Sophie cleared the table, then set out the cheese platter. "Christian and I and our daughters have lived in Brittany for only the past three years. But I have learned how to cook like people in this region: a lot more fish, vegetables, and fruit, and lots of pork. There are many pig farms in Brittany."

"In the winter months, do you ever use frozen vegetables?" I asked. I was thinking of the convenience of frozen vegetables in lands that experience cold winters. Sophie looked at me with surprise.

"No, just fresh. The one thing that I still do from my years in Cahors is to use fresh basil and olive oil in my cooking. This is not the norm for folks in Brittany."

"Where is Cahors, exactly?"

"Just to the east of Bordeaux—maybe a bit southeast."

I was trying to get my bearings, as she had mentioned so many unfamiliar town and city names. We continued talking about foods and wines, and Sophie mentioned a favorite wine they used to enjoy in Cahors.

"It is called Fenelon. It is a specialty drink made with walnut wine, black currant liquor (*crème de cassis*), and wine from the Cahors area. Very little of the first two ingredients are used, but it is sooooo good." I made a note to check into this.

As we were finishing the cheese platter and awaiting the cake to be served, the doorbell rang, and Alice rushed to the door. With a crash and a bang, and wearing roller skates, a friend of Alice's appeared. He had come to join us—and to see "the American." He appeared to be Alice's age, and despite his unsteady entrance and quick flump into a chair, was polite and eager to be part of our little party. Nothing like showing up for dessert. *Timing is everything,* I thought. And he was delightful.

Josiane turned to Clemence. "Do you understand what has happened in the national elections?"

"Oh, *oui,*" Clemence responded shyly.

"What do you think will happen now?" I asked. It was clear the election was an open topic. For all the French, young and old.

"The danger in this second election," Sophie replied, "is that people, thinking that Chirac will win with an eighty percent score, will simply not go to the polls, and thus give Le Pen a chance to succeed." Josiane nodded vigorously. I pondered this predicament and wondered if my own country was at risk.

As we took a break from the table and politics, Sophie and Clemence gave us a tour of their house. I had already been charmed by its attractiveness. It was relatively new, but like many new homes, small—or so I thought, until we climbed the steps to the second floor. There must have been four bedrooms upstairs, and a spare bedroom downstairs. The girls each had their own room, which reflected their unique personalities. And like me, Sophie is very fond of the sea. She talked of her love of going to the beaches and to Belle-Ile during the summer. She had spent many wonderful childhood hours there and enjoyed returning often with her family. Their house reflected her love of the sea, with tasteful aquatic touches throughout. If I hadn't known better, I could have sworn I was on Cape Cod or in my home in California. Sand dollars, starfish, little photos of the girls at the beach, seashells everywhere. They were all proud of their home, yet even more excited to take us to the site of their "new" home. It was being built that very day. Before heading out the door, we returned to the table for coffee and the special cake Clemence had baked.

At the table, Sophie began to share some family stories she remembered about World War II. "My uncle Jacques went to America," she began. "And my grandmother didn't receive news from him for one full year. There were no means of communication like we have today, and it was during the war.

"He did finally come back. He was my father's brother. My paternal grandparents had four boys and one daughter. My father, who was born in Lorient in 1930, lived in Brest, and is now in Niort, where I was born."

"That would have made him ten to fifteen years old during the war," Josiane said. "When your father talks about that period, does he mention it being difficult or terrifying? Was it as dramatic as it was for so many?"

"I think my father's family experienced a real drama," she answered, "so he talks very little about it. My grandmother talked much more about it. They were lucky to be in the Free Zone, and live in the country, so they had some fruits and vegetables to eat. My father told my children that they used to make their own butter and soap. Plus, there was little or no coffee and few potatoes. Everything was very difficult. The grandchildren, incredulous, looked at him with wide eyes."

Josiane turned to Clemence. "What do you remember from your grandfather's stories?"

"It was not like it is now," she said. "It was very hard, for they had nothing. The Germans wanted my great-grandfather's bed. They were waiting for him to die."

Sophie nodded. "It is important to keep in touch with history and to understand history, so that it will not be repeated. But I can see we are moving away from talk of the traditions." She sensed that the conversation was disturbing Clemence and shifted the topic.

Josiane spoke quietly. "It is part of life. It influences the traditions. And after the war, the question was, would people go back to their old traditions, or would they establish new traditions?

Sophie answered quickly. "The new generations have not experienced any of war's dramas. They have forgotten. Or never knew. And here we are, seeing a surge of fascism in our country. The new generations see only the problem of security in their life, the high rate of unemployment. We understand why some people may have voted for Le Pen. He has promised to solve all these problems. He is anti-abortion, wants to reinstitute the death penalty and intensive immigration policies. In cities like Strasbourg, where six hundred cars are burned by vandals in a year, the surprisingly high rate of votes for Le Pen is a way to let our leaders know that some situations are no longer acceptable. It truly is a case of intensive immigration in one area."

This flew in the face of what I thought I had learned of Strasbourg when Josiane and I were there. None of this had come up in our conversations, which were—when? Only a couple of weeks ago? I realized how little I as an outsider knew or understood. Especially when these same people had suffered so dramatically under the Germans in World War II.

I decided to change the subject. "Sophie, how did you and your husband meet?"

"I met Christian in Limoges. We worked together for ten years and even helped to manage summer camps for children together. I also worked for five years in the French Administration in Evereaux, a military town, but it was not close to Paris. Christian studied in Evereaux with me but commuted to his job in Paris. After two years of commuting, he transferred to Cahors, where we lived for ten years. I learned to love truffles, big porcini mushrooms (*cèpes*), walnuts, cakes with walnut oil, fruits—strawberries, kiwi. Plus, *confit*—duck or goose *foie gras*—and excellent wines. As I've told you, the wines of Cahors are very distinctive . . . red wines only. They are so good!

"Cahors was a very small town of twenty thousand. But this area of Rennes where we live today offers much more for our family, partly because Rennes is 300,000 (with 60,000 college students). Also, there are more social and cultural avenues available. Plus, when Christian was given an opportunity here in Rennes, it was one he could not say no to. He could not turn down any more promotions and remain on the job. So, we moved here, and we love it. The promotion was more favorable for us financially," she said, "but it was a difficult decision to move."

Sophie sighed. "Cahors was near the sea. And, of course, the sea is where my heart lies. My childhood vacations were always on the Isle de Ré. Now, when our family gets together in the summer months, we have twenty-one cousins from throughout France who gather together. Family is very important, and the summer holiday is an occasion to celebrate. It's almost always a time with family and a trek to the sea."

I clearly resonate with her passions.

CHAPTER EIGHT

I Was Born in the Middle of the Sea

"Me zo gañet é kreiz er mor"

*W*e returned to the Manoir de la Roche Torin in Normandy for one last night before heading to Marcelle's homeland. We were excited about going to Vannes the next morning—Marcelle's hometown. That had been our original plan—to take Josiane's mother back home for her last visit. Alas, that trip was not to be, but our promise still rang true.

Before turning in for the night, Josiane made contact again with Christian about his internet research. She seemed jubilant that he had made some progress. Up to that point, we had kept this search for Marcelle's identity a secret among the three of us—Josiane, Christian, and me—but it was always pressing on our minds. Marcelle had been born on November 11, 1918, the last day of World War I, but never knew her father or where her last name, Pourrez, had come from. She had wanted to find this out years ago, but only in her final months had she enlisted Christian's help.

Before we left the manor in the morning, I asked Josiane

to return one last time over the waterway to the Mont to take photos. The morning was crystalline, a pink glow rose in every direction, and an air of expectation hung in the cooling mist. While standing on top of a wall facing back toward land, Josiane, always one to regale me with French myths, babbled, *"Le Couesnon dans sa folie, a mis le Mont en Normandie."*

I looked at her wide-eyed, without a single idea of what she'd said. I blinked.

She laughed out loud. "That means 'The Couesnon, in its madness, has put the Mont in Normandy.'"

"And what does that mean?"

"Wherever the River Couesnon runs into the sea, that marks where Normandy ends, and Brittany begins."

Trying to imagine how disconcerting that might be for mapmakers, tax collectors, or anyone else, I scanned the shoreline for the elusive river which, if Josiane was correct, should literally be emptying at our feet. I could see evidence that the river had flowed to both the left and the right sides of Mont St. Michel. The border between Normandy and Brittany moved with the rains—the tides—and the flooding of the river.

"Normandy is very proud because the Mont almost always lands on the Norman side, but, of course, nobody knows when the next change will take place. Perhaps, to Brittany?" Josiane said with a coy air.

"Mais oui," I replied. "Where else could it go?"

Josiane tittered. *"C'est vrai.* But, of course. Where else would it go?" Josiane seemed more jubilant than in days past, and more relaxed. She jumped up on the wall with me and said, "I find that to cross over the River Couesnon from Normandy into Brittany is a journey like no other." She breathed in the fresh air. "Today you and I are joining with my mother's Breton history."

"Then we should get a move on," I said.

As we skittered back to the car, I thought back on the days of sitting with Marcelle at my kitchen table as she spun joyous tales of her youth in Vannes. And the marvelous Breton recipes she had shared with Josiane and me.

As we began to drive, I recalled Marcelle's soft resonant voice, as she created images in my mind of Brittany— "a most beautiful and ethereal place." It did not surprise me to feel her presence in the car with us.

To say that Brittany's past belongs to its present is not a paradox. The Bretons remain faithful about preserving their origins. Brittany retains, within its soul, its own language, history, customs, and legends. And these legends, whether natural or supernatural, form an integral part of the region. Knowing that at any moment an elf or, as Sophie's girls had delightfully explained, a *korrigan,* could spring into view amidst the heaths of flowering gorse and broom, was enough to make me sit up and clean my glasses to see more clearly . . . just in case.

"Do you know much about the mythology of Brittany?" I asked as we wended our way along the coastal roads. GPS Peggy was vocal again, spewing directions with a mind of her own. Unlike yesterday, when the chips were down in the middle of Rennes and she'd lent no help whatsoever when we were mired in that little dust-up.

"Mythology? Not a lot. How about you? Have you researched this?" Josiane said.

"Well, a little bit," I admitted. "After talking with Sophie and the girls yesterday, I wanted to know more. While you were on the phone with Christopher, I googled it. I found that the *korrigans* are traditional Breton gnomes. They're neither good nor evil and are said to come out at night and entice people into dancing and dancing. Only at the break of day do they release them. That must have been what Sophie was alluding to, don't you think? Did your mother ever mention them?"

"No, but I think she had a bit of the *korrigan* in her too, don't you?"

I laughed. "I think that's part of why she fascinated me. She reminded me so much of my own Irish mother. Before I left home, I also looked up the legends of King Arthur (King of Brittany), the Forest of Broceliande, Lancelot, the Knights of the Round Table, Merlin, and Viviane, who also supposedly came to life along these paths. In Brittany. Not in England. That was a real surprise to me. I also remember learning about Tristan and Isolde and their torrid twelfth century tale of love and passion. It was written here. Right here. And I ran across the legend of the City of Ys, which is the story of the King of Cornouaille. That story sounded so familiar . . ."

"That's one my mother told us about, perhaps because Cornouaille is close to Vannes where she grew up. But don't you remember the story? Supposedly the King built a city for his beautiful daughter, Dahut, and called it the City of Ys, which was built on a spit of land out in the sea. But as the legend goes, when she began practicing the ancient Celtic rites to lure handsome men to visit her, the God of the Roman Catholic faith intervened, and destroyed both the City of Ys and her.

"Even now, the ringing of bells at night brings Bretons to their windows to peek out in anticipation of this ancient city rising once again out of the sea. I can imagine my mother thrusting her head out of the window listening to the bells of the sea."

"Oh, yes, yes! I love that. It must be the Irish in me," I said. "But how much of an impact do these stories have on the Breton people today?"

The question fell into the silence as we contemplated the possibilities.

"Then again," I said, "I can imagine my mother responding in kind. She wove stories and legends for my brothers, sister, and me while we were growing up. If truth be known, I may have chosen this trip because I missed my own mother."

"Other than the City of Ys story, which Maman told us, I didn't pay much attention. Plus, I didn't live in Brittany. Yet I remember my mother spoke often of Brittany and always longed to return, especially to Vannes. Even after all her years of living on the other side of France, she always wanted to come 'home.' And now, here we are. She would have loved this trip."

I reached over and touched Josiane's arm. How her heart must have been breaking. "I hope this trip becomes a salve for you, Josiane—a trip of healing." She smiled but kept her eyes on the road.

As my thoughts about Josiane and Marcelle continued, the road curved and undulated up and down the hills and through the tiny villages along our route. The Breton character, which I had witnessed firsthand in Marcelle, was formed from this land and legends. I knew it was the intertwining of a devout Catholic faith, with the fervent belief in the mystical, that I had witnessed in her. Add in the independent will of the people of Brittany to remain steadfastly "Breton first, French second." Perhaps I was hoping to capture a glimpse in the people of Brittany the same personality I had come to know in Marcelle.

As we ventured further into Brittany, rain fell gently, off and on, light and misty at times, always changing with the wind. The April air was cool but not cold, and as we traveled around the fringes of Brittany's coastline, we popped in and out of the car, enjoying the seascapes. As lunchtime neared, we veered off toward the walled city of St. Malo.

"'A crown of stone above the waves' wrote Gustave Flaubert of this magnificent city on the sea," Josiane announced.

But it was these very ramparts (the crown) that caused us great consternation. After not one, not two, not even three times of circling and searching for access onto the island where the old city lay, we were unable to reach the center of the city itself. The bridges were being repaired, and entrance to the island city was elusive. We parked outside the city walls and began walking along a quay-side park in the Saint-Servan area (named after a Welsh monk who came there in the seventh century).

The tide was extremely low, and old tugs and sailboats listed heavily to one side with their keels resting in the mud. The locals walked along the sea wall with their dogs, stopped to chat with friends, disappeared through the city gates and beyond the majestic Solidor Tower, or merely sat on park benches to smoke and ponder the day. Sea gulls and pelicans skulked about the edges of the water in search of lunch, as the smell of salt, sea, and seaweed wafted up to us.

"Hear that?" I said. "I believe that's my stomach's growling. *J'ai faim.* I'm hungry."

Josiane, always the perfect tour guide, rose to the challenge. She moved quickly into her take-charge mode, and off we went. *Vite! Vite!* Off to several little *cafés* that paralleled the water. Unfortunately for us, it was nearing three o'clock, and the *cafés* were preparing to close for the afternoon. Not to be daunted, Josiane asked for suggestions, and we were directed through the city walls and up the cobblestone street to a little *crêperie*. As the door swung open and we entered the tiny shop, we were hit with the sweet smell of sizzling *crêpes*. The banter between the owner and his patrons was thick with talk of the national primaries that had taken place earlier that week.

"After eighteen years of flipping *crêpes*," the owner regaled his customers, "I've just made the decision this very week to sell my business." He was thinking of leaving the country as well. Brittany, I took it, was not far enough away from the fray of presidential politics.

"Nothing good could possibly come from either presidential hopeful," he intoned. The runoff was due in another week. He was preparing *crêpes* at a fast clip as he bemoaned the thought of having to sell, but then, what is a Frenchman to do? Enough is enough.

Having never had a Breton *crêpe* (and there I was in Brittany, the *crêpe* capital of the world), I decided to order two. They are small, I thought—a savory one with a bit of ham and cheese, and a sweet one made with a red berry *confit* with butter drizzled throughout and sprinkled with powdered sugar. I was salivating at the thought. Each was steaming hot, and those brown lacy pancakes literally melted in my mouth. Did I even chew? A quick cup of coffee was definitely needed before heading out the door. But, while I was totally engaged in eating, Josiane, like the Frenchwoman she still is, was more interested in debating the issues of the upcoming runoffs.

"I've heard people are planning to go to the polls with

clothespins on their nose—just to show their distain." She chortled. They all chortled, but still the voices remained raised.

"That's a Frenchman for you," she said as we walked out the door. "We never miss a debate about politics." She loved that about her people and I, too, loved the passion I was seeing in each French person I was introduced too.

We had hoped to stay in St. Malo for the night and get to know the city, which for centuries, Josiane pointed out, was known for its maritime prowess. But, alas—another trip, another time. We hadn't made reservations, so we continued to wander on down the road. Josiane felt confident we would find something, and we wanted to see more of this famous coastline before cutting south across Brittany for Quimper tomorrow. The sun began to pour through the clouds as we headed up the Côte d'Emeraude.

"Even on stormy winter days," Josiane said, "when the rain pelts the moors, the Côte d'Emeraude honors its name. The sea is never slate gray, but a deep emerald green."

Today was no different, and with the sunlight dancing across the water and the surf crashing along the rocky shoals, we were shielding our eyes from the flashes of blinding light as we continued west down the country roads from Dinard to St. Brieuc. In and around inlets where ancient fishing villages were cradled into protective coves, we continued. Up and around bracken-covered cliffs as heather stretched its purple fingers over the hillsides, we rattled along. Josiane was determined that I see the wild and windy peninsula of Cap Fréhel and Fort la Latte.

"Fort la Latte, a fourteenth-century castle, is poised on two rocky promontories of pink granite high above the sea," I read from a Breton guidebook I had on hand.

"The castle is connected to the mainland by two draw-bridges over rifts in the cliffs and despite being besieged numerous times during its lengthy history, the castle continues to maintain its noble integrity. Legend has it that there was another castle built on this same site in the tenth century to fend off the Normans, but the present castle was built by one of the oldest Breton families, the Goyon-Matignons. Originally called the Roche Goyon, the fort was besieged in 1379, in 1490, and again in 1579. This last time it was plundered, devastated and set on fire. Only the impenetrable 'keep' was left intact until Louis XIV rebuilt the castle in the seventeenth century."

We parked and left the car and stumbled down the long gravelly slopes that angle down—down—down—and out to the promontories. We had just stepped back almost six hundred years. My breath caught in my throat. This was astounding.

We continued to meander around the grounds of the crenellated fort, which was surrounded with battlements, circular towers, and of course the extraordinary "keep" I had just read about. I peered through the slits in the door and gulped. It still showed signs of war.

Stepping up on one of the outer walls, we gazed westward out to sea. With the wind whipping our faces with sea spray, and the bitterns and seagulls swooping nearby, we lamely struggled to imagine what life might have been like living here—so far removed from civilization, and so far out on a precipice with the seas crashing only two hundred feet below.

"I remember Maman used to quote an old Breton adage," Josiane said. "'*Me zo gañet é kreiz er mor,*' which means 'I was born in the middle of the sea.' This statement expressed how far removed from the rest of France the people of Brittany felt. They are certainly far removed—remote."

We climbed back up the hillside to the car and began driving again down the road. The sky was beginning to darken. We whipped past a Neolithic menhir (standing stone) called Doigt de Gargantua (Finger of Gargantua), and Josiane mentioned it in passing.

Quickly I looked up the history in my guidebook and began to read: "'According to an ancient legend, at the time humans lived with the *korrigans*'. . . oh, here we find the *korrigans* mentioned again . . . 'they all lived together along with the giants, and the *korrigans* had to fight the giants because the giants were ravaging the country. To manage this dilemma, humans would bait the giants who fell into a trap and then, were beaten by the *korrigans.* Giants' body parts were flung out in all directions, and the large Finger of Gargantua or the Giants. . . .'—I looked up at Josiane, whose face was gripped by a frown—'. . . ended up right back there.'" She giggled at the conclusion of my recitation. Unfortunately we couldn't see much of anything. We continued past some rocky cliffs covered with gorse, before dropping down through pine woods and into a valley by the sea.

By that time we realized it was getting late, so we stopped in the next village—L'Etapes sur Mare—and fortunately found a motel room and a recommendation for a good restaurant. We were directed to Saint-Quay Portrieux on the water and a folksy little restaurant stuffed full of locals. Must be good food, we thought, and indeed it was. In fact, I'd swear that the steamed mussels with a cider-based broth and topped with thick salted cream were the best I'd ever eaten. "We must be in Brittany—it's the cream," Josiane said.

"I thought you said that about Normandy," I said, with a wink.

"There, too." She chuckled.

We laughed and talked the night away. After the pleasant repast and a bottle of wine between us, we made our way back to the car and started driving back to our motel. "But where was it?" we asked out loud. And what was the name of the place? Had we picked up a business card? Was the name written on the key card? As I began digging through my purse for some form of motel identity, we realized it wasn't just our blurry wine-induced vision, but a dense fog that had wiped out our visibility. We could barely make out the road, much less see a sign that would hopefully lead us back to our rooms.

"Do you think we'll have to rely on a *korrigan* or two?" I asked.

"It might be helpful," Josianne grinned. "Maybe they have their fog goggles on."

After more than twenty minutes of driving about—which should have taken less than five—and with Peggy on the GPS, we caught sight of the motel. We breathed a sigh of relief. We had found our home away from home.

CHAPTER NINE

Off to Damgan

The next morning, we rose to a gloomy, rainy day. Coastal fog had not lifted from the night before, and we had many miles ahead of us. But as we began driving down the road once more, we both commented on the feeling of not being alone.

"As close as the clouds are to us," I said, "it feels comforting, doesn't it?"

"It's odd, but yes, it does," Josiane said. "Maybe we're allowing the legends to accompany us. Do you think that was part of why we got lost last night? You realize, we didn't find our way home until late." She giggled. "Was that you dancing with the *korrigans?*"

Again, my thoughts slipped back to the impish smile on Marcelle's face when she talked about her childhood here in Brittany.

"I do believe your mother is continuing to lead the way."

After a few hours of circuitous driving, having cut south across the whole of Brittany, Josiane, adept at navigating the roads with her trusted Peggy—except when the roads seemed to disappear at night or in the fog—brought us into the center of Quimper. I'd read about this beautiful town and looked forward to discovering some of her history and, of course, sampling some traditional foods. It was, fortuitously, almost lunch time.

Josiane squealed into a driveway in downtown Quimper to hopefully gather information from the local tourist bureau before it closed. As it turned out, she'd parked not in a driveway, but on the sidewalk.

"No matter," she said with a flip of her hair and disappeared into the tourist office, leaving me sitting in the errant car. Visions of our traffic snafu in Rennes clouded my thoughts. I contemplated what I might say to a *gendarme* should one happen by, but fortunately Josiane soon jumped back into the car. Unfortunately, she backed straight out into the middle of oncoming traffic. But, as Josiane is wont to do, with a smile and a wave of her hand, she headed the car back across the road—and off we went in the opposite direction. I figured when I entered heaven—shortly—I would simply plead ignorance. Josiane, with full awareness, exuded bliss. I am slow to learn, but learn I did, that when in the company of Josiane, you enter her world. And (try to) relax into the moment.

It was almost eleven o'clock, so Josiane decided we had time to see the sights before lunch.

"Quimper," she said, "is the capital of the department of Finistère and is also well known as the French Cornwall, or Cornouaille. It is a city over a thousand years old and carries the prestigious label of Ville d'Art et d'Histoire . . ."

"Wait," I interrupted. "Weren't we talking about the city of Cornouaille yesterday?"

We had parked the car and were making our way down the cobbled streets. Tapping my purse with my fingers, I stopped in the middle of the street.

"Aha! The City of Ys. We talked about it yesterday. Remember your mother telling us about Dahut, King Gradlon, and the doomed City of Ys?"

"Yes, she mentioned it was known as one of the most beautiful cities in the world. Until the tragedy happened. As my mother told us, the legend of the submerged city of Ys is perhaps the most romantic and imaginative of all Breton legends . . ."

Just then, the sound of a train whistle jolted me into reality, and Le Petit Train pulled up near us. I love Petit Trains. They're a wonderful way to get to know towns and villages by touring on a little train with a backdrop of historical explanation. Of course, I can't always understand what is being said, but once we hopped aboard Josiane planted herself next to me, so I didn't miss a thing. It began to rain again, but the train was covered with a colorful top, so we huddled into the center to avoid the rain blowing toward us from the open windows and to enjoy our tour. The legend of Dahut was left behind for the moment.

Le Petit Train traversed back and forth through the ancient alleyways, passing through the three main areas of the old town. As Josiane translated the melodious message from French to English, she pointed out that one section, known as Locmaria, has an eighteenth-century church, and tucked behind it were lovely gardens that skirted the banks of the Odet River. Another area was known as the Town of the Dukes of Brittany. It held great charm and numerous half-timbered buildings that sagged precariously against each other, as if seeking the support of an old friend. In the third area, known as the Bishop's Town, was the magnificent Saint-Corentin Cathedral.

"According to legend," Josiane translated from the audio

tour, "King Gradlon"—she grinned at me, as we were back to the subject of good King Gradlon and Dahut— "met Saint Corentin on a nearby mountain, Ménez-Hom. The king was so impressed by the strength of the man's religious faith that he invited the then-hermit to become Bishop of Quimper. The cathedral replaced an old Romanesque church which was supposedly built in . . . oh, say in the sixth or seventh century."

"Oh, you've got to see this," Josiane said, jumping out of the almost moving train. She grabbed my hand and literally dragged me to the west side of the cathedral.

"Look up there," she instructed. She waved her hand high and pointed.

The west façade of the cathedral was graced with two tall spires and a beautiful Gothic portal with a series of angels decorating the arches. Above them, a statue of Christ loomed over them all as he gave a blessing while holding a globe. He seemed to be standing on a grimacing demon. But at the top of the arch, balancing between the two spires was—could that be . . .?

"Yes, it is a statue of Good King Gradlon," Josiane said with pride. "Our legends continue, and always there is the mix of mythology with the Roman Catholic faith."

The statue of the king, the noted sixth century founder of Quimper, was not easy to make out from the ground level, but there he was set upon his horse. So yes, Good King Gradlon was a real person, but how did Marcelle's childhood memories fit in with him? I'll save that for later. It was lunch time, finally.

We made our way into a crowded and obviously much appreciated restaurant where plenty of traditional favorites were being served: buckwheat *crêpes*, of course; Guinea hen in cider (*Pintade au Cidre*), Breton onion tart (*Tarte Bretonne à l'Oignon*), and a hearty pork and vegetable stew with buckwheat dumplings (*Kig ha Farz*). I was extra hungry and curious about the *Farz*, which was described as buckwheat cooked in a cotton sleeve with the meat and vegetables, then rolled until it was fluffy like couscous. It was delicious, with full, rich flavors from the many vegetables, bacon, ham hocks, plus smoked sausages. Obviously, a nap would have to follow this heavy spread. I prepared to order coffee to stave off the nap, but Josiane propelled me out the door and around the corner to a lovely patisserie known for its *macarons—Les Macarons de Philomene*. The glass cases were filled with jewel-toned delicate cookies in light green pistachios, strawberry pinks, chocolates, lemon, lavender honey, vanilla, and a special favorite—the caramel salted-butter *macarons*. This *"macaronerie"* had reinvented the delicious pleasures of the small round almond sweets, and each melted delicately into our mouths upon first bite. Like a cloud on the tongue. Poof! Did I even eat it?

Then, truly in need of a nap, I followed Josiane as she led me back out the door but not back to the car. We went to the Musée de la Fäience, which featured Quimper's world-famous traditionally hand-painted pottery. Each piece was a work of art, and there was no way of leaving Quimper without purchasing several pieces for our homes. Yes, we were an easy touch. The traditional patterns of Breton characters and costumes enriched the plates, platters, butter dishes, and water jugs in deep greens, blues, and yellows . . . so difficult to choose.

"I suppose we better get back on the road," Josiane said after a time. "We are headed to my friend Micheline's home, to spend the next few days. I've been giving her enough time to get home from work, so we won't arrive before her. I know you will enjoy the drive."

Careening again down the E60 from Quimper and along the Morbihan Bay, which skirts the south shores of Brittany, we made our way toward the coastal village of Damgan. Micheline Thionet, or Mimi, for short, had been Josiane's grade school friend, and in the past few years had become a dear friend to Marcelle as well. She had eagerly agreed to be our tour guide in and around Vannes, Damgan, and the surrounding area of Brittany.

"Micheline was born in '45 in Damgan, the village where we're headed," Josiane said.

"So, she is our age," I interrupted, looking out to sea as we flew down the thoroughfare.

"*C'est vrai.* She lived part of the year in Damgan, the town where her father grew up and where her paternal grandparents resided, and the rest of the year in Piennes with her maternal grandmother. A few months after her birth, and once World War II was over, her parents moved to Paris to find jobs. Mirroring my mother's life, in which my mother was delivered to her maternal grandparents to be raised in Vannes, Micheline was delivered to her maternal grandmother in Piennes, far from her parents. She lived in Piennes for the winters of at least her first eight to ten years of life. That's how we met and became close friends.

"But it was during those warm summer months of her childhood, when she was sent to Damgan, where she got to know her parents and, of course, Brittany."

"Somewhat like how your mother got to know her own mother, right?" I asked.

"*Oui.* Even though Mimi only spent summers here, her connection to Brittany was strong. She remained wrapped in the embrace of her family, old friends, and her childhood memories of living near the sea.

"We share many memories of our early childhood together. And it was in Piennes that she sought the comfort of our home and my mother's kitchen."

"What brought her back to Damgan as an adult?"

"A long story I'll cut short. She spent most of her adult years in Paris, where she married and had three sons. But after she was widowed, she and her sons moved to her Breton roots to help her ailing father in Damgan. After he died, she remained in his childhood home near the sea—where we will be staying. She wanted to remain near where her grown sons were living, plus she wanted to live close to some of the dear friends she had known during her childhood summers. A friend in Mimi is a friend forever."

We entered the village of Damgan and drove from its center through residential streets toward the sea. As we slowly pulled through the blue wooden gates and into Micheline's circular driveway, we entered a yard filled with flowering trees and flower beds—pale violet crocuses, bright yellow lilies, green ferns, rhododendrons, daisies, and deep blue hydrangeas—all growing with wild abandon. Up the white mortar and sandstone outer walls of her house grew deep green fingers of ivy, which spread up and around the doorway, around the windows, and about the house in a gentle embrace. A matching blue front door was tucked back into a portal with a niche high above holding a small stone statue.

"Who is the saint above the door?" I asked.

"That's Sainte Anne—the patron saint of Brittany and the protector of all houses with blue doors," Josiane quipped. The same blue that coated the gate and front door framed the windows and peeked through the foliage.

Josiane waltzed into the foyer and called out Mimi's

name. I lagged sheepishly behind. We were met at once by a very happy-to-see-us small, spunky bulldog named Lulu, who jumped up and down excitedly. Micheline popped her head in from the kitchen. She had strong, northern-European good looks—blonde hair, deep blue eyes, and a fair complexion. She greeted us warmly. It had been a while since Josiane and Micheline had seen each other, and they embraced like sisters. Excited French chatter and shrieks of delight raised the roof. After a moment, Micheline and Josiane apologized for ignoring me. "Welcome!" Micheline exclaimed. "Let me show you around."

She led us through her house, which was filled with quiet touches of elegance—antique armoires, tables, chairs, and paintings—interspersed with comfortable, low-slung contemporary sofas, along with colorful, braided rugs, and a sleepy cat in the back window seat. A large bank of windows and a sliding glass door from the family room opened onto an expansive back yard and garden. Stepping onto the flagstone patio, Micheline proudly pointed out the new additions to her garden. Carefully constructed rock gardens were overflowing with sweet alyssum and miniature pink roses. Flowering shrubs and raised flowerbeds of cyclamen, impatiens, and geraniums abounded. Birdsong was broken only by the unmistakable sound of crashing waves from the sea—not visible, but less than a block away.

Lulu bounded outside to get our attention. It was clear by the leash she held between her teeth that she wanted a walk. Micheline had arrived home from work only a few minutes before our arrival and had not had time to take off her coat, much less walk her dog. Josiane and I volunteered for duty. As Micheline shooed the three of us out of the house, she began to busy herself making appetizers for later. Lulu, who wasn't serious about leaving her mistress behind, scampered back into the house, leaving us two women to make our way down the road.

The cottages we passed were modern and designed for year-round residency. "Reminds me of Carmel in California. *Et vous?*" Josiane asked. I nodded and pulled a scarf out of my pocket and wrapped it about my neck. A cool, sharp wind was coming off the water.

The sea was a murky green from recent storms, and the wind whipped across our faces, so we clamored down along the rocks and crunched through a million seashells—mostly mussel shells that had washed up onto shore. We sauntered along for quite some time, taking in the fresh air and watching the lapping of the waves. This was the bay where Marcelle had grown up. We passed two young lovers huddled together on the rocks near a couple of closed lifeguard stations. All of us were waiting for the warmth of summer.

On the way back to Micheline's house, I needed to quicken our pace. I must have picked up something bad in the food in Quimper, because I suddenly required a bathroom and a bed.

Indoors, I was hastened into Micheline's own bedroom. "I can't believe it," I wailed to Josiane. "Here I am in this beautiful home, the guest of a woman I don't even know, and I've taken over the best bedroom in the house."

"It's the closest bedroom to the bathroom. She's just fine with it," Josiane said.

Josiane and Micheline made me as comfortable as possible, and occasionally, late into the night, I awakened to their laughter and banter as they caught up on their lives. As I lay in the unfamiliar bed, I heard the calling of a hoot owl and the ever-consoling sound of church bells that tolled every hour through the night. I was pleasantly reminded of the church bells of my childhood, and I slid somewhat comfortably back into sleep each time they woke me up.

In the morning, bright sunshine greeted me through the lace curtains, as did the wet nose of Lulu burrowed under the covers. *Perhaps I'm in her bed,* I thought. I must have had a simple twenty-four-hour "bug." I was still a little shaky but felt much better than the night before. Plus, I so looked forward to seeing Vannes that day. Since Marcelle had so beautifully described her beloved place of birth, I longed to see it firsthand.

"How are you feeling, Carole?" Josiane poked her head into the bedroom.

"Much better. I'm so sorry for last night. I don't know what hit me, but I'm so grateful to you and Micheline for putting up with me. Did you two get caught up on everything?"

"We were up late making toasts to our pasts," she laughed. "Are you ready to head to Vannes?"

"I wouldn't miss it. This is like putting the final pieces of your mother's story into place," I said, kicking the blankets back and hopping out of bed.

Brittany

CHAPTER TEN

Marcelle Comes Home at Last

Vannes

*A*fter a quick Breton breakfast of breads, salted butter, jam, and a bowl of *café au lait*, the three of us scurried out the door and into Micheline's car. The air was crisp and sparkling as we drove along the beach heading out of Damgan. Again, we observed a rough and rambunctious sea.

"The market in Vannes," Micheline said, as she drove at a fast clip, "attracts several thousand visitors every Wednesday and Saturday for its fresh vegetables and meats. And because it lies on the Gulf of Morbihan, it is noted for its fresh fish. We'll start at the traditional market, which is held in the Old Town near the ramparts, just inside the city gates."

My eyes lit up. After parking the car, the three of us scooted across a bridge that connected the "outside world" to the inner city through Porte Poterne, one of the portals or ancient city gates. Before zipping down the steps from the top of the ramparts and into the market, we stopped to catch the view. Micheline pointed out the most sought-after landmark, the Cathedrale Saint Pierre, and below us, the lovely flower-filled moat.

"There they are, Carole," Josiane said, pointing to a row of old buildings below us. "The *lavoirs*."

I was delighted. I had become enamored of the *lavoirs*, the public clothes-washing troughs Marcelle had spoken of often. These ancient washhouses, with their thatched roofs, were bent low over the Marle River and looked much like a group of old women hunched over, enacting their timeless job of washing clothes.

I closed my eyes and slowly opened them again. Standing at this spot and overlooking the *lavoirs* was part of why I had come to Vannes. Marcelle had described how she spent hours here helping her grandmother. I envisioned Marcelle as a child chasing around the legs of the women busily scrubbing their clothes. Vannes was where Marcelle had begun her story, and if she had had one of her last wishes, this was where her story could have come to a peaceful end.

"Vannes may have been the only place your mother knew contentment," I said quietly. Micheline's eyes widened as she looked to Josiane for an explanation.

But Josiane simply said, "*C'est vrai*, Carole. That's true. And like my mother told you, that's the same building that was used for generations by the cobblers in my mother's family. They took water from the Marle River, boiled it in large cauldrons, and worked the sheets of tanned leather also on that very spot."

She sighed as she looked at the buildings, her own history lying below us. Popping up above the washhouses were half-timbered residences with wooden window boxes filled with bright red geraniums.

"*Oui. C'est vrai.* This was probably my mother's favorite place. If not, it certainly held fond memories."

"I wonder if your mother would have been surprised to

know this has become a place of honor in her town," I said.

"They say the washhouses are the most photographed buildings in the city," Micheline said.

"Aw, a thing of beauty is a joy forever . . ." I quoted John Keats.

"But I do not think this was originally considered a thing of beauty," Josiane tittered.

"I imagine the washer women thought of this as a place for backbreaking work. And, maybe a bit of gossip," Micheline said.

"But the smell from the tanneries? Eee-yeew!" Josiane laughed.

Just then a mix of land and sea aromas commingled in the air, and the three of us breathed in, then picked up our pace, crossed the bridge, and shambled down the stairs into the square below. People were everywhere and a cacophony of noises belched forth. Old friends greeted one another with excited calls, hands reached out and were shaken, cheeks were brushed with kisses, and chatter swelled. Gestures were dramatic, as hearing was next to impossible and progress was slow. Children chased each other through the streets and then, disoriented amidst the crowd, called out in alarm to find their parents.

We turned at the Place des Lices and passed through a neo-Moorish archway, beautifully decorated with brightly colored enameled bricks. We entered an immense indoor marketplace, which Micheline said was a blessing in inclement weather—which occurred often in the winter months. Throughout the massive room were aisles filled with vendors—the butcher, the baker, the vintner, and the dairy farmer.

"Typical Breton products are sold here, such as goat

cheeses or, more unusually, *pie-noire* cheeses made from the milk of the Breton cow," Josiane said.

"Ah, Carole, look there." Micheline pointed to several women seated quietly on a bench near the side door.

"They are known as the *'p'tites dames au beurre'* or the 'egg and butter ladies.' They come each market day from surrounding villages with their wicker baskets filled with freshly churned butter and large farm eggs. There's nothing better."

On tables and in cases, *Galette-saucisses* (grilled sausages wrapped in buckwheat *crêpes*) competed alongside Breton Onion Tarts, *Far Breton aux Pruneaux* (flan-style cake with plums), and *Kouign Amann* (extremely rich butter cake). Groups of jabbering women waited in long lines for their share of the tall stacks of freshly made *blé noire*, or buckwheat *crêpes.*

"It looks as if homemade *crêpes* are becoming a thing of the past," I said, rather smugly. "Convenience has once again taken a bite out of tradition."

"But are we not so different from you, dear Carole?" Josiane asked, with a smile and a shrug.

I nodded and grinned. *"C'est vrai."*

Before we knew it, Josiane and I had entered the fray, following quickly behind Micheline as she gathered up fresh bread, sweet buns, and local cheeses. We sampled wines and cider and were charmed by salesclerks in traditional costumes and jaunty little hats. Josiane and Micheline took turns purchasing specialty *charcuterie*, including Morlaix ham and *Andouilles de Bretagne,* then we darted out the door toward the fresh vegetable and flower markets. Time was of the essence—the fresh vegetables were being plucked up quickly. I did my best to keep up, even though I was writing notes and taking photos as I skittered along behind.

"Why are you writing all this down?" Micheline asked. She was becoming slightly annoyed by our delay. "Aren't all markets the same?"

"Carole wants to know what my mother's life was like growing up in Vannes. She's obsessed with Maman. Aren't you, Carole?" I grinned but remained silent.

Micheline shrugged her shoulders and continued the race down St. Vincent's street, where we arrived at the Place du Poids-Public.

"This," Micheline pointed out, "was once the center for weights and measures for the King, and is now the center for fresh vegetables, potted plants, and flowers. I'm sure your mother, Josiane, came to this market every single week when she was young. Does that help, Carole?"

"Yes, it does, Micheline. Thank you. And I'm sorry if I'm moving slowly, but this is an incredible experience for me and I'm just trying to absorb it all."

A panoply of bright spring flowers was stacked in tiers along the street, calling suggestively to buyers. The orange and yellow chrysanthemums were so vibrant they seemed almost obscene for the season's transition from winter. While Josiane and Micheline purchased a potted mum, the only flower suitable for placing on Micheline's father's grave, my eyes traveled up above the flowers to the distinctive houses surrounding the small square. These houses had reigned over this marketplace for more than four hundred years and probably witnessed the comings and goings of one little girl named Marcelle.

With too much in hand already, we finally reached the fish market, a freshly restored nineteenth-century hall. We threaded our way through the aisles, where table after table, continuing the full length of the hall, was covered with ice and topped with sundry fresh fish pulled from the waters off Quiberon. On other tables were mountains of clams, cockles, scallops, winkles, spiny lobsters, crabs, shrimp, and langoustine. Many of these creatures I had never seen before (or tasted), and when Josiane and Micheline attempted an English translation, they came up short and burst into laughter. We picked up a dozen oysters and three filets of sole, all for the day's *déjeuner* back at Mimi's.

We raced back to the car, dropped off our purchases, packed the fish into a cooler, then returned to the main portal and the harbor, known as Port de Plaisance. There we ducked into a dark little bistro to soak up our surroundings and drink cider (and a cup of hot tea for me). As we sat overlooking the square, Place Gambetta, we watched dozens of sailboats bob in the breeze along the quay.

A clock in the bistro chimed and all three of us swiveled in its direction. It was one o'clock. We paid our bill and strolled into the square. As we arrived at the Gates of Sainte Vincent, we noticed people disappearing off the streets. The markets had closed for the day, the main stores in town were also closing, and people were heading home for their *déjeuner*.

"*Bon*," said Josiane, "it's a perfect time for us to wander the streets at leisure. Now we can really show you the city of my mother's youth." *The moment I was waiting for.*

As we passed from the port through the Gates of Sainte Vincent, I couldn't help but notice the immense statue of the saint lurking above us.

"Is this what your mother was talking about, Josiane? Is this where she used to play?" I asked excitedly.

"Yes. Do you see how Sainte Vincent has his right arm raised as if to hold back the sea? That's part of an old legend, and you know they love their legends."

I stared at the statue. "Didn't your mother tell us that the day St. Vincent's arm bends back down, Vannes will be invaded with water?"

"You have a good memory," Josiane said.

"It is said that this terrible punishment, which was once placed on the glorious City of Ys, haunts this city, too," Micheline said. "Somewhere in the town, there is an inscription which says, 'Do not be too proud, people of Vannes; avoid resembling those of the City of Ys, who did not listen to the wisdom of Guénolé.' He was a monk; those who travel by water, pray to him."

"I doubt my mother held many good thoughts for Guénolé." Turning to face me, Josiane said, "Guénolé was the vicious monk who tried to turn King Gradlon against his daughter, Dahut. Remember her? He caused the King to be late in reaching Dahut in time to save her from the sea."

I couldn't believe my ears. I was prepared to have these myths debunked, but they kept tumbling into our paths. I turned to Micheline. "Marcelle mentioned Dahut on several occasions, and I wonder if you could tell us more about this mythology? Perhaps tonight?"

"I'd love to," Micheline said, as she walked a few steps beyond the gate.

"Actually," Josiane said, stopping in her tracks, "Carole and I were wondering about what my mother told you of her childhood—or her life in general. I know you two became quite close."

"Micheline, the truth is I've started writing a book about Josiane's mother," I blurted, "and we were hoping you could fill us in on memories or details she might have shared with you. Memories explicitly about growing up in Vannes."

Micheline's eyes widened again, but she smiled. "Okay.

I'll try to think of some of our conversations." She reached down and plucked a small stone from the bottom of her shoe. "I'll have to think about it, though, as it was a few years ago when we talked."

"Any memory would be helpful," Josiane said, "as I'm trying to sort out much of my mother's life. She left me with some wonderful journals and letters, but there are many holes in her history, and I have many new questions, as she asked me to find out some history on . . . on her father. But Micheline, if it feels like a breach of confidence, hold tight to it. You were a very good friend to her."

Micheline, deep in thought, stared at the cobblestone street below her feet.

"Well, I did go to the Hall of Records to look up her birth certificate like you asked me to do several weeks ago. But, sadly, I found nothing."

"Nothing?"

"Nothing, as she was born on Armistice Day—November 11, 1918, the end of World War I. I guess there was so much celebration, they failed to record her birth. In fact, no births were recorded for several days thereafter. I'm sorry. It seems like an idiotic blunder, but a blunder all the same. I have nothing on that front, but I will try to think about your questions, Josiane. She was a special woman and truly like a real mother to me."

Josiane put her arms around her friend and hugged her close. "It's all right, Mimi. We'll find the answers. I'm sure of it."

"Wasn't it near here that your mother talked about playing tag with her friends?" I asked, shifting the subject from heavy to light.

Josiane whirled around and stared up at the ramparts we

were leaning against. "Yes, up there on top of the ramparts. She said she preferred to be King Gradlon, but she lived more the life of Dahut. Even though she didn't say it, she must have felt like she, too, had been cast out of her family as a teenager and into an unsympathetic world. Those are my words. Not hers. She rarely spoke of her life disappointments with me," Josiane said, shaking her head sadly.

"I suppose that's the reason I knew so little about her. I never wanted to intrude on her personal pain, but now I feel she has guided me here to find out what happened to her . . . and to her father. Micheline, did my mother ever tell you anything about her father?"

"What I remember," Micheline said, "is that she said she never knew her father or his first name."

"Well, we're here to see the village of Vannes," Josiane said, changing the subject. "We'll chat more tonight." She brushed her hair back with a quick flip of her hand. It was clear to me she wanted to know more but was also reticent.

"For now, we are on a mission to see the house where my mother grew up. I can't recall where it is. Did you ever know where she had lived?"

Micheline nodded, and the three of us began our hike up the streets to find Marcelle's childhood home. Passing by the closed fish market and the farmer's market once again, we continued an upward climb into the hills of Vannes.

"Let's take this street," Micheline said, veering onto a side street. "Rue Noé climbs up the hill toward St. Patern, the district where your mother spent her childhood. I never walked this way with her, but she talked about it often. She certainly could weave a story, couldn't she?"

Josiane's eyes smiled at her good friend. "Yes, she could. I believe that's how Carole became charmed." She walked a few more steps. "I've been up there before, but it was many years ago."

As the hills grew steeper, it became more difficult to walk and talk. I stopped to get my breath. "By the way, what does Rue Noé mean? Steepest hill in the city?"

Josiane and Mimi tittered.

"Almost. It means Noah's Street, like Noah's ark. Obviously, another reference to getting up and away from the rising tide," Josiane said.

Finally, we reached Valencia Place. Josiane stopped and pointed out the bas-relief images of "Vannes and His Wife" on the façade of the opposite building. She, too, was out of breath and leaned against the ancient wall.

"Wow! I read about this in my guidebook," I burbled. "It's known in local history that if you pass between the houses of Sainte Vincent and the plaque of Vannes and his Wife while making the sign of the cross, you will receive many blessings. It seems good to pay attention to these legends, don't you think, Micheline? Who's to say which ones are actually true?" I asked as my fingers made quick touch points of a cross on my upper body.

Micheline shook her head and laughed. "I hadn't heard that one, but you certainly have done your homework." She, too, crossed herself, just in case.

"Oh, Micheline, you don't know the half of it," laughed Josiane. "And you'll love this one, too, Carole. I remember being told this when I was a kid. The corner we are standing on is called 'the corner of the bigots.' It's also translated as 'the corner of the overly-devout.' Despite lying in close proximity to the cathedral, it always made me ponder how it got its name." Her eyebrows lifted and disappeared under her fringe of bangs, as in mock surprise.

"But the street down there," Micheline pointed out, "is called the Street of Benevolence and the public garden tucked behind the garden gate is called the Garden of the Bigots. One can only imagine that this is the place where, after mass ended, the men would go off to the local bistro, while the women sat in the garden to chat. Don't you think?"

Josiane let out a gale of laughter. "I can imagine it happened just like that." She looped her arm through Mimi's and mine and off we went. With the streets empty except for us, her voice and laughter ricocheted off the buildings. Giggling as we wandered back up the street, we headed to Cathedrale Saint Pierre.

"This was the place of my mother's baptism and her first communion," Josiane whispered as we entered through the massive doors of the Gothic-style cathedral. "Again, Carole, can you imagine what this great church meant to Maman?"

We wandered through the austere church, peering through the dim light at the altar and up through the stained-glass windows. The massive rooms held tightly to the damp and chill, and even though we wanted to remain longer, after only twenty minutes we rushed outside to catch some of the sun's warmth radiating off the outer stone walls.

"I can't imagine how frigid that place must have been during the cold, cold winters," I said.

"Your mother told me how bone-rattling cold she used to get sitting in this church," Micheline said. "Also, in the church nearest her home at St. Patern's."

"No wonder she wandered off from her ritual attendance," Josiane said with a shudder. Micheline flashed a look in her direction but continued walking slowly along the streets ahead of us.

"I'm sorry, Micheline," Josiane said. "I know the church

means a great deal to you and has been a real comfort, especially after the loss of your husband and father. It simply had a different impact on my *maman*—even though she wove a great deal of spirituality into her everyday life. Remember how we used to go to church together in Piennes? But I, too, walked away from the church, once I got a divorce. Not that I had any choice at that point . . ."

"Not to worry, Josiane. I'm not judging you or your mother. In the world of turmoil, I grew up in, and having lived with a difficult husband through most of my adult life, the church was my only constant. My rock."

We continued up the cobbled streets, seeing but not seeing, our minds each a thousand miles away. We passed through the Porte Prison Gate without comment. Then I stopped short.

"Is this the ancient gate left over from the third century AD? Is this the gate Marcelle passed through on her way to St. Patern district?" I spun around looking in all directions. Before I could get an answer, I felt almost giddy, as I had passed into the oldest part of the city and closer to Marcelle's first home. I felt like an archeologist on the last legs of a dig. Certainly not like searching for the Holy Grail, but . . . This was where I hoped to find some answers. I can't say to what questions, but I had a hunch.

"Yes," Josiane replied, "remember how Maman would talk about helping to push the laundry cart up, up, up from the *lavoir*? She said they would go through the 'cart gate,' which is unique."

"Ah, *oui*," Micheline chimed in. "This district is the original site of the old Gallo-Roman city." She and Josiane walked to the side of the gate. "It says on this plaque, Carole, that this is 'a remarkable example of a fortified gate, controlled by a double drawbridge system, one for the cart gate and the other for pedestrians.'" She continued, "It says, too, 'Saint Patern's has not ceased to confront its past, for the traces of memories still remain.'"

I nudged in beside Micheline and stared at the French inscription. This was exactly what Josiane and I had been seeking: to confront the past. I turned and before us was the home church of Marcelle's youth, St. Patern's. I stared up at the building. The exterior of cold, gray granite was starkly austere and more rough-hewn than the elegant St. Pierre Cathedral we had just visited.

Micheline continued reading. "'During the fifth century, St. Patern, one of the original seven saints who fled to Brittany from England, established this as a place of worship. This current church was rebuilt in the eighth century, and it still preserves the patronymic memory of this saint.'"

"No wonder the church looks so old," Josiane said.

Micheline turned to face us. "Patern was the first bishop of this city and was later made a saint. People still call upon him when there is a drought."

"A drought? On the bay? What is this story about St. Patern?" I asked.

"The story goes that when St. Patern left the city for a few years, the rains in Vannes stopped," Micheline said. "But after his death, when his body was returned to Vannes and he was interred here, the rains immediately began to fall. Thus, whenever there is a drought, you will hear great outcries to St. Patern."

"How remarkable that there are so many ancient images and stories about water here," I said.

"I'm certain my mother called upon him many times, but probably not for rain. I think she mostly called upon Sainte

Anne d'Auray throughout her life. But I know that St. Patern—and this church named after him—was a real touchstone for her."

"I remember Marcelle telling us how she had lived so close to St. Patern that she felt she could reach out of their upper-story windows and touch the stones of the church across the street. That certainly would make it her touchstone, so to speak." I grinned proudly.

We moved around to the side of the church. The bell tower, which overhung the small narrow streets, was bordered by half-timbered buildings. One in particular, at the corner of the streets Saint Patern and Place du Général de Gaulle, displayed the decorative richness of fifteenth century architecture. Just then the church bells began to chime the hour, which startled us all.

We giggled and looked up to catch sight of the moving clapper within the bell.

"My mother said the church bells would awaken her every morning. Oh, how she longed to come back here before she died—right here—to hear those very bells just one more time." We stood, absorbing the reverberations of the chimes. Nothing was said. It was simply for Marcelle.

"So exactly where did she live?" I asked finally. "It must be very close."

"Right up there." Josiane pointed up at some windows in a dilapidated half-timbered building. On the bottom floor of the building was a business that appeared to be closed for the day. We inched closer. The store windows were streaked with dust and grime, and through the mottled glass we could see the store was empty and hadn't been open for quite some time. The dark green paint on the outside timbers had chipped and peeled, baring the original wood of the fifteenth century. A green-weathered side door, slightly ajar, led up dark, rickety-looking steps to the apartments above. Nothing was visible above the fifth step. The darkness was total.

Josiane moved toward the door to peer up the steps. She pushed the door slightly, and a loud creak resounded through the empty hallway. She jumped back, then smiled sheepishly.

"Did your mother ever tell you who she thought her father might be, Josiane?" Micheline asked. The question came like a bolt out of the blue.

"No. Like I said before, she never talked about it. I never asked, because I was afraid it would hurt her."

"I just now remembered a time when we were together at your house in California, Josiane, and we were talking about questioning paternity. I don't remember how we got onto that subject, but she said, 'I remember when I was still living in Vannes, some of the kids in my class used to tease me about being sisters or cousins with another boy in my class. Of course, I said that wasn't true. I even fought with one of the girls who made the claim. But the truth was, I didn't know. He certainly looked like me. I remember sneaking a peek at his father one day as I wondered if . . . well, maybe he was my papa, too. But their last name was not the same as mine. And I could never bring myself to ask *ma grand-mère*. So, I never knew.'"

"Wow, Micheline," Josiane exclaimed. "I wonder how this fits with the information I will receive from my nephew Christian?"

We all stood on the corner looking completely perplexed. Suddenly the heavens opened and the skies, which had been threatening rain all day, gave way to the spirit of St. Patern. Instead of going into the ancient church of St. Patern, we scurried down the streets, clattering over the same cobbles that Marcelle must have run along seventy-five years before. Laughing like schoolgirls, we raced through the rain, dodging under overhangs on buildings along our route and all the way back to Micheline's car, where we jumped in and zipped back to her home.

CHAPTER ELEVEN

Unpacking Mimi's Memories

Damgan

*A*fter hiking up and down the crooked streets of Vannes all morning and part of the afternoon, then racing to the car in pouring rain, we were famished. Back at Micheline's home in Damgan, she prepared an elaborate lunch, beginning with champagne and shucked oysters, followed by the fresh sole with new potatoes and asparagus we had purchased that morning. The three of us lazily savored the briny but succulent flavors of the Breton land and seas, as we drank more and more wine and wiled away the rest of the afternoon.

During one of those languorous moments, I asked Micheline to tell me about her summers in Damgan as a child. She poured three more glasses of wine from a second bottle, and we adjourned to the living room, where we settled into the comfort of her sofa. She began slowly at first, tipping her head back against the cushions, her blonde hair spreading around her flushed face, and soon vivid and animated memories began to flow almost as easily as the wine.

"I remember taking the night train from Paris with my parents to Vannes. We would arrive in Vannes early in the morning and take a bus to the very small village of Damgan, where my paternal grandmother lived. We were so tired and sometimes we had to wait a long time for the bus. When it finally arrived, it was like seeing an old friend. It was this very old green bus that picked up vacationers at the train station and was always heavily loaded down—with people, valises, and even luggage loaded on the top of the bus. Things were strapped to the roof—bicycles, lounge chairs for the beach, wicker chests, picnic baskets, big suitcases . . . All of this the driver handled with great gusto as he lashed summer treasures onto the top.

"I had come to spend the summer with my grandmother, which I did from the time I was seven or eight until I was fifteen years old. As I recall, children were out of school from July through September—three full months. Right, Josiane?"

"Yes, part of the reason was so children could help with the harvests, so school was usually delayed until the beginning of October. I remember waiting and waiting for you to return to Piennes, Micheline." A wistful smile spread across Josiane's equally flushed face.

"Thank you, Josiane. I, too, looked forward to that. Anyway, my parents and I remained on the bus until the very end of the line, which was here in Damgan. It would take perhaps an hour before we arrived, which seemed very long for me. We would get off the bus in front of a little *café* in downtown Damgan and unload our luggage and treasures. It was like a great party because many people were there to meet their families and friends—and, indeed, my grandmother always came to greet us wearing her traditional long black dress and white *coiffe* (headdress). She would be pushing a wheelbarrow, like everyone else, to carry all the suitcases from the bus.

"Back then, Damgan was a little village of 300 to maybe 350 people. There were many farms in the area, as it was a rural community, and I remember the smell of the farms was sometimes . . . quite strong. Especially in the heat of summer. But no matter, because this was also a community by the sea, and many people came to spend their vacations in little seaside cottages.

"We would arrive at my grandmother's house. It was an old house with a very big yard. The first thing we did was to put on our summer clothes, and I remember everyone wore the same type of shoes—*espadrilles*—made of hemp. I was crazy with joy to be there! I loved the carefree summers—three full months where I could run and play with friends whom I had not seen since the summer before."

Micheline stopped her story. "You know, I am still friends with these same girls from my childhood, and now we all have children and grandchildren of our own."

"I imagine the reason I am here today is because of the rich friendship you two formed," I murmured.

"*C'est vrai*, Carole," Josiane said. "That's so true. We have been fortunate to have known each other most all our lives." Josiane shifted in her seat and pulled her feet up under her.

Micheline nodded and continued. "At that time, people came to Damgan by train and bus, but now everyone makes the trip by car, so those old ways are gone. I remember my parents bringing me to my grandmother's house, but then they had to return to Paris to work. But they traveled to Damgan on weekends and also spent their vacation month of August with us."

"Micheline," I interrupted, "was this the only time during the year that you saw your parents? Like Marcelle's mother coming only a few times a year to see her in Vannes? Did you ever talk to her about this?"

"Yes, I did. That was one of many things we had in common. As you may know, I spent my winter months with my maternal Polish grandmother in Piennes. During the Christmas holidays, I would sometimes get to see my parents, but most of the time when I was young, I lived without them."

"Sorry. I didn't mean to stop your story," I said. "Continue on."

"My grandmother lived in the same house as her great-grandparents from generations before. Her home was one of the few stable places I knew as a child. And, like me, other young children would arrive to spend summers with their grandparents. They came from Paris, from all over France," she said throwing her hands into the air, "and we would always meet at the same place every summer—under the eaves of a little cottage by the sea." She sighed and took a sip of her wine.

"After pulling on our summer espadrilles, the next 'first activity' of the summer was to get the bicycles in order. And then we would gallivant around on our bicycles going everywhere—down all the little paths, all the little streets. We were free to go everywhere, and everyone was on a bicycle, as there were not many cars back then.

"Of course, we spent a great deal of time on the beach. In fact, every afternoon until at least seven o'clock in the evening. At the beach, there were all these *catkins*—white flowers like little balls of fluff on long stalks. We liked to collect them and take them home."

"Like cattails?"

"No, not like cattails or pussy willows. They had much more fluff."

Josiane joined in. "I remember the fields of buttercups were always beautiful in the spring. The cows had not been allowed to go into those fields yet, but once they did, the fields were immediately empty of buttercups. And do you know what happens to their milk?" She laughed at our quizzical look. "It turns a beautiful shade of yellow. Do you remember, Micheline?"

I wondered if Josiane had had too much wine. But Micheline said, "Ah, yes. I remember we used to take a yellow dandelion and rub it under our chins—to see if we were in love."

"I only did that with buttercups, Micheline, but I couldn't be in love after the cows came by." They both giggled.

"So, back to the beach?" I urged.

"While we were at the beach," she continued, "we spent our time fishing among the rocks. We would fish for pleasure, but also for food. We took great pride in that! Some of my most special memories are going fishing with my father. We would fish for shrimps with an *haveneau*, which is a net used to catch the little shrimps."

"What exactly is this net like?" I asked.

Micheline jumped up and grabbed a small piece of paper. Puffing her lips in and out as she worked, she carefully sketched the net, indicating a contoured net with a long handle. Josiane leaned over and offered some help on the matter, then got up and refilled our glasses. At that point, I was grateful that I was recording the conversation, as I could barely see my pen and paper. The wine had blurred my vision. It had also wrapped us in an envelope of heat. Josiane must have been feeling it as she walked to the sliding glass door and opened it to let in cool air.

"Okay, here it is," Micheline said. She held up the picture and explained how her father wielded the net to catch shrimp. It reminded me of a handmade net my great-uncle used to catch catfish.

"My father would also fish with a harpoon. He would

look around the rocks and eventually find the conger eel. They were about two meters long and very difficult to catch, but because he was raised here, he knew all the best tricks. I thought he was wonderful, and I was so proud of him." She leaned over and turned on a lamp; her eyes were glistening in the telling.

"We children would stand in the water when we fished with our fathers and gather the mussels and oysters. The crabs were also easy to catch. We would lift the seaweed and, with a special hook, wiggle it about and shuffle the whole thing. The crabs would venture out and we would catch them. There were some places—special fishing holes—that were a little better than others. We also used special crab pots that were barrel shaped, where the crabs could go in but not get back out. Sometimes we would place old fish in the pots to attract the crabs. Oh! It was great sport!" She clapped her hands as if she were that gleeful child again.

"When we took the fish home, my grandmother would make soup. Especially a *matelote*, which is a fish soup made with conger eel. But this soup is loaded with bones—very, very fine bones. It was difficult to eat without straining it through our teeth." She gritted her teeth to indicate what they did and inhaled with a slish-slishing sound.

"Did you learn to make your grandmother's fish soup—the *matelote?*"

"No. It's a lot of trouble, but I do enjoy making her *co-triade*. This is a fish stew, which in Brittany is typically made with potatoes and onions cooked in butter or lard. I remember the recipe and it is one where I use a great deal of shellfish. That's the main difference between *bouillabaisse* and *cotriade*."

"There is no *roux* used in *cotriade*, which is that russet thickening sauce made with olive oil and tomatoes commonly used in *bouillabaisse.* As you may know, *roux* is used as a base for the Mediterranean soups cooked only in Marseille or Provençe. We don't use *roux* in Brittany; we simply use the best mussels and oysters we can find."

"Did you learn to cook from your Breton grandmother?"

"I think so. My grandmother was a good cook and she always had a big garden, so we had plenty of fresh vegetables and wonderful fruit from our own trees. This was a real pleasure—and a difference from my subsistence in Piennes, where food was difficult to come by.

"Do you want family recipes, too? There is a cake that is very important in Brittany. It used to be if you went to someone's home for coffee or a small meal, you were to bring a *Far Breton.* Have you heard of that?"

"I believe so, but I don't think I have a recipe," I said.

Micheline jumped up from the sofa and disappeared into the kitchen. She came back with a handful of recipe cards. "Here it is," she said. "My grandmother used to make her *Far Breton* using fresh pears instead of plums. I suppose that was because she had so many pears in her yard and the plums were very expensive."

"I also have a great recipe for a cake made with pears," Josiane said. "It's much like a cobbler, and it is always a success. Come to think of it, I believe I got it from my mother. I wonder if it was a Breton recipe. I remember my mother saying there were no cherry trees in Brittany, so instead of cherries, they used pears."

"Yes, the fruits we use in Brittany are plums, apples, and pears. Those are the most common fruits here. And they are scrumptious!" Micheline smacked her lips. "Shall we have dessert?"

"Oh, in a few minutes. That would be lovely," I said.

"Okay. I remember, too, that the nearby farms were very small and had only a few pigs, cows, horses . . . They would sell their milk to the villagers and make butter—much like we saw the women at the market today, the *p'tites dames au beurre*. Every day trucks came to the farms to take the milk and butter to the cities. These were very small farms—only ten or twenty cows."

"Like at my brother Martial's farm. Very small," Josiane said.

I was busy listening and taking notes, but I happened to glance up just in time to catch Micheline's face, which was simply glowing. *She's no longer sitting across from me,* I thought. *She's back in her childhood.*

Micheline continued. "The area around Damgan did not have a large variety of vegetables. It must have been the lack of good soil, as we are so close to the sea.

"Now, we have what you would call the 'farm produce shops,' where people drive to the farms and buy their produce directly from the farmers. It is a very nice experience—much like when I was a child—because you get to know the farmers who grow the products, and you get to know how to prepare them. You can buy direct from the farm, products such as a suckling veal to *foie gras*, eggs, honey, cider, chickens, flower-pot jam, venison, and ostrich meat—right from the farmer."

"How do people find these farm shops? Are they just for the locals?" I asked.

"Oh, *trés simple*. You look for signs that say '*Bienvenue à la ferme*,' which means 'Welcome to the Farm.' These are open only during the summer seasons and the tourists love them because they can see the farm production." She laughed. "What now seems charming to tourists was a very real part of my past. I guess I should feel old."

"What about fresh seafood?" I asked. I was determined to capture as much information as I could. "Are there special places to find that other than the Saturday market?"

"People go directly to oyster farms, or to the fishing boats to buy their oysters directly from the fishermen. They also buy their shrimps, and mussels . . . They appreciate the work that is done, as they can see how tough it is. This type of buying is relatively old, but the buying from the farmers market at the farm is relatively new."

At this point, we decided to take a break from the conversation. It was time for a nap, as all three of us were dragging. *Perhaps another walk along the beach and maybe some answers about Marcelle,* I thought.

An hour later, Josiane and I invited Micheline to join us in a walk along the sea, but she was busy catching up on weekend chores and email. The wind had picked up and the water was etched with vivid whitecaps. The brackish green water coursed up onto the shore. If there had been a sunset, it would not have been visible, as the sky was slate gray with the darkening clouds. Overhead a helicopter hovered, circling and circling over the water. Small search boats followed the helicopter, also circling and searching. It was an ominous sight. As the winds increased and began to howl, Josiane and I were stricken with the realization that the lifeboats had returned once . . . twice . . . three times, and the bodies of three fishermen were stretched out on the shore, side by side, awaiting ambulances to take them to the morgue. Church bells began to ring, sounding the knell.

When the ambulance drivers arrived, Josiane eased up to talk with them. I hung back awaiting word but fearing the worst.

"The drivers tell me," Josiane returned to say, "these fishermen are strangers to this area. No one seems to know them, yet their lives have been extinguished. This is so sad." We stood silent with shoulders slumped. A prayer passed between us. To have died in an accident close to home and familiarity would be tragic enough, but to have died far from home seemed a colder death to fathom.

"It seems even more tragic," Josiane said, "that no one knows them." The sea at that point had lost its appeal, and we trudged back to the house silently, again sending up prayers for the men on the beach.

"I imagine this is a common occurrence for sailors and fishermen alike," I said. My thoughts were on my husband, who often casts out to sea for a good sail.

"Oh, yes. My mother used to talk about the dangers of the sea, as she knew many who had lost their lives."

When we returned, we settled down for a cup of tea and began to talk once again. This time the discussion was about Micheline's family and her grandmother in particular.

"How would you describe your grandmother, or the women in Brittany?" I asked. "I have some idea from Marcelle, but I would like to know your thoughts."

Micheline thought for a moment. "For one thing, they are not very tall; in fact, they are on the short side. A little bit round! They have high cheekbones, with almond-shaped eyes. I guess they look a lot like me, but with dark hair. Not black, black hair, but dark brown. Yes, I would say the women of Brittany usually have dark brown hair and very blue eyes."

"Would that describe your mother, Josiane?" I was trying to remember Marcelle's eye color.

"All but the very blue eyes. Hers were dark brown, but the rest of the description fits her."

"What were their clothes like, or their costumes? You

mentioned your grandmother wore a long black dress and her *coiffe* to meet you at the bus station."

"Lace played an integral part in Breton national dress, particularly in the most immediately recognizable items, like the lace *coiffe* or ladies' headdress. Each region of Brittany can be identified by the style of the *coiffe*. For instance, Pont-Aven has a great starched sweeping lace collar plus the *coiffe,* which is a lace crown with lace streamers down the back. In Bigouden, the *coiffe* used to be quite small until 1930, but now, curiously, is very tall. Quimper's *coiffe* is small and worn on the crown of the head. And Plougastel has a traditional medieval appearance with ribbons tied on the side.

Brittany possesses costumes of surprising richness and variety. The fine clothes are prized and cared for and passed from one generation to the next. It was once customary for a girl at marriage to acquire a costly and magnificent outfit, which she would wear on all Sundays and at all public occasions. After the headdress, the most striking feature of traditional dress was the apron, which revealed how well-off the family was by the richness of its décor. The aprons, of every size and shape, were made of velvet or satin and were brocaded or trimmed with lace.

"The men wore long waistcoats, with black pants, and a black felt or velvet broad-brimmed hat with a wide velvet or grosgrain ribbon draping down the back, about to the waist."

"Do you remember seeing people in these costumes?" I asked.

"Oh, yes. They were very common, especially for church services, weddings, and festivals. And we loved our festivals. Women now wear their traditional clothing only for *Pardons*—pilgrimages—and special occasions. Very rarely do the older women wear their traditional clothing or *coiffes*." She paused to think. "I guess twenty years ago it was more common to see this style. But my grandmother always wore the dark dresses and *coiffe*. This tradition died out when these ladies passed away."

"Did you ever wear the traditional clothing—either of you?" I asked.

"I never wore it, and neither did you—right, Josiane?"

"Oh, no, and my mother never did either," Josiane replied. "In fact, I believe the tradition began to fade shortly after people began to leave the region and live elsewhere—such as in Paris. I'm told my grandmother did not wear the traditional dress after World War I, because she left for Paris, but my great-grandmother wore it until she died."

Just then the bells began ringing again down the street. I asked Micheline to explain, as they had been chiming off and on while we had been talking.

"When someone dies, the church bells in the village begin to ring. Seven bells for women. Nine bells for a man. People stop and say a prayer, and within an hour everyone in the community knows who has died. Of course, in the old days, it was almost always told 'mouth-to-mouth.' The burials were usually performed the next day, and everybody in the village came, whether they knew the dead or not. It was the custom to drop whatever you were doing and go. Now the newspaper reports the death and lists when the burial will take place.

"My good friend, Janet, who lives nearby, never misses a funeral. But one time she was terribly embarrassed, as she showed up at a funeral of someone she never knew, and the few in attendance were certain she had come strictly for the repast that followed the funeral. How we howled about that later!" she said, throwing her head back and laughing. "Janet is a dignified, refined woman and she would never attend for that reason. She learned the hard way."

"Janet is Micheline's dear friend," Josiane explained. "They met because she is the mother of one of Micheline's childhood friends who now lives far away. Just like Micheline became friends with my *maman*."

"Yes," Micheline said, trying to compose herself once again. "Janet used to open up her home to all of us children during the summer months when I was a child. We still talk about how she used to play with us and loan us old costumes for play. As I recall, the costumes came from the attic, and we would act out pieces of theater up there and even jumped from the attic—out the window—holding to an old broken umbrella, like a parachute. Fortunately, we didn't break anything. We must have been very lucky. And in her garden, there was a very old rabbit hutch, and when the weather was not so nice, we would go into the rabbit hutch to hide.

"Aha!" she said, with a gleam in her eye. "I remember when I was twelve—I received my first kiss right there in that rabbit hutch. Mmm! Such sweet memories. Or maybe I was fourteen. It doesn't matter. I was so in love with him."

"Micheline, which holidays, birthdays, or summer events did you celebrate here in Brittany?"

"I was lucky because I always got to celebrate my birthday, the 26th of August, here in Damgan. It was also a special time because my parents were here for the entire month of August from Paris. That was a special treat! My mother always made the *Quatre Quart,* which is another special cake made with lots and lots of butter. All my friends would be invited to the party. It was a wonderful time!"

"How did people celebrate weddings in Damgan?"

She reflected for a moment, "I saw the last grand wedding

in the area. It was a very, very big wedding of the daughter of the owner of one large farm to the son of the owner of another large farm. The wedding took place in an open field, with two or three hundred people. The tables of food were set up outside. For the wedding feast, the butcher killed two cows, a couple of pigs—oh, there was a lot of meat, and it was all cooked outside. And each guest brought his own table service or silverware. This is actually a medieval custom. And we sat on boards, which were supported on large stones because there were not enough seats for everyone to sit down to eat. The musicians were in their Breton costumes playing the *bombarde*, the *biniou* . . ."

She saw my confused expression. "The oboe and the bagpipes," she said.

"Wedding celebrations lasted about one week. There were fewer people on each one of these days, but for the grand feast, there were at least three hundred. Some nights everyone went to the villages to dance in the streets, and we would dance in front of each *café*, moving from one to the next. We were eating and drinking the whole time. It was great fun! My friend Janet and I still talk about that wedding because it was so spectacular. And that was many years ago."

"I asked about weddings because I read something about a 'milk soup' tradition at Brittany weddings. Do you know anything about this?"

"Oh, I do know about that. After the wedding, the bride and groom are not left alone for many nights of the celebration, and so they have absolutely no peace . . . and they can't go to bed! None of that! I believe the milk soup is prepared with milk and some garlic and spices. Originally, it was to represent a marriage, which has its smooth days and spicy days. But, on the last of these days, the soup is very spicy, indeed, and meant to tease and make great fun with the newly married couple. I've heard it can get quite raucous, at times. I wasn't married here in Brittany, and I'm glad I wasn't." She covered her mouth with her hand and giggled.

"Has that changed over the years?"

"Yes, it has changed a lot, as now families do not have as much money. They have simple weddings, one-day affairs. That is ordinary now. Everything became too expensive."

"I know I'm asking you a lot of questions, but I find the traditions here in Brittany so interesting, so charming," I said. "And also, because Marcelle told me about a special Breton tradition that involves the *Pardons*. Have you participated in any?"

Micheline sat up and grew very animated as she spoke.

"Oh, these are wooonderful! A number of special *Pardons* are held in Brittany that I remember, but my favorite and the most famous is still held every July 26 for St. Anne. She is the Patron Saint of Brittany."

"Carole," Josiane said, "the little statue above Micheline's front door is Sainte Anne d'Auray. The same St. Anne."

"Oh, you will love this," Micheline said. Excitement lit up her eyes. "The *Grande Pardon,* which takes place at the chapel in the little village of St. Anne d'Auray, is only three miles from the town of Auray in the Diocese of Vannes. It is also not far from Damgan. In very early times, Christians dedicated a chapel in her honor. I believe it was around the end of the seventh century that the first chapel was destroyed, but the memory of it was kept alive by tradition, and the village was still called Keranna, which means Village of Anne. More than nine centuries later, at the beginning of the seventeenth century, St. Anne is said to have appeared several times to a simple but pious villager and commanded him to rebuild the ancient chapel. The apparitions became so frequent, and before so many witnesses, that the Bishop of Vannes finally gave permission for rebuilding the chapel. Anne of Austria and Louis XIII enriched the sanctuary with many gifts, among them a relic of St. Anne brought from the pope. In the meanwhile, pilgrimages or *Pardons* began and became more numerous, year after year. The Revolution did not even put a stop to them, but the chapel, indeed, was plundered again.

"It was the Carmelites who were serving the chapel at the time, who were driven out, and the miraculous statue of St. Anne was burned at Vannes in 1793, yet the faithful still flocked to the chapel. There is an old Breton saying: *Sainte Anne d'Auray, c'est notre mere a tous; mort our vivant, dit-on, a Sainte-Anne, une fois, doit aller tout Breton.* Saint Anne is the mother to us all. We say that any Breton, whether dead or alive, must at one time go to visit Sainte Anne.

"So, what is this *Pardon*, you asked? It's carrying the statues of the saints, and the banners of every church from the surrounding areas, while the pilgrims arrive wearing their Breton costumes, which are worn only at weddings and these special *Pardons*. The *Grande Pardon* begins in St. Anne d'Auray, at the church, where a mass is heard early in the morning, perhaps at 4 am. The people come to give thanks to St. Anne or present her with a request. Some people used to go on their knees to St. Anne in thanks for granting their requests from the year before. Following the mass, a procession begins, and this is the most picturesque part of the *Pardon*. I wish you could see this, Carole.

"The procession is led by the bishop and all the other diocesan priests, who are followed by hundreds of people. Into this procession join all of those whom the intercession of Sainte Anne has saved from peril and danger. The sailors are there with fragments of their boats, upon which they escaped shipwreck; the lame are carrying on their shoulders their own crutches; those who have been rescued from a fire are carrying a rope or ladder showing the means by which they escaped the flames. And the fishermen carry a small reproduction boat, which was made by them and carried only during this procession. This was the fishermen's way of thanking God as well as asking for protection, for safety, and for a good catch in the coming year. More people continue out of the chapel carrying the many statues, called '*ex-votos*', made of painted wood, and are very, very old. Sometimes when they were made of basalt and were so heavy, they would be carried on a plinth with at least four strong young men. And of course, always there is Breton music and religious songs. Do you understand now what a *Pardon* is?"

"Yes, I believe . . . it must be very beautiful and meaningful for each participant."

By that point in the evening, we were exhausted from talking and sipping wine. And around nine o'clock, after eating a late omelet—made by me, of all people, the only non-French woman among us—along with a salad, toast, and jam, we finally trundled off to bed.

"Tomorrow," Josiane said, "will be another busy travel day. So, get some good sleep!"

I wasn't sure that would happen, as visions of traditional music, dance, weddings, and *Pardons* danced through my head for some time before I drifted off to sleep.

There's a communion of more than our bodies when bread is broken and wine drunk. "

—M.F.K. Fisher

Basse-Normandie

Île-de-France

Brittany

Pays de la Loire

Loire River

Fontevraud

Azay-le-Rideau

Angers

Valley

Loire

Chenonceau

Chinon

Richelieu

Centre

Poitou Charles

N

0   25 mi

0   25 km

Limousin

CHAPTER TWELVE

*One Thousand Years of History
and Truffle Farms, Too*

*A*s Josiane began to pull out of the driveway early the next morning, it seemed appropriate to call out to Micheline, *"Kenavo, au revoir,"* as she had taught me to say in Breton. *Goodbye for now.* I was surprised to find that despite our short time together, I had formed a warm friendship with Mimi and would miss her.

Josiane drove down the route Peggy had given her and began to head out of Brittany. I sat quietly, reflecting on the connections I had made over the past few days, both physical and emotional. I couldn't help but notice that I felt a strange mystical pull—back to the parts of Brittany we had just visited.

Unable to address this feeling, I asked Josiane, "Are you also having a difficult time leaving Brittany?"

She gave me a sidelong glance, and a sad expression graced her sweet face.

"It's curious that you ask, but I've always felt that. Like a large magnet pulling me back. I don't know what it is; it's like I'm leaving 'home' and I feel compelled to immediately turn around and return. I thought it was just me."

"No wonder your mother struggled when she was away from her home. But there's also something that feels . . . Well, I can't describe it . . . it seems elusive."

"Like a *korrigan?*" Josiane giggled.

"Maybe. When I try to understand your mother's character—which must be the embodiment of the Breton people—description slips away from me. It's like attempting to separate the color blue from water. It feels palpable, yet ethereal at the same time. Maybe I'm trying too hard."

My fingers were tapping a tattoo on my chin as I attempted to sort out this enigma.

"Even when someone, like my mother, has been away from Brittany for long periods of time, this magnetic pull—this hold and belief system—seems to linger on. That's why my mother wanted us to return with her—one last time."

We rode in silence, contemplating this dynamic, viewing the remaining bits of Brittany as it flashed by the car.

"And another thing," I said. "I find it remarkable that Micheline's childhood story mirrors your mother's in so many ways, and she carries some of the same characteristics—such strength and independence."

"I think the two of them shared a lot in common. I'm sure that's what drew them together."

"Josiane, I know your mother shared a close relationship with Mimi, but no one could replace you in your mother's heart. No one! I could see that in how you two were with each other the short time I spent in your company. It was a joy to witness, believe me!"

"Thank you, Carole. I do so miss her." As Josiane started to tear up, I changed the subject.

"Where are we headed today?"

"Oh," Josiane said, as she dabbed her nose with a Kleenex,

"we're headed through the Loire country. We will make a stopover for lunch in Angers." She negotiated a tricky turn onto N165 toward Nantes.

We continued to chat and laugh about conversations from the day before, especially the comedic retelling of St. Anne d'Auray's story. Before we knew it, we crossed the River Mayenne and were in the city of Angers in the province of Anjou. Josiane pulled into a parking lot facing an immense castle—the Chateau d'Angers.

I stared out the window at the fortress before us, counting the towers (seven that I could see from the car), which rose at least two hundred feet above us. It was only mid-morning, so Josiane encouraged me to take a tour of the castle.

"The last excursion of the morning will probably begin shortly. I must make some phone calls to arrange for our next stay, so why don't you go ahead. I'll be back to pick you up in a couple of hours and we'll have lunch."

I was somewhat used to navigating on my own, but I felt timid about attempting, one more time, to sort out the language. I proceeded over the drawbridge across the moat and to the entrance gates of the castle. I purchased my ticket, which included an English-speaking tour—thank you—and stood in the inner courtyard near the formal gardens awaiting the time to begin. Sunlight fell on my shoulders and warmed my chilled body, as I continued to reflect on conversations over the past few days. Oh, the wonderful history we had covered, from Celtic to present day, and now I would be reaching back again, but into medieval history.

The visit took me into the feudal fortress built of limestone and schist that was occupied by the notorious medieval counts of Anjou in the ninth century, the Plantagenet Kings of England's extensive rule in the twelfth century, King Louis

I of Anjou in 1360 and Louis II in 1410, followed by Good King René of 1450–65, and on past the Huguenots' rule, to King Louis XIV in 1652. The fortress, our guide informed us, had remained grim in color and design until succeeding monarchs, such as King René I, added charm to the castle with gardens, aviaries, and a menagerie.

"The outer wall is over 9.5 feet thick, extends for about 2,170 feet and is protected by seventeen massive towers. Each of the perimeter towers measures 59 feet in diameter and the château covers an area of 220,000 square feet. Two pairs of towers form the city and landward entrances of the château. Each of the towers was once 130 feet in height, but they were later cut down for the use of artillery pieces. The Tour du Moulin is the only tower which conserves the original elevation," the guide continued. I scribbled notes down as fast as I could, but actually, I was moderately curious.

But then she said, as she turned directly toward me, "Even though the fortress faced many enemies throughout the centuries, it was the Allied bombers who wrought significant damage to the building during World War II, as the Germans were using this space as a munitions base." I have since read that the damage was done by the Germans themselves, but I immediately felt fully responsible, as if being from the U.S. made me complicit in this castle's demise.

"But now," the guide said, as she continued walking, "carefully restored parts of the building house one of France's most famous tapestries—the Apocalypse Tapestry. It's very similar to the Bayeux Tapestry, but not quite as old. This one was woven in the fourteenth century for Duke Louis I of Anjou. The carefully crafted woven panels illustrate St. John's visions of the end of times, from the Book of Revelations."

Standing before the 338-foot masterpiece, I couldn't help

but feel the hopelessness created by the images of the devils devouring all of Babylon. Frankly, feeling the weight of destruction on my back, and with the prospect of war looming outside the castle after the 9/11 attacks, all of life seemed foreboding to me. Humankind's need to bring more devastation onto itself was more than daunting.

I plodded through the dark, gray hallways with the other tourists, climbed the uneven steps up onto the parapet, and attempted to peer out into the outer courtyard (I was too short.). Again, I felt overcome with the threats of war and death all around me.

I decided to break away from the group and wandered down to the garden and back onto the drawbridge. I peered over the gates and down, down the 36-foot walls to the verdant floor below me. Geometric gardens with ornamental borders filled the 100-foot-wide swath of the former moat. My eyes swept over the beauty of the gardens and then were drawn once again up the fortress walls. It was difficult to imagine that almost eight hundred years of history had played itself out here . . . all the way up to and including the devastating explosion brought on by the Nazis storing munitions here during World War II. *Unfathomable,* I thought. *What human foibles have been encountered?*

A small cloud of butterflies hovered over the colorful bushes below when . . . a horn honked close behind me, and I turned to see Josiane waving from the car. I waved back, rejoiced at seeing a friendly face, and quickly joined her. She was in high spirits and excited about some of the calls she had made while I had been busy slogging through history. She had talked to Christian again and he was going to join us at her brother Martial's in a few days.

"And even though I was not able to secure a hotel room

in a troglodyte cave for the evening," she said, "Madame Gaulandeau has room for us to come one day early to her truffle farm."

"A truffle farm?" I had no idea what a troglodyte cave was, much less a truffle farm, but the latter sounded delicious!

"Just so you have the experience of these caves, after lunch we will head through Saumur toward a troglodyte village, where we will stop to see them before we head toward Chinon and south toward Richelieu.

"You'll love all these places—especially the truffle farm. You will find it quite surprising," Josiane gushed. She pulled away from the curb and took a left onto Boulevard du Roi René. En route, we stopped for a short lunch—probably one of our shortest, at one and a half hours—at a fine hotel/ restaurant called Aubérge de la Rose. The sign outside indicated *Cuisine Traditionnelle et Raffinée.*

"Have you been here before?" I asked. I was doing my best to keep up as she rushed me to the front door.

"No, but when I see a sign like that, I know we will find good traditional food inside. That's what you want to sample, *n'est-ce pas?*"

"*Mais oui,*" I said, "and what is *raffinée?*"

"That is the key word, *mon ami.* It means refined or sophisticated. Sound good to you?"

"But of course," I burbled, as we were quickly escorted through the dining room. White tablecloths covered small intimate tables; glass chandeliers sparkled above; mustard-yellow provincial print wallpaper covered the walls, and matching damask curtains separated the dining area from the hotel. We were seated in the center of the dining room.

"After we share a plate of *Friture de la Loire*—it's like

french-fried smelt but is local fish from the Loire River—we will have to share a plate of *Rillettes du Mans*, which is usually a paté of shredded potted rabbit or goose. In this case, I believe it is rabbit, which the menu says is served along with garden greens," Josiane said, and placed our order.

The French have a splendid way with anything french-fried. I don't know how they can turn a plain potato, or anything for that matter, into the most delicate of foods with a simple and brief glancing through hot oil, but they do. The food was feather light and delicious. And I was hungry. I needed to replenish my fortitude, I told Josiane, having marched through eight hundred years of history before lunchtime.

We declined the cheese course when it was offered, but Josiane insisted we try a local dessert called *Crémets d'Anjou*. A small crown of soft creamy pudding, made of whipped double cream and egg whites, was presented to each of us, ringed with enormous fresh strawberries. Certainly, more than we needed, but again, *délectable!* And it did not contain apples. After cups of cappuccino, we hit the road again.

"Next I will take you to Rochemenier, a village built into the porous limestone of the Loire's ancient river valleys, called 'tufa.'"

"That must be why the wines taste so good from this area," I said. "In the southern reaches of Tuscany where my husband and I stayed for ten days, there were entire ancient Etruscan villages dug out of the tufa, surrounded by miles and miles of vineyards that yielded—my, oh my—some of the best Italian wines we've ever tasted."

"*Bon!* Then you are familiar with this. Here they have some excellent hotels and restaurants that still reside inside the caves. I was hoping we could stay in one tonight, but my favorite is booked. Too bad! You would have enjoyed the experience. And people to this day still live in these little warrens. We'll see some carved-out chapels, dovecotes, wine cellars, along with homes and stores. Some of these caves have been in continuous use since the twelfth century. Quite unique, don't you think?"

"Do people still live in the caves we'll be visiting?"

"No. But I think we will get an idea of how families used to live here."

We rolled into what looked like an open field adjoining some farm buildings. We walked across the flat, dusty field to a small hut to purchase our tickets. We were led to a large, inconspicuous hole where, as we climbed down, down into the earth, the air temperature was much cooler than on top, yet the air smelled—oddly—fresh. The tour guide said the caves had been in use for at least a thousand years, he thought. As we continued to descend, we squeezed past large lift systems that had been rigged up to raise and lower farm products from the farmyards below (along the river). Although the floor seemed dusty, the owner said that this was from lack of use. When the caves were inhabited, the floors were usually swept clean and the families who had lived in these carved-out rooms were quite comfortable.

It was an experience worth thinking about, but Josiane decided she wouldn't have made a very happy "cave rat," as she called it. "I suppose it was better than nothing. And it is not so much different from the cave dwellers north of Santa Fe, New Mexico. I think the time period of cave dwellers in the American Southwest was around seven hundred years ago. So, these caves may be older."

"Good point," I said. "I wonder if these caves were occupied during World War II. This would have been a perfect place for your fellow countrymen to hide out. And we know that the Germans roamed all over this area. I believe the tour guide mentioned the Chateau d'Angers was bombed by the Allies because it was being used for German munitions."

"Layers and layers of history are here," said Josiane brushing the dust from her clothes and heading back toward the car. She had seen enough. "We need to make our way to the truffle farm before it gets too dark to see."

We popped back into the car, where Josiane shifted into gear and into her role of tour guide once more (Which, for her, was every waking hour, poor thing!).

"This area of the Loire Valley is best known for the magnificent chateaux built by French royalty over the centuries. We will tour some of them tomorrow, as I know you will find them fascinating. More so than that grim fortress you just went through. And those caves." She blew dust from her jacket. "These all come with kitchens." She grinned.

I had done no homework to prepare for this region, so I sat back and listened to Josiane as I took in the beauty of the multiple tributaries that flowed into the Loire River. Broad, fertile plains undulated in sensuous turns above the rivers. Reed beds and flooded meadows inched up toward the roadway. I rolled down my window to catch the call of a redwing blackbird and waterfowl that had made the riverfront home. From the waterways rose soft hills covered in a mélange of vineyards. Row upon row of vines were hitched onto bamboo poles that marched like soldiers, up and out of sight over the hills beyond. Josiane eased around turns in the road where forests sprang up out of nowhere with magnificent oaks, horse chestnuts, pines, and beech trees. Then open spaces appeared once again, for the sole purpose, she said, of capturing a good view.

"We didn't stop in the village of Saumur in order to catch

the troglodyte caves, but remember the name for wonderful wines," Josiane said.

"I do," I said. "You chose one the other night at the manor near Mont St. Michel."

"*Mais oui!* Perhaps this evening we will sample some in . . . well, wherever we end up!" We continued along the Vienne River and through the historical city of Chinon, hung a right, and headed south on a route toward Richelieu.

"I think it's around here somewhere," Josiane said as she fumbled through her maps as she drove. Peggy had become cantankerous—she was not familiar with this road and continually barked orders. *"Retournez! Retournez! Vite!"*

Despite Peggy's remonstrations, Josiane soon shouted, "There it is," pointing to an immense white stone chateau surrounded by a small forest of oak trees. Beyond the fortified walls, decorated turrets atop cylindrical towers poked above the trees. Corbelled walkways, possibly used during battles, skirted the upper stories along the dormer windows.

"This is wonderful! This is so grand!" I blurted.

"Actually, that's not where we're staying. The truffle farm is back over there." She pointed to a few low-to-the-ground stone buildings.

"The truffle farm is housed in those farming buildings attached to the chateau. Sorry to get your hopes up, but I believe you will be pleased."

"I believe you also used the adjectives 'surprised' and 'pleased' when you spoke earlier of coming here. You've yet to steer me wrong—so far." I grinned broadly at having quoted a favorite quip of Homer Simpson's.

When we climbed out of the car, on the back lot of the property, a frenzy of barking rose from inside the gates. Be-

yond the outer gate, which led to an inner gate and courtyard, scrabbled two boisterous dogs.

"There's our welcoming committee," Josiane said cheerfully. She began walking toward the gate, with me lagging
reluctantly behind. I wasn't sure about the dogs . . .

"I think we should check in before we drag our luggage
through there, don't you?" she said.

"Good idea!" I put a small bag back into the car and we
walked together to the wooden gates. We saw a woman inside
the farmhouse beckoning us to come in. The dogs immediately
quieted and raced off to the side to play in the garden. Madame
Gaulandeau greeted us in the grassy courtyard with a hearty
smile.

"Don't worry about the dogs," she said. "They sound
much fiercer than they are. They are supposed to guard me,
but they seem to have more fun challenging each other. Welcome."

At the word *chien* (dogs), the two bounded up again. The
older, smaller, black and white border collie was clearly in
charge. With nips and barks, she was demanding that the
dark brown, bright-eyed, scruffy spaniel settle down. It was
clear she had her work cut out for her. Finally, success. We
couldn't help but laugh.

"These dogs are not just our guard dogs," Mme. Gaulandeau said. "Poof!" she exhaled. "No. No. No. They are our
truffle dogs. They are most important to our operation.
Zabou, the older, has the gift of a most incredible nose and
for many years has led the *cavage* parties—that's the term for
scouting for the fragrant tubers—or truffles."

She motioned us through one of the doors leading into
what had been the livestock quarters centuries before. The
stone-on-stone walls, which appeared ready to fall in, sup-

ported an ancient, low-hanging, red barrel-tile roof, green with years of mossy overgrowth. We stepped through a deep-set doorway, past a Dutch door and into a large open room, which was obviously Madame's living room. A black leather sofa sat against one wall, with a colorful tapestry stretched across the wall above. Large overstuffed chairs sat opposite the sofa and antique side chairs were throughout the room. Over the old ceramic tile flooring were red Oriental rugs, and in one corner was a television set and numerous bookcases. She led us through another deep-set doorway into a dining room. At a long wooden table that would easily accommodate twelve were place settings for two—for our breakfast in the morning. She handed us keys to our rooms, then invited us to return for tea once we got settled.

Josiane and I discovered we each had our own room. Both were immaculate and nicely appointed with a four-poster bed with blue and white gingham bed curtains, matching sitting chairs, and a clean, modern bathroom.

We headed back to the car to retrieve our luggage. "Josiane," I said, "I think this is one of the nicest rooms I've ever stayed in. It is simply lovely. Yes, you were right! I'm surprised and quite pleased."

My buoyant attitude started to slip a tad as we dragged our luggage over the gravel driveway, through the double gates, hoping not to let the dogs out, and across the grassy courtyard. By the time we stowed our bags into the rooms, I was exhausted. And ready for tea.

"Grab your notepad, Carole, and your tape recorder. This may be the time for our interview. I set it up in advance, but I'm not certain if it will happen today or tomorrow."

We ducked back into the main house—of course followed by two overly curious dogs. Just as the large spaniel set one paw inside the door, Mme. Gaulandeau turned and stared him down. Zabou nipped at the young upstart, as if he knew his counterpart was in trouble. Clearly, he was saying, "Didn't I tell you, Mutt-face? I knew she wouldn't let us in."

Mme. Gaulandeau set up the tea service in the living room. Once we settled into our chairs, she served us hot tea and small sweet biscuits and settled in across from us on the sofa. She said she would be happy to talk with us about her truffle business, but she had an engagement early that evening. While Josiane was writing down recommendations for that night's dinner in Chinon, I relaxed back into my seat, which was close to the door. The door was slightly ajar. Out of the corner of my eye, I noticed the lower half of the Dutch door slowly, slowly begin to swing open. I'm sure a look of surprise flashed across my face. I poked Josiane to take a look, and we both burst out laughing. There, standing on the threshold were both dogs sheepishly staring in at the *tête-à-tête* before them. Although all eight paws were comfortably outside the door frame, one of the collie's paws was stealthily easing open —centimeter by centimeter—the lower half of the door.

"Oh, you scamps!" Mme. Gaulandeau snapped, then stood up and firmly closed both sections of the door. She began to apologize but could see we were enjoying this comedic interlude. She smiled, shrugged her shoulders, and sat back down.

"So, to begin," Josiane said, "when did you start your truffle business?"

"Our first plantation was started twenty years ago. My husband and I had read a lot about this area, and learned that in the past, there had been many truffle farms near here. But that, of course, was long, long ago."

I looked up from my notepad. "How long ago?"

"I believe it was before the Revolution in 1789. At the

time there was only one oven in a community to bake the bread. After the Revolution that law changed, and everyone in the village could have his own oven. That was wonderful and much more convenient, but as a result there was a lot of deforestation. People needed wood not only for baking, but also for heat. Many of the oak trees, which are essential for truffles to form, were eliminated.

"On the land that had been cleared of oak trees, people began to plant grapes. Then in the 1860s, phylloxera attacked the grapes, destroying the vineyards. The winemakers, knowing that after you have grown grapes on a piece of land, there is very little that can be successfully planted, began again to plant oak trees. They used the acorns to start the trees. They continued to work the land with the remaining grapes, but after a while people realized that truffles were growing on the roots of some of the oak trees. The mycelium of the truffle—which is the starter of a truffle—exists in most soils, except in some area such as the Alps, the Massif Central, or the Vosges. Our research found that the mycelium in the soil in the regions south of the Loire River were significant. To start a truffle, it needs a support, and the support within the root system comes from the oak trees." She took a sip of tea and bit into a butter biscuit.

"In this region," she continued, "the production of truffles reached as high as two thousand tons in a good year. But that is quite extraordinary."

"What exactly does that mean?" I asked.

"Poof!" she said, waving her hands in the air. "Well, to give you an example, France, in an average good year, harvests about sixty tons of truffles. Last year, there was a very small production of about eight tons, as a result of poor weather conditions, plus straight winds and such."

"That is harsh!" I exclaimed. Madame G. nodded.

"How many truffle farms are in this area?" Josiane asked. She popped a biscuit into her mouth.

"Until 1914, there were many farms producing truffles. And then, during World War I, the women had other things to do than produce truffles, and when the men returned from the war, a lot of tree trimming needed to be done. You see, the trees of a truffle farm must be trimmed so that enough light comes through the leaves. When the trees were neglected during all that time, they had become too thick and the production of truffles dropped very low. Then after World War II, the trees completely ceased to produce truffles. So, when we began twenty years ago, there were only two farms."

"Were truffles always considered a delicacy?"

"Yes. People always knew the culinary value of the truffles. They were using them as vegetables, whereas now they are only used as a condiment. Back in those days, the cooks would prepare a stuffed capon and use two kilos of truffles. And when you think that last winter one kilo of truffles cost 5,000 Francs . . ."

"How much is that, Josiane?" I asked.

"*Trés cher!* Around $800 per kilo," she chortled.

"*Oui!* That's why we now tend to use truffles only to season our food," Mme. Gaulandeau said.

"How did you get started with your farm?" I asked.

"First, we bought a young oak tree impregnated with mycelium and planted it. It was about one foot tall. It takes a long time before a truffle farm can produce—around sixteen years."

"One has to wait sixteen years before a return on the investment? Who can do that?" Josiane asked.

"Crazy people like us. It must be a passion. We have to be

creative, patient, and hard workers. At harvest time it is like a treasure hunt. No two years are alike. We never know if we will have a crop or not. And the size of a truffle varies: it could be the size of a pea or the size of an apple."

"Do you enjoy hunting with the dogs?" I asked. I could still hear the two dogs cavorting like puppies in the courtyard.

"Oh yes, very much. The work of the dog is marvelous. It is the same as the dog working with a game hunter. The dog is your leader. And a dog is more convivial than a pig and much more interesting. Oh my, yes! In this area, there are not many people who work with pigs. In the Perigord Region, older people still use pigs to hunt for truffles. We tried at one point, but our pig weighed about three hundred pounds, so it was difficult to train. And if it pulls on you, you are in trouble, as you are not stronger than the pig. We found it horrible! Once, we had a sow that pulled my husband across the snow and icy ground, before she escaped. That whole day we looked for that ungrateful sow, only to find her late in the evening. When we were able to get close to her— like three or four meters . . . we could almost touch her, and then she would bolt and run away again and again. I could have killed her!" Her face turned red with the frustration she had felt years ago.

"In any case, that is the way she was finished! She made a tasty ham and *rillettes*, I must say." She slapped her thigh and laughed.

I laughed along with her and tried to imagine her frustration with the animal they had counted on.

"Was this business a partnership with your husband?" Josiane asked.

"Yes. When we started our adventure, we knew nothing

about truffles. In fact, the only truffle I remember from when I was a kid, is the piece of truffle in the can of *foie gras* at Christmas. At that time, manufacturing regulations required that the truffles be heated for many hours, which destroyed the flavor of the truffle. That little piece of truffle in the center of the slice of *foie gras* had no taste whatsoever and was like chewing on a piece of rubber!"

"I never experienced the pleasure of smelling or tasting real truffles," Josiane said, her face open with anticipation.

"I'm so sorry we don't have any for you to sample. Last year was very poor for truffles. But the flavor of the truffle is very powerful. The first time my husband came home with a truffle in his pocket, I smelled it right away. If you are interested in just smelling the truffles, you should go to a shop in Paris, just near Fauchon during the truffle season in winter. There you will see and smell the truffles. The people from Fauchon come here to buy our truffles at $350 per kilo, and then they sell them in their shop at $500 per kilo."

"Are the truffles white?" I asked.

"Yes, ours are always white. It is not necessary to cook them at all, so you can use them in *carpaccio*, steak tartare. Whatever."

"I imagine you slice them thinly, correct?" I asked. "By the way, how do you cook with truffles?"

"Yes, you slice them paper-thin. People who have never used truffles should use them for the first time with eggs. It is the easiest way." She placed her teacup down and began to demonstrate with her hands. "You put one truffle in a box of twelve eggs, which have not yet been cooked, and seal a plastic bag around them. We keep the eggs and truffle in a bag for four to five days. The flavor of the truffle goes directly into the eggs. Then you can cook the eggs, soft boiled or any other way. You can prepare scrambled eggs with thin slivers of truffle. You can even crush fresh truffles and mix them with butter and spread the truffle-butter on a piece of bread that you dip into the soft-boiled egg. It is *délicieuse!*"

"So simple," I said. "And sounds delectable! You should write a book of your recipes."

Mme. Gaulandeau blushed. "I would not know how to do it. And there are so many recipes—and so few truffles. Truffles and caviar are the last two remaining delicacies at the highest level in gastronomy. Chefs love to work with truffles. But looking back at our last ten years of production, I concluded that we had only four wonderful crops. The other years were simply acceptable."

"It's a tremendous gamble," Josiane said.

"Mais oui! We never know. In April through June of each year, the truffles are born. They grow in July, August, and September. They need the summer rains. In October and November, they ripen. From December to February they can be harvested. This last year, because October through November was very dry, they didn't ripen, and in December it was too cold for them to ripen. That is why the crop was so poor."

"When you can harvest them, how do you sell them? Do people come to you, like those people from Paris?"

"Oui. We have long-time clients. Sometimes people come for an afternoon, and they go hunting for truffles with my husband and the dogs. When they come back, I prepare the truffles they've just harvested, for a late afternoon snack or an early dinner. It is quite convivial!

"As for the restaurants, they know about our production. They beg us for truffles. When the crop was as poor as the last one, it made many people very unhappy. But Mother Nature made the decision. But to answer your question, our customers usually call us. Oh, for a nice appetizer, you can prepare croutons with olive oil, and a thin slice of truffle, with a dash of *fleur de sel.* It is also *délicieuse*."

"And, once again, *trés* simple! What are some of your favorite truffle recipes, Madame?" I asked.

"Oh," Madame said with another Gallic puff, "you can prepare *potage* with mushrooms, *foie gras, crème fraiche,* and truffles. Prepare a cream of mushroom mixture, to which you add slivers of truffles. Then add the cream. In serving, use individual terrines or earthenware, preheated; add the uncooked *foie gras* cut in small pieces. Pour the *potage* on top of the *foie gras* in the terrine and serve."

"Not too many calories there," laughed Josiane. "Oh, Carole, I see you salivating. Me, too!"

"Another recipe of *potage*? Are you ready?" Madame Gaulandeau said, looking at me.

"Oh yes!" I turned the page in my tablet.

"This is *Potage Valery Giscard d'Estaing*, named after a former French *President de la République.* The president's chef, Bocuse, invented the recipe. It is made with chicken stock, shredded carrot, a little piece of celery stalk, and chicken breasts cut in small pieces and sautéed. Cook these ingredients. Then cut small cubes of *foie gras*, one truffle per dish cut in two pieces. Be sure to brush the truffles under cold water to clean them. Then put all the ingredients in individual terrines, one truffle per terrine; wrap the terrine in puff pastry dough to completely seal it. Once the dough is baked, serve the terrine. As you break through the dough with your fork, all the flavors are released. Yummmmmy."

"This is marvelous, Madame. I hope to try some of these wonderful recipes you have given us."

"But first to find some truffles," Josiane said.

"I am not finished. I have a recipe for another appetizer: *Foie Gras Truffé.* If you prepare fresh *Foie Gras Truffé,* it will keep between four to five days. No longer.

"Usually we use two lobes of fresh *foie gras,* uncooked. Place one layer of *foie gras* in the bottom of a terrine; make a second layer with thinly sliced truffles. Repeat once more. Place it in a double boiler and cook it at a low temperature about 100 degrees Celsius, (215°F.) for about 35 minutes. Now, if you want to do it faster . . . I rarely talk about this way of preparing it, but I use the microwave. It makes the *foie gras* only half-cooked and it is perfect. I put the *foie gras* in a small terrine and place it in the microwave for only one and a half minutes. Then let it rest and repeat. It is delicious. I usually do not tell people I use the microwave, but it gives very good results with some recipes."

"That's true," I said. "Sometimes chefs pretend they do not use microwave ovens, but . . . for restaurants it is necessary."

"I use the microwave to reheat, but rarely to cook—except for *foie gras,*" Madame said. "Are you ready for another recipe? I have one with soft boiled eggs, Faugeron-style. Like with any soft-boiled eggs, first let the eggs absorb the flavor of the truffles by putting them in a sealed bag or container for four to five days. Soft boil the eggs, then serve them with mashed truffles. For four persons, use 120 grams of truffles (a little more than 4 ounces), 30 grams (1 ounce) of *béchamel* sauce, 40 grams (1.5 ounces) of *crème fraiche,* and some butter. Mix these ingredients over low heat and beat the mixture until very fluffy. Serve the soft-boiled eggs, and on a plate serve a little bit of this preparation. Mix one spoon of the soft-boiled egg and one spoon of the sauce. *Délicieuse!* It is my husband's favorite dish."

"Would you care for a little more tea?" she asked, jumping up and rushing to the kitchen. I looked at Josiane and we both stared at our forgotten cups of tepid tea. We quickly drank them before her return.

Mme. Gaulandeau returned, clutching a sheaf of recipe cards and carrying the teapot. She poured the tea, sat down, and began again as if there had been no break.

"It must be difficult to keep your girlish figure with all these rich foods," Josiane said.

Mme. Gaulandeau grinned. "I am on a diet now and have been for two to three weeks. I had gained 15 kilograms . . . about 35 pounds." She shrugged her shoulders and continued.

"Here is a recipe for a filet of beef wrapped in dough. First, sauté the filet in a pan to give it a nice color. Cut the long filet in two pieces. On one piece arrange a layer of thinly sliced truffle, *foie gras*, and again more *truffle slices,* salt, and pepper. Tie it together, strongly. I prepare it in the morning and let it drain until evening. I first wrap it with *filo* dough, and then wrap it again with a *Paté Feuillettée . . .*"

"Which is puff pastry dough," Josiane said to me as an aside. I nodded in acknowledgement. I was writing as fast as I could, attempting to write the names phonetically, so I could catch up with some of the words later.

"The *filo* is going to soak up the blood, or juice. So be sure to make a little chimney on the top of the roast. Bake in the oven and serve with the same sauce I just described. Oh, and with mashed potatoes, Robuchon-style."

"That is potatoes mashed with butter, more butter, and much more butter," Josiane explained.

"So, just before serving, you add crushed truffles uncooked to the mashed potatoes. You can prepare a big seven-bone piece of meat in the same way. Cook it in a stock, like a *pot-au-feu.* Tear the meat apart, into small strings. Add a little bit of stock to moisten, and truffles. Make mashed potatoes Robuchon. In a ringed dish, make a layer of meat with truffles and meat mixture, then a layer of the mashed potatoes. Decorate the top with a flower of truffles. It is all black. And still serve with the same sauce."

"My goodness," I gasped. "After all these recipes, I am starving."

"Yes, Madame Gaulandau," Josiane said with a laugh. "Do you think you could make reservations for us at that little restaurant in Chinon you recommended? We are, indeed, getting terribly hungry."

"But of course. I need to head out myself." Madame Gaulandau looked at her watch.

"Thank you for the tea, recipes, and conversation," I said. "Would we be able to ask you more questions tomorrow?"

Madame Gaulandeau looked surprised. "You still want to talk some more? I would love too. We will work it into your touring schedule. I'm sure you will want to see some of our marvelous chateaux first, *n'est-ce pas?*"

"Yes, of course. But today, we thank you for your valuable time, Madame."

CHAPTER THIRTEEN
Chinon and Beyond

*J*osiane and I cleaned up in our separate rooms—they were so charming—and soon headed out the door and back toward the city of Chinon. Arriving from the south, we caught a glimpse of the Chateau de Chinon—the Chinon Castle—perched on the top ridge of the city that overlooked the River Vienne. The setting sun left a lingering glow of amber that glanced off the ancient walls of the castle and looked much like a golden crown of light above the city. We drove straight toward the chateau, crossing the River Vienne, turning left, and following along the Quai Charles VII.

"You do know the history of this town, don't you Carole?" Josiane was back in tour guide mode and ready to dispense more tidbits of history.

"Nope," I grumbled. "I am once again an historical moron. Where are we now?" I was beginning to wear a tad thin and could tell I was missing my afternoon nap. Plus, I was hungry after all that truffle talk. *Who wouldn't be?*

"Remember when we first headed out of Paris to Reims in the champagne region, and I took you to the cathedral where *Jeanne d'Arc* brought the Dauphin, Charles VII, to be crowned?"

"Yes, but we're quite a distance south of Reims, aren't we?" I struggled mightily to keep up my verve, but I had run out of steam. *I apologize, dear Josiane. I am also trying to sort through my memory of cities that begin with 'R' in France that have a connection to Jeanne d'Arc, like Rouen, where she was burned at the stake.*

Josiane turned a corner and headed up a winding road to the top of the hill, where we passed the chateau. "This, dear Carole, is where *Jeanne d'Arc* shed her costume as a peasant and took up the role of warrior in order to convince the Dauphin to become King of France. To fight against the British. Right here! That's why this place is so important," she finished with a note of triumph and a flourish of her hand.

At that, my ears perked up and I sat up straight. Josiane drove slowly along the long limestone walls of the fortress. She pointed out some of the buildings inside the fortress walls, such as the chateau, the fourteenth century clock tower, the Great Hall, and one of three remaining citadels.

"I'm sorry I was so grumpy, Josiane. You know exactly what I love and what I'm interested in. I apologize. And are we going to be coming here tomorrow?" I asked with renewed interest. "Will we be able to climb into the clock tower?"

"I think we will run out of time, no pun intended, as to-morrow we have plenty of *chateaux* to see. Too bad! This chateau does have a marvelous history. Not only was *Jeanne d'Arc* here, but in the tenth and eleventh centuries, this was the castle where Henry Plantagenet lived and died. Just a few years later, his son, Richard the Lionhearted, was laid to rest in—I'm thinking 1199. If I'm not mistaken, much of England was ruled from this very location during the Hundred Years' War. That's why *Jeanne d'Arc* found the Dauphin hiding out here in the first place."

"Speaking of time," I said, "our reservation is for 8 p.m. We must go."

Josiane gasped and spun past the chateau parking lot. She turned around in the street and we rattled over the cobblestones and down to the base of the hill. Once locating the restaurant known as The 30s on Rue Haute St. Maurice, we parked and hiked quickly back up the cobblestone street and into the establishment.

The small restaurant was in a row of buildings tucked back into the actual tufa or hillside below the chateau. Only five to eight tables were slipped in and around the pillars that divided the petite place. An art deco theme with black and gold-fringed lamps, damask wallpaper, and dramatic swag draperies from the 1930s set the tone. Two waiters raced in and out of the dining room, and we could hear them pounding up and down a staircase out of view but obviously going to the kitchen upstairs. They bounded back again, huffing and puffing, with an array of local cuisine that left a thin cloud of aromatic steam in their wake.

Beginning with *escargots* in garlic butter, and *salade au chèvre chaud*, Josiane and I opted for at least one dish apiece with pungent flecks of truffles wafting up from our plates. Josiane chose roasted duck with truffle sauce; I chose fillet of beef with truffle-infused gnocchi. Both were accompanied by fine red Chinon wines. Ah, sweet decadence!

By the time the cheese cart rolled around, we were feeling no pain and we sampled the *Crottin de Chavignol,* one of the most famous local Loire Valley cheeses. But the *pièce de résistance* was dessert: a true Loire Valley classic: *tarte tatin,* with caramelized apples in a delicate puff pastry. We had experienced a plethora of apple desserts on this trip, but this one took the cake. Or the *tarte,* so to speak. As we dug in, the pastry chef strolled by and introduced herself. She was Sylvie Preteseille, and she had overheard Josiane regaling the waiter with compliments to the chefs. After a brief conversation, we were served a specialty wine to accompany the dessert, followed by an invitation to join the chefs in the kitchen after dinner.

It was after 11 pm when Josiane and I were led up the long staircase to the kitchen. Patrice Morcel and Sylvie Preteseille, the husband and wife team who ran the restaurant, escorted us into a side office, where we all sat down at a table, and where Josiane immediately switched into translator mode and snapped off a question to me.

"Questions, Carole? Do you have any questions for them?"

I could barely focus my eyes due to the amount of wine and the need for sleep, and I had failed to bring my tape recorder or notepad. (What kind of writer was I? I didn't realize I was on 24-hour duty.) Josiane slapped a stack of thin white paper napkins before me, handed me a pen, and the interview began.

"How did you begin to cook and what were your influences?" I asked.

Patrice sat back in his seat and slipped his toque off, swiped at his sweaty forehead, and blinked his dark blue eyes. He could tell this would not be a short interview, so he signaled one of his lingering wait staff to bring a bottle of good Chinon wine, a Crémant de Loire. He poured four glasses and settled back into his seat, facing the two of us and with his wife at his side.

"I was born in Casablanca, Morocco," he said. "Many of my influences came from my childhood. But once I began to cook for a living, I worked all over, including the French Antilles. After the Antilles, I decided to really invest time into becoming a chef—not just a short order cook. So, for seven years I apprenticed, working two years for a chef in a very small restaurant to learn more traditional ways. That is what our focus is at this restaurant—the traditional ways of regional cooking."

My ears perked up. Right up my alley!

"By accident, we both came to work in this tiny bistro and fell in love with this job . . . and each other," Sylvie said with a smile. "I think we both had a passion for cooking since we were quite young. We worked together for four years here, and then two years ago our boss sold us this bistro after having built up the clientele for eighteen years. We have been able to hold most of his clientele, and add many of our own, who come from all over. Like you . . ." She nodded toward me.

I was busy scribbling back and forth across the napkins, up one side and down the other, trying to keep up with Josiane's translations. I almost missed the smile and nod in my direction.

"We were recommended to you by Madame Gaulandau. Do you know her?" Josiane said.

"*Mais oui!*" they said in unison. "She notifies us when they have excellent truffles. They were not able to get many this past season, but we appreciate that she calls us first—even before the Parisian restaurateurs call or arrive."

"We were not able to sample truffles at her home, but she told us much about the business. We were only too glad to be able to taste them here," I swooned. "Our dinner was superb!"

"*Merci,*" Patrice said. "I'm glad you enjoyed them. I have a great many ideas about how to use truffles. I guess I was influenced by my boss, who had many restaurants. But for me, cuisine is something that comes from the inside. You have to love what you do to give pleasure to others."

"You've managed that well," Josiane said. "What other ingredients do you enjoy using in your cuisine?"

Because Patrice was head chef and Sylvie the pastry chef, he immediately answered. "I love to pick mushrooms each morning and gather the fresh ingredients for the restaurant. Here, we do not provide foods unless they are made with fresh ingredients, plus education regarding the produce is very important." Sylvie nodded her assent.

"I teach my apprentices the old ways of cooking. For instance, I have them prepare the gratin of pasta. It's important to bring to the family."

"Gratin of pasta?" I asked Josiane.

"Ah, *mais oui!* It is like your macaroni and cheese, but much richer and moister."

"Sounds delicious! Speaking of family," I asked, "did your family teach you to cook?"

"Yes," Patrice said. "I was lucky as I had two grandmothers who both loved to cook and were willing to teach me. One had a vegetable garden, rabbits, and lots of recipes; the other made big family-style meals—they were from a little village near Nancy."

"Josiane, weren't we near Nancy when we visited your brother Jacky?" That seemed like years ago but had been only a few weeks earlier.

"Yes," she said. She turned to Patrice and Sylvie. "I, too, was raised not far from Nancy . . ."

In the blink of an eye, the translation dropped and the three conversed rapidly in French, leaving me to look from one face to another trying to sort out the conversation. The three laughed and became animated, but no English was forthcoming. I sipped my wine and hoped I had not diverted them for too long. Finally, Josiane brought the conversation back to traditional foods and began translating again.

"So sorry," she giggled. "We got carried away!" A small hiccup burbled out.

"Quiche Lorraine was a favorite recipe of the family," Patrice continued. "I learned to master some of the old favorites of my grandmothers—the traditional dishes came first —before I ventured into new cuisine. One old favorite was *pâté brisée*."

"He helped me improve on my pastry dough from the influence of his grandmothers," Sylvie said. "I use those methods from his grandmothers almost daily."

"When I was working in Sainte Maarten in the Caribbean," Patrice said, "I started to learn the new cuisine, but my heart has always been with the traditional ways of cooking."

"How about you, Sylvie?" I asked. "Where were you living when you began to bake?"

"I was raised here in Chinon, but I worked for a time in Lyon and Vendu."

"Were you born here, Sylvie?" Josiane asked.

"I was born in the French Alps, but my family moved here when I was quite young." She twirled a blonde curl back from her glistening face and grinned. "I guess I, too, was lucky to have a papa with a vegetable garden. I also learned my cuisine from my grandmother. She focused on the traditional ways of baking, as that was her forte. With her influence and careful attention to my attempts in the kitchen, she encouraged me to become a real pastry chef. I hope to be as patient with our own children."

"Do you have children?" I asked.

"We would like to have time for a family . . ." Patrice began.

"Yes," Sylvie interrupted, "we are still in the family spirit even though we work long hours and many days straight. We do want to have children, but right now, our job does not leave time for a family."

"So, you work long hours and many days straight," I repeated. "What do you do to take time for yourselves?"

The couple looked at each other and blinked. "Well, we try to keep our family traditions. We incorporate our holiday traditions here at work and, whenever we can, we get together with our families." They both sighed, slumped down in their chairs. They looked exhausted.

"This is such a tough business," I said. "But your passion for what you do shines through."

"Ah, *mais oui*," they said in unison, rising in their chairs. "We do love what we do!" Sylvie said.

"And I am creating dishes in my head all the time," Patrice said. "I love to cook for other people. I love simple cooking. I believe I prefer the cooking of my mother and mother-in-law to the *haute cuisine* of Michelin-starred restaurants."

"It seems many of the French feel as you do," I said. "As we've traveled through France in the past weeks, we found that traditional methods and recipes are still being used and that the basics of *cuisine pauvre,* or peasant cooking, are still valued. Just like you said. And they are superb!"

Patrice's eyes brightened. He smiled and nodded. "*Bon!* I'm glad to hear that! *Bon!*"

"How has your business been this year?" Josiane asked.

"There used to be more tourists," Sylvie said. "In fact, too many tourists in the summer months, but now the tourist trade is down—due to 9/11." She looked cautiously at the two of us from America. We nodded in acknowledgement.

"I'm sorry that has happened to you," I said. "This tragedy

has impacted so many people. Hopefully that will change again shortly."

They nodded their heads. "Actually, the blessing for us," Sylvie said, "is we find we have had more time to learn more creative dishes. Repetition in our foods is not always good. We need energy and input from all who work here. Patrice and I work together," she said, touching her husband's hand, "because we share the same passion for our work. And when we prepare something new, the whole staff participates, and they make recommendations."

"Yes, we are open to criticism," Patrice said. "That's the only way to improve."

"Say," Sylvie said, jumping up from her chair, "would you like to see our wine cellar? It's unique and we have some of the best wines in all of the Loire Valley."

"Most certainly," Josiane said, slipping gracefully out of her seat.

"Sure," I said, stacking all my ink-covered napkins into a pile and shoving them into my purse. Ordering my notes would have to come later—much later.

Sylvie headed out the door in a quick bound, waltzed through the kitchen, and instead of heading down the stairs to a cellar, she proceeded up a few more steps and lifted a heavy latch to an old wooden door. Immediately, cool air hit us full force. She beckoned us into a long, narrow hallway with a barrel-vaulted ceiling that reached beyond the yellow arc of lighting from the bulbs above us.

"This," she said with glee, "is our wine cellar."

"I wouldn't have expected a cellar up here," Josiane said, looking around her.

"Is a wine cellar still considered a cellar if it's in the attic?" I asked. No one was listening.

Sylvie reached down and rummaged around at her feet and came up with a dusty bottle of red wine, which she forced into Josiane's hands.

"Oh, this is too much," Josiane protested.

"Do you know where you are?" Sylvie asked with child-like excitement.

We shook our heads in bewilderment. We assumed we were standing in the wine cellar.

"We are under the moat—the moat of the Chateau de Chinon!!"

We gasped.

"What a perfectly marvelous idea," Josiane exclaimed.

"Only the French would think of such a perfect place for wine," I said, shaking my head and smiling. "Only the French . . ."

A half hour later, having left Chinon far behind, Josiane pulled into the darkened farmyard of the truffle farm. We looked at each other. There was no light outside the gates and no moon claimed the sky.

We had walked through the double gates only a couple of times before, and in our somewhat inebriated state wondered if we could find our way. Giggling, we inched out of the car and began stumbling over the rocks in the roadway, just as the dogs began to bark and howl. "Zabou," Josiane called out, and the older one quieted down. The youthful hound continued to howl, and Zabou must have nipped at his heels, because the noise stopped quickly and the two bounded away from the interior gates. We struggled to lift the latch of the outer gate, then walked through the interim yard to unlatch the inner gate. Following the sound of two dogs gallivanting in the center courtyard, we managed to find our way. Suddenly a light flashed on, and Mme. Gaulandau waved from the door. A quick exchange of greetings filtered through the night air, then we each entered our separate rooms, glad for the safety and sanctity of our private spaces. Sleep followed within moments.

The next morning, over croissants and bowls of *café au lait*, I switched on my tape recorder and, with Josiane's help, began to interview Mme. Gaulandau again. Josiane had laid out plans for a busy day of visiting famous and infamous chateaux throughout the Loire Valley, so I wanted to grab these few moments with Madame.

"I would like to focus on where you were raised," I began. "I would like to know what influenced your traditional food choices."

"Oh, *mon Dieu*," Mme. Gaulandau exclaimed with a note of surprise. "Well, my father was always sick, so we lived on a diet of Vichy water, lean ham, no eggs, and no desserts. My pleasure for cooking came as a reaction to this regimen of my family. I was fifteen years old when I began to cook for my friends."

"Where were you raised?" Josiane asked.

"I am from the area of Loire et Cher Rivers; actually, the Blois on the Loire River, next to Blois. You probably know of the goat cheese from Selles sur Cher that is very famous—round-shaped, not too thick. I was born in Selles sur Cher. Maybe you have heard of it?"

"I have," Josiane responded. "How long did you live near Blois?"

"Twenty years in Blois. Have you been there? There is a very beautiful castle near where I lived. There are four wings in that castle, representing four different eras. One is from Francois the First's time frame; it is the most representative and well known. Another wing was built under Francois d'Orleans. Chambord is more the castle of Francois the First, than of Blois."

At that point I was too confused to try to track what information had just been given and asked another question.

"May I ask again about how you learned to cook? Did your mother like to cook, or did she have to cook only the foods your father could eat?"

"My mother didn't like to cook, but my great-grandmother did. She was a chef in a castle from 1870 to 1900. I know very little about my great grandmother. Only when I showed an interest in cooking did my father tell me his grandmother had been a good cook and a chef."

"Do you have any recipes from her?"

"No, and I am sorry I don't. There was, in particular, a recipe I liked very much. It was a potato pancake, made with a puff pastry dough, using potatoes instead of flour, and a lot of butter. It looked like a *galette* or pie for Epiphany. It was so good. I really regret not having that recipe. There are certain flavors, smells, tastes in your childhood that remain forever in your memory, and that was one. My grandmother lived in a farmhouse with no heat, no comfort—the floor was of clay, nothing more. I remember sleeping at her home in the winter, under a big down comforter, and in the morning, there was frost inside the windows. I still can see her, stooped in front of the wide-open fireplace, heating water over the fire, and on the side, she was toasting bread for my breakfast. That smell of grilled bread is imprinted on my memory."

"Josiane, that sounds like your mother's description of her grandmother," I said.

"Yes, it does."

"I also remember," Madame continued, "the huge Comtoise clock, and its tick . . . tock. Tick . . . tock. The pendulum was so beautiful. When my grandfather passed away, the clock went to my cousin. I was so sad."

"*Comtoise?*" I asked.

"She means it comes from the region of Franche-Comté," Josiane said in explanation, ignoring my blank stare.

"Did you have a good relationship with your grandmother?" I asked.

"Not with that one. She was so tough—with herself and with others. Times were very hard for her. Her husband was away at the war. At age eighty, she still was climbing the ladder, with her wooden shoes on, to get hay from the attic of the barn for the goats."

"What about the other grandmother? Was she nicer?"

"She was very nice. She was my mother's mother."

"Do you have special memories of her?"

"Yes, a lot. Her smell . . . She always used lavender soap and an *eau-de-lavande toilette*. It still is fabricated, and if I smell it somewhere, I recognize it instantly."

"What else do you remember about your grandmother?" Josiane asked. "Did she also live a long time?"

"They both passed away in 1968. My mother's mother was younger. She was married to a military man who was in Africa during the war. He rallied the forces of General de Gaulle. While he was gone, the Germans took away all her belongings, and her five-year-old daughter died of hunger and cold. She was my mother's oldest sister. My grandmother's older son died at the end of the war while jumping with a parachute that failed to open. And my grandfather died of a heart attack when he learned of the death of his son. In four years, she lost three important members of her family. I think she was not very close to my mother, but she became very attached to me. She said I was the continuation of her life. I think that I loved her more than my mother." Madame bowed her head, as if ashamed.

After a moment she continued. "My grandmother loved to embroider, and she had lots of hobbies like knitting and crocheting. She embroidered the tapestry in your bedroom, Carole. I am left-handed, so there are some hobbies, like crocheting and knitting, I am not able to enjoy and am not good at. At school I was the first one to write with the left hand. The teacher tried to change that, but I cried so much it was impossible. I think that my handwriting was affected by that —I spent so much time trying with the right hand. There are so few tools specially made for left-handed persons. It really can be a handicap."

"My daughter shares your left-handedness. And you are right—we need to do more for the left-handed," I said.

"What other things do you remember about your grandmother?" Josiane said, trying to keep us on task.

"My grandmother loved desserts, and like I said, my father was not allowed to have them. After he died, I remember her buying many pastries at the bakery. Then she would invite her friends to pass some time at her home in the evening, and they would eat the pastries. I remember being there during summer vacations and being so shocked when those ladies ate two to three pastries. That made a lasting impression on me."

Just then the phone rang, and Madame excused herself from the table and went to the phone.

"We better get a move on, if we are going to see some of the *chateaux* today," Josiane said, scooting her chair out from the table and carrying her cup and plate to the kitchen. We waved our thanks to Madame, as we disappeared from the breakfast room.

The next two days were indeed filled with beautiful and luxuriant castles, the likes of each one exceeding the last. The first was the graceful Azay-le-Rideau chateau, a sequel to the original medieval fortress built at the end of an island on the Indre River. The original fortress was built with two loges or buildings on either side of the fortress, with pepper pot towers at each corner overhanging the river below. It was built during the early part of the reign of François I in 1515, and was an expression of the owner, Gilles Berthelot, and his ascendancy into the social graces of that day and age. Unfortunately, his benefactor was considered corrupt and was executed in the Bastille, and Lord Berthelot made an escape, leaving his lovely bride to care for the castle on her own.

The castle regained prominence in 1791, when Marquis de Biencourt purchased the property, and over several generations the castle was returned to a more abundant splendor. In the courtyard, the dominant feature of the main building was the monumental open stairway. In the center of a return wing, a passageway led over a drawbridge that crossed the old moat to the garden. The façades, all symmetrical, accentuated their height. Pilasters, giving the appearance of columns, framed every window, and decorative lattice work became a hallmark of the designer. Over the outer façades, a sentry-way ran around the outside in a cornice as decorative with its numerous moldings as it was functional. The rooms were filled with elegantly embroidered satin tapestries from Louis XIV's time frame, and Italianate furniture that dominated the Val de Loire in the sixteenth century. Formal gardens in the English style featured exotic trees, flowers, and plants that were reflected in the slow-moving Indre River.

The next chateau, the overly grand and regal Chenonceau, which was built during the same reign as Azay-le-
Rideau and under similar methods of financing, was known
not only for its French Renaissance architecture, but for the
history of at least two extraordinary ladies: Diane de Poitiers
and Catherine de Médicis. (Catherine, who hailed from Flo-
rence, Italy, did seem to get around.) When the castle fell
into the same financial distress as Azay-le-Rideau, a settle-
ment was reached, and the property fell into the hands of the
Crown and Francis I. Diane de Poitiers, widow and lady-in-
waiting to the Queen, aroused passion in the young Dauphin,
the future Henry II. She became Henry II's mistress, even
though he was nineteen years her junior, and he eventually
bequeathed the Chenonceau property to her in the pretext of
honoring her deceased husband. Using her natural beauty
and her intelligence to her advantage, she set her ambitions
on restoring the castle to greatness. She not only handled the
oversight of architectural changes, she undertook and managed the production of wine from the vineyards, silk from
the silkworms, produce from the gardens and farms, and
made Chenonceau a profitable and enviable entity.

But on the death of Henry II, Diane de Poitiers was forced
to cede the property back to the Crown, and to his widow,
Catherine de Médicis. Daughter to Lorenzo de Médicis, duke
of Urbino, and mother of Francis II, Charles IX, and Henry III,
Catherine brought to Chenonceau her own Florentine embell-
ishments. What her rival Diane de Poitiers had done for the
castle, grounds, farms, vineyards, and silkworm production,
Catherine did more—and did it better. Drawing on her Italian
flair for gardens, she created a splendidly balanced garden in-
corporating flower beds, citrus groves, grottos, pergolas, and
fountains, all along the beautiful Cher River.

Josiane showed me first through the extraordinary gardens, then across part of the Cher River to the castle beyond. Room after room was filled with the accoutrements of both the French and Italian Renaissance, with fifteenth and sixteenth century Flemish tapestry wall coverings, fifteenth century French credenzas and bed frames, sixteenth century Italian cabinets, beautiful inlaid parquet flooring, ornate marble fireplaces, paintings in baroque gilded frames —and then we disappeared into the massive kitchens. These were, to me, the heart of the house—though I loved the history of the women of this castle. Built in the hollow core of the base of the towers, the kitchen's stone floors showed the five hundred years of constant wear, and the walls were covered in hundreds of copper pans of every shape and size. A massive fireplace, with large spits and hangers for pots, was evidence of meals prepared and enjoyed. The stories of glorious parties for hundreds of guests, along with licentious merrymaking, must have had some of their beginnings in that very kitchen.

As we started back up the kitchen steps, Josiane led me to the enclosed bridge-gallery. "Do you know that during World War II, this gallery was an entry point for those moving from occupied France to the Free Zone?"

"What do you mean?" The very mention of World War II took me right back to Marcelle's stories of her valiant attempts to save her darling sons by fleeing from Paris to the Free Zone in the Auvergne. The Auvergne was the final region we would be visiting on this trip.

"This very gallery, which stretches across the River Cher, begins in the occupied part of France, but if a person could make the break, they could enter into the free part of France by continuing all the way to the end of the gallery and jumping onto the left bank of the river and into what they thought would be freedom. Some extraordinary stories took place right here—right in this room."

At that point, Josiane walked solemnly out of the expansive home of the rich and famous, and back to her car, deep in thought, with me in her wake.

Like I said, over the next two days, we visited one extraordinary chateau after another, each new one blurring into the last. Then Josiane took me to the Abbaye de Fontevraud, where the Loire and the Vienne Rivers meet and where the small market towns of Candes-Saint-Martin and Montsoreau come together in a wooded vale. There we found the largest group of monastic buildings still standing in France. Surprisingly, this collection of four monasteries/abbeys, built in 1101, was for men and women, with women holding the reins of power over the men for many centuries. During the twelfth century, when the Anjou region held royal sway, the Abbey came into protection under the Crown, and it was here that some of the tombs of the *Plantagenets*, the Kings of England, came to rest. In the nave of the church lay polychrome copies of the recumbent figures of Henry II Plantagenet, Eleanor of Aquitaine, Richard the Lionhearted, and Isabella of Angoulême. This had been the English royal necropolis until the end of the twelfth century, when the kings were later buried at Westminster Abbey in London.

"Isn't this amazing?" Josiane said as we walked around the tombs. She pointed to the figure of Eleanor of Aquitaine. She was stretched out like the others but appeared to be quietly reading a book.

"Good use of time," I said. "So, they were laid to rest here in the twelfth century, but what happened here after that?"

"Well, first of all, she may have finished her book,"

Josiane said. "But I believe the abbeys were used for school-ing the royal families, and as a place for meditation for men and women. Then the Revolution came, and the place was gutted and remained empty for years until Napoleon used parts of it for a prison. I'm not certain when renovation be-gan to restore these buildings to some of their former glory, but the project didn't include the main monasteries or abbeys."

We wandered out of the abbey church, through the chap-ter house and the refectory, out into the cloister gardens, and into the famous medieval kitchen, which was topped with the pyramidal Evraud Tower. Staring up at the tower from inside the kitchen, I could see how remarkable in size and construc-tion it was, with a central octagonal space covered with an open-air ventilation grid. I had seen a similar construction of chimneys in Istanbul at the Topkapi Palace and one in the Palace of the Popes in Avignon. Extraordinary design.

"This kitchen chimney was used for smoking meats and fish and for ventilating the kitchen during the heat of sum-mer," Josiane translated.

"Speaking of smoked meats, I'm starving," I whispered as we left the kitchen, which had filled with tourists.

"Good. I have a special place for us to try here in the vil-lage of Fontevraud." And off we went to the exemplary Michelin one-starred restaurant La Licorne—The Unicorn. Built in the 1700s before La Révolution, the restaurant oozed grace and opulence. We decided it was late enough in the day that our main meal would be right there. After a couple of flutes of champagne, I ordered a filet of beef flavored with smoked pork and shallots, and Josiane ordered roasted *sandre,* a type of perch, with spicy peppers and crayfish-stuffed ravi-oli with a morel mushroom sauce. We shared an exquisite warm chocolate tart with pears and lemon-butter sauce, and several glasses of regional Saumur wines. Neither of us remembers much about the return trip, back through Chinon and south to the truffle farm, but the luncheon at La Licorne was one exquisite memory. And it helped that I took copious notes, but none on thin paper napkins.

The following morning was bright with sunshine that radiated through the crisp, lace curtains and cast a variegated pattern of light across the red brick floor. I rolled over, stretched, and once again admired the beauty of the appointments to this simple, sweet bedroom. Light blue and white gingham curtains hung from the bed frame above me and were tied to each post of the four-poster bed. A white crocheted coverlet, made by Mme. Gaulandau's grandmother, laid over me. Satin tiebacks, in the same blue as the gingham curtains, complemented an upholstered chair in the corner, and a blue and white handmade rug lay by the bed. On the wall above the bed was a lovely tapestry also made by Mme. Gaulandau's grandmother. And the separate bathroom had every convenience of home. This ancient barn, I thought as I lay there, had quite the rich history. I crawled out of bed and headed for the shower. It was May 1, and we would be heading toward the home of Martial, Josiane's oldest brother. Just a couple more days on the road, and I would finally see what I had come to France to see: Fontanières—Marcelle's home.

As we finished breakfast and were preparing to leave the Truffle Farm, I turned to Mme. Gaulandau to thank her once again for her hospitality.

"Before I go, I'm curious about one thing. How old is this farm and farmhouse?"

Josiane translated, and Madame disappeared and returned a few minutes later with a tight little scroll of paper in her hand.

"This is a document I found while cleaning one of the ceiling beams," she said. "My dust cloth ran across a loose knothole, and when I pulled on the plug of the knothole, it came out, and behind it was this rolled up piece of paper."

"What does it say?" I could barely contain my excitement.

Josiane began to translate the document. "It says . . . why, I think this describes a payment of debt. It is dated—hmm, I think 1665! Wow! This is something, isn't it?"

Mme. Gaulandau smiled about her special find. "And there's more to it than meets the eye," she said.

"Carole, I'll do my best here, since this is written in old French." Josiane began to read.

Translation of the Document Found in the Walls of the House of Mme. Galandeau

Document Dated 1665

1. *To you, René REVILLAUD, ploughman, by request of*
2. *Vincent BESNARD, residing in Champigny, who has*
3. *declared "his domicile" the house he lives in*
4. *by virtue of an obligation agreed upon in the front of DUCHESNE, Notary*
5. *Royal who was in good health in continuing*
6. *I give you the imperative order*
7. *by the law of the King, our Sire, to pay and to give*
8. *forthwith and without delays to the said BESNARD*
9. *or to me to take to him the amount of sixty*
10. *and ten pounds the remaining to pay in cash*
11. *the said obligation . . . I summon you*
12. *to appear next Monday*

13. *in front of Mr. . . . The Seneschal of Richelieu, on the*
14. *hour of the change of guards to see yourself condemned*
15. *to the interest of the said amount until*
16. *complete payment, without prejudice to appeal*
17. *for its principal as it would be,*
18. *to be done. Established in me, Sergeant Royal, undersigned*
19. *. . . and JEHAN*
20. *REB. . . witnesses residing in the said Richelieu*
21. *Who do not know how to sign and . . . the seventh day*
22. *Of August one thousand six hundred sixty-five.*

"Wow! This is incredible. 1665!" I exclaimed. "And what does the rest mean?"

M. Gaulandau smiled and said, "The reason that no address is given, and only partial names, is because of the strong belief in witches at the time. Actually, some believe in them even today. But during that time, the belief was that if you wrote down your own address, the witches would know where to find you, thus . . ." She shrugged.

"So, you are saying that the farm was here long before this document was signed—or at least, sometime before, and this scroll was wedged into that knothole?" I asked, as I looked up at the dark weathered beam above my head.

"That's extraordinary, isn't it?" Josiane murmured. "To find this treasure in your home and to determine the date of your house based on this discovery is . . . amazing!"

"Yes. I like to think so," Madame Gaulandau said proudly. Her hand quickly moved to cover a blush. Pride was not an emotion with which she was comfortable. We hugged her good-bye and left her home, carrying a copy of the document she had printed for us. We were floating in a sense of awe.

CHAPTER FOURTEEN
A Night at a Forest Chateau

As Josiane headed south from the farm, we drove through the elegant city of Richelieu. "This is the city that was named in the document Madame Gaulandau showed you this morning, as the place where the document was to be signed and witnessed," Josiane said. She was turning her head left and right as if to catch the action of an event that had taken place in the 1600s.

"Yes," I said, "and didn't the document imply it was to be signed at the changing of the guards? What guards? Was there a castle or royalty about? Why does the name of this town sound so familiar? Richelieu. Richelieu."

"Probably you're familiar with the famous Cardinal Duc de Richelieu who lived here during the seventeenth century—probably before the paper was drafted. What was that date?"

I reached into my notebook and thumbed through the pages. "August 7, 1665. I'm glad Madame Gaulandau made a copy for us."

"I believe Cardinal Richelieu had come and gone by that time, as I think he died in the 1640s, if I remember correctly. But his palace may have been near where this document was to be signed."

"Palace? I thought he was a cardinal."

"Again, I'm trying to rely on my memory. But if I'm not mistaken, at the age of twenty-one he was made a cardinal and from there rose to become head of the Royal Council and the first prime minister of France. The king at that time was King Louis XIII, who was known to be a weak ruler. Richelieu slipped into power to fill the void and ran the empire by giving the king advice. Richelieu was a clever politician and strategist, and he expanded the royal power, punished dissent harshly, and built France into a great European power. At the same time, he supported the arts and education and founded the famous French Academy. You may have heard of him through novelist Alexander Dumas's *The Three Musketeers*, where Richelieu was made into a crafty villain. Richelieu's name has become synonymous with political intrigue and ambitious power from 'behind the throne.'"

"You're a walking encyclopedia, Josiane. I'm sure that's where I heard the name. I can't believe you remember so much of your country's history." My eyes swept back and forth hoping to catch a glimpse of a palace.

"I suppose that the document," I said, "if actually signed, was signed right near here—at the appointed hour. That's so interesting, isn't it?" I continued to crane my neck. Certainly, there was at least a guardhouse of sorts around here somewhere.

Josiane rolled on down through the main part of the city, then hung a left and headed to the east as we started out of the city. In the street, next to the curb, two small boys stood near a table set up with an umbrella and two plastic chairs. The smaller boy held a bouquet of flowers in his hands, waving to passersby.

"What are they selling?"

"His sign says '*Muguets.*' He's selling lilies-of-the-valley.

Oh my, this is May 1, isn't it? This is a national holiday—Labor Day, and I . . ."

"I know about this one, Josiane. This is when you purchase a small bouquet for someone you love, isn't it? Stop the car, will you? I want to buy a bouquet."

Josiane pulled off the main road, and I jumped out of the car and headed toward the boys. Suddenly it dawned on me I had no idea what to say. I turned and humbly waited for my intrepid French translator to once again bail me out. In the meantime, the older boy leaped up from his chair, almost knocking the younger boy over to reach us: their two prospective customers. Being the big brother—he looked at least eight years old—he must have decided he could handle this sale. But upon reaching us, he stood with his hands stuffed up his coat sleeves in the chilly morning air. The smaller boy, probably five years old, began to wail at his brother, but made his way over to us, pushing his brother aside. Prominently displayed on a thin cardboard sign that hung around his neck and laid limp on his red and blue parka, were the carefully written words: MUGUET – 2,00 Euro. His hand clutched a small fistful of flowers. He smiled shyly, revealing a missing tooth, and held the flowers aloft for us to see. And, to smell.

"I must have a picture of these two," I said as I raced back to the car for my camera. "Do you think it would be okay?" I yelled over my shoulder. "Should we check with their mother?"

Josiane in the meantime had bent down to talk with the boys. "We would like to buy two bouquets, if you have them. And could you ask your mother if she would give permission to have an American *journaliste* take your picture?"

"Our picture? By an American?" they said in chorus, their dark blue eyes bulging with excitement.

"Yes, by an American." The two almost knocked each other down again as they scrambled toward the open window overlooking the street. Both bellowed into the window to get their mother's attention. A curly-haired woman—presumably their mother—poked her head out from behind the lace curtains. A look of surprise swept her face. Josiane walked over to the window and asked permission from the woman, who smiled and nodded vigorously. By the time Josiane returned to me, the boys were already posing for the camera. One inched forward, pushing the other behind; the older one ruffled the younger one's red hair as he squawked in protest; then the older boy poked the other's hand to pull it down and out of sight. The two finally fidgeted into place and faced me, toothed and toothless grins spilling onto my lens, a small forgotten bouquet hanging limp in one clenched fist.

"Perfect! *C'est parfait! Vous êtes adorable*," I said to the boys. I handed them several euros for two bouquets. They blushed, then bounded back to their table to fetch the flowers and make change.

"Ah," said Josiane, "isn't life sweet?"

We two friends drove happily down the road, having exchanged bouquets between us. I babbled on and on about the encounter with the boys. Within an hour, the lilies-of-the-valley had wilted on our laps, but their lovely scent perfumed the air. It made for joyous memories for years to come.

"So, where are we headed, today?" I asked, as the city of Richelieu disappeared in our rearview mirror.

"We're scheduled to stay in a chateau tonight near

Thalmiers—the one you located on the internet—and it's halfway to my brother Martial's, which is our last stop. Plus, Christian is hoping to get to his father's house two days after tomorrow."

Josiane adjusted her course, with the help of Peggy, who was cantankerous as ever, especially since she had been ignored over the past few days. As we headed down some side roads, the much-needed maps we had brought did not have the fine detail we were hoping Peggy could provide. Ah, but she would make us pay first. After several— hmmm, should we say deliberate misdirections? She finally led us down the correct path toward Châteauroux and beyond.

We stopped for lunch at a little truck-stop *café* near Châteauroux and were reminded that people in some parts of France still smoke. I can't tell you what we ordered, as it was more important for us to eat and leave. Shortly, we were back on another country road when I spotted a sign with some words I thought I recognized: Musée d'Arts et Traditions Paysannes.

"Traditions? Peasants? What is this, Josiane? Something we should stop to see?"

Josiane slammed on her brakes, backed up, turned down a dirt road, and followed the route indicated by the sign. "I don't know where we are, but *voilà*—we must be here!" She pointed at another sign. "We are in the municipality of Saint-Hilaire-en-Lignières, in the department of Cher. The museum is called Le Château du Plaix."

She waved her hand with panache as we stepped out of the car. We trudged past some rundown farm buildings and up a long path toward a large yellow castle, all with the requisite pepper pot towers, angular rooflines, and towering chimneys. Once we crossed what appeared to have been a moat, we continued across a small bridge that led to the entryway of the castle door. It was closed and locked.

"Is this the correct place? Are we trespassing?" I whispered. I was becoming a little wary, as we hadn't seen anyone on the grounds.

"No, I think the staff are at lunch. Since we're here, let's wander around and see what we can find."

I was nervous, but Josiane began to walk around the courtyard, peering into locked windows. She disappeared around the back of the castle, where a small river fed into an irrigation ditch and then sent a gentle rush of water through a sluice and to a nearby field. I tagged along but kept a watchful eye over my shoulder.

Shortly we heard a truck door slam and a dog bark, and we headed back toward the front door, where we were met by a kindly woman dressed in a costume from the early seventeenth century. With a large key she unlocked the heavy door and forced it open so we could enter the interior of a once lovely country estate. She and Josiane began chatting and in no time at all she consented to give us a full tour—even though it was only two of us—and even though I had no tape recorder or camera in hand. We began the tour. The woman spoke no English, so slowly we inched through the house—through living rooms, bedrooms, kitchen, and pantry—and then on to the farm buildings, with Josiane translating all the way.

After over an hour of traveling back through well over three hundred years of time and discovering the methods of farming, cooking, and living in those quarters, we drove back down the dusty country road and away from the Chateau du Plaix. I was giddy with delight.

"I can't believe we found this wonderful place. It was like we were meant to visit. Everything was right along the lines of what I want to know: traditions, methods—even the cooking ideas were great!"

"It's a good thing you had your eyes open and saw that sign."

I felt a sense of pride rise in my chest. It was rare I caught much French on any signs along the way, as I was so dependent on Josiane.

I continued to babble on as we headed toward the main roadway. Billows of dust fomented from the back of the car, until we entered traffic on the paved highway.

"Where to now, Josiane?" I asked, as I was finally winding down.

"On to the chateau you found on the internet. I have no idea what we will find, but off we go. To Chateau de Thaumiers."

"Is it near here? I can't remember where we were headed before I forced us onto our side trip."

"We were headed to George Sand's, but now that it's after four o'clock, we'll catch that tomorrow. Tell me again what road or highway the chateau is on. I need to pull off and load the coordinates into Peggy."

Josiane pulled to the side and the two of us fished through the paperwork to find the address and a map for our overnight venture. After a short delay, and some careful coercing of Peggy by Josiane, we were back purring along the route, passing through Saint Armand Montrond and back east along the D951. After a few false starts and stops, Peggy found her way—and acted as if she had intended all those missteps. Josiane patted the dashboard as if to acknowledge all the horror we had put Peggy through.

We passed through a small village—which did not appear on any map we had, so no wonder Peggy had gotten lost—and then we turned down a narrow lane that led us back off the road through an oak and hickory-forested area that eventually opened onto a clearing. Before us appeared an immense stone chateau, and for an instant it was captured in the glow of afternoon light, with rays of gold radiating around the fringes and defining its regal outline. Once again, we were arriving at our destination just before sundown. The castle, with at least three pepper pot towers crowning the roof lines, appeared to be of the same vintage as the other castles we had visited—sixteenth century, we estimated. But this would be the first night we would sleep in one.

We drove across a moat, through an ornate black wrought-iron gate and into a sand-covered courtyard, where Josiane pulled to a stop. We stepped from the car and looked up at the five-story L-shaped structure. The golden light that had almost blinded us before was now behind the building. The white shutters, which opened onto the courtyard, revealed darkened rooms behind the white stone walls of the castle. Twelve third-story dormer windows peered from the black slate roof. Nothing about the exterior gave a hint of life or color to this house. No flowers in pots. No rows of blooming hydrangeas. No bright red geraniums along the dark-gray slate walkways. No indication of a main doorway. Only one small white plastic chair propped up on the walkway hinted that someone had been there or thought about sitting there. No sound came from the house. No dogs barked a welcome. And no one answered the door. After much knocking and looking for a doorbell or buzzer, we hesitantly pushed open a side door, stepped into a dark, cavernous, and frigid hallway, and called out to announce our arrival.

I pulled my jacket around me as we moved cautiously down the long hallway. "It's freezing in here. Maybe they aren't expecting us."

"No, no, no," Josiane said, putting on an air of having been there many times before. She puffed into the air, as if such things happen often, and a small plume of white breath escaped her lips. She began to giggle. "Ooh, it *is* cold in here."

An undeniable nervousness soon overtook us, and we began to titter then laugh uproariously. What a predicament. Standing in a chateau that might or might not be the bed-and-breakfast we had signed up for. We were trespassers, possibly. Then, from way down the hallway, back through the living room, the dining room, and the kitchen, we heard a small voice calling out to us.

"Yes, I will be right there. I'm on the phone. *Un moment, s'il vous plaît.'* In English and French, the voice echoed off the walls and back to us. Following in the direction of the disembodied voice, we walked down the corridor and hesitated at the entrance to a once elaborate but now somewhat dilapidated living room. The outdoor shutters were hinged shut, and the darkened room, with walls covered in dark brown print wallpaper, felt oppressive. Staggered across the wall were large portraits of presumably former owners, in gilt-edged frames that were no longer golden, but dusty brown. The blue velveteen sofa and window treatments leaned toward threadbare and held only a hint of their former color. Only a white marble mantelpiece and a scattering of white provincial chairs with fuchsia cushions gave light to an unusually grim, yet once ostentatious, room.

Just then a woman with slightly disheveled blonde hair

and light blue eyes appeared in the doorway leading to the dining room. "Ah, there you are. I'm so sorry I wasn't outside to greet you. Just as you arrived, of course, the phone began to ring. It was my husband . . . I'm so sorry. I'm Madame de Bonneval. And you must be . . ."

"Josiane." Josiane stepped forward and kissed our hostess on both cheeks. "Josiane Selvage. And this is my American friend, Carole Bumpus."

I stepped forward and reached out to shake hands with Mme. Bonneval. She responded in kind and welcomed us warmly. As she led us through the dining room, she spoke in both French and English, sliding back and forth as if they were one language. She walked directly to a long walnut table and picked up some paperwork. "Let's get the business out of the way and then I'll show you to your room. I have a splendid room for you on the third floor."

After the papers were filled out and signed and money changed hands, she said, "You may come down for tea any time, or I can bring it up to you. And dinner will be at 7:30 pm sharp. My husband is out of town or he would help you with your luggage. I hope you don't mind tending to your own things."

I inwardly groaned. "Three stories up? Oh, how I wish I had packed for only one week and not six," I muttered to Josiane as we walked back to the car. Our suitcases were getting heavier as each day and week progressed.

Once we arrived back inside the darkened hallway with our luggage in tow, Mme. de Bonneval led us up first one extra-steep stairway and then another—envision twenty-foot ceilings to each floor—then down a long hallway that skirted along the third story facing out onto the front courtyard, then down almost the full length of a hallway across the front

of the house and into our room. The room—actually rooms—
were immense. Mme. de Bonneval said they had been the
quarters of the nurse and part of the original nursery. The
bed was to be shared, but it was two queen-sized beds pushed
together and layered with one, two, maybe three comforters.
Faded mauve wallpaper covered the walls, and a coat of yel-
lowing white paint stretched across the wooden doors and
along the baseboards, but all was very clean. The floorboards
creaked and moaned as if in pain as Josiane walked across the
room to put her suitcase down. She giggled. Mme. de Bonneval ignored her and led us through a separate door to a
large bathroom, which like most bathrooms in sixteenth century houses, had been an afterthought. In the very center of
the room—standing like a white porcelain albatross—was the
bathtub. Smack in the middle of the room. The toilet and
bidet were hiding on the other side of the tub, and along the
entire back wall were expansive windows—large drafty, windows—with no curtains. Both of us shivered as the windows
rattled with a slight breeze that seemed to have eked its way
into the bathroom.

Back in the bedroom, I walked over to another bank of
windows that also yawned out onto the back of the house.
Woods extended for what looked like miles, but only a
canopy of dark green leaves was visible. As I looked down, a
black truck pulled away from the back entrance and sped
down a winding driveway from the house.

"Would you like for me to bring tea to you up here?"
Madame suggested.

"That would be lovely," I said. "A cup of tea, a nice
warm bath, and perhaps a nap . . . You said dinner was at
7:30 sharp. Will there be others for dinner?"

"Oh my, yes. There will be at least—hmm, let me think

—yes, there will be one other woman. She's from Switzerland. I believe she said she could join us," Madame Bonneval said as she backed out of the room.

We settled in, even though the rooms were terribly chilly. No, they were downright cold. And I did attempt a hot bath. Turning on the hot water in the tub, I went to the adjoining room to undress and gather my toiletries. My feet, I noticed, had turned dark brown from walking around the grounds of the Chateau du Plaix and I was certain that the rest of my body needed great attention, too. I looked forward to slipping into a hot soapy soak for about an hour and then washing my hair. No such luck. The water, which was momentarily lukewarm, came out in rusty blasts of cold water jettisoned into the tub. In one or two fast and frenzied motions, I washed my feet and body before leaping from the tub. There I stood, dripping on the cold tile, without a floor mat, and my towel on the other side of the room. Just then, I felt—not just heard—the breezes careen again through the crevices around the windows. I made a mad dash to the towel, wrapped it about me, and rushed into the warmer bedroom, where a hot cup of tea awaited. Immediately after finishing my tea, I fell sound asleep.

Josiane, on the other hand, had been busy attempting to connect her laptop to the internet. When I awoke, I found her on her hands and knees, reaching under the bed to make the electrical connection. After several trips up and down the back staircase, she somehow succeeded.

"*Voilà*," she shouted to the lump in the bed next to her. I turned onto my side. "I have conquered all my demons and arrived at Nirvana."

"More like Nerd-vana," I said, grumbling from underneath the blankets.

At exactly 7:29 pm, Josiane and I appeared in the dining room. To both of us, the light lunch in the smoky truck stop around noon seemed like weeks before. The Swiss guest was already seated at the head of the table and waved the two of us to join her. She was in her early forties, lithe of build and movement, with blonde hair and blue eyes. Propped prominently on her thin and angular face was a pair of silver metal-rimmed glasses that reflected the light from the dimly lit chandelier above her. Gretchen Muir had been chatting with Mme. de Bonneval, but Madame, she said as she introduced herself, had just disappeared into the kitchen to silence the ringing telephone. Ms. Muir said she had been visiting some of the countryside while she was on a business trip to the city of Bourges, which she said was just north of the chateau. She worked in marketing for a Swiss banking firm and made regular trips in and around Europe enjoying the sights and sounds of each country. She seemed pleasant enough.

Although the table was large enough for fifteen, four places had been haphazardly set. Josiane and I had just taken places on either side of Ms. Muir, when Madame de Bonneval burst forth from the kitchen bearing four small plates of *terrine* she said she had just made. She dashed back into the kitchen and then reappeared with a basket of bread slices and a bottle of Sauterne. I assumed the *terrine* was *pâté de foie gras*, but after smearing the concoction onto a small slice of bread and popping it into my mouth, I wasn't certain. The pinkish-gray mass, which had the markings of having been just cut from a tin can, had a distinctive flavor that I couldn't pinpoint, but it permeated every morsel. I had in the past sampled and purchased fine *pâté* that had come in a tin, but for some reason I played with this food on my tongue. I hesitated to ask Josiane what we were eating, because for one of the first times on our trip, everyone at the table spoke English. Furthermore, Josiane had tucked into her plate of *terrine* with gusto. I decided to follow suit but chased it down with massive swigs of Sauterne.

Once Madame joined us at the table, the conversation turned to a discussion about the Chateau de Theirault. All three of us were eager to hear the history of the castle.

"Please, Madame, tell us about this marvelous home," Josiane said as she bit into another slice of bread.

"To begin, this chateau has always been in my husband's family—the Theiraults—and has been handed down since it was built in the early fifteenth century. It was originally built as a fortress of sorts, then was updated and rebuilt in the eighteenth century. I'm not certain how many rooms it once had, but it now has 45 rooms and 247 acres of forests and streams around it.

"Originally," she said, starting to take a bite of *pâté*, then setting the baguette slice back on her plate, "the land holdings, I am told, were much more extensive, as it was quite necessary to work the land to support the chateau. This included all the small outlying farms that are still along the edges of our property on the other side of the moat. That's where the swimming pool is now. Maybe you didn't have a chance to see it yet. *Oui? Non.* Perhaps tomorrow you will have time to walk around the grounds."

"How long have you lived here?" I asked.

"Oh, my," she said, as she stretched her arms and sat further back in her seat. "I moved here many years ago. It was 1977 when my husband and I, along with our three small children—one just an infant of two months—decided to move from Paris to my husband's grandmother's home. As the eldest son, my husband had been given the chateau by his grandmother. He had always been quite close with her and had spent many holidays and summers here as a boy, and he loved it very much.

"Big family gatherings had always been held here when my husband was a boy, and he had come from a large family—four boys and four girls. Once we moved here, he regularly regaled our children with tales of his life here as a boy. He especially loved summers here, as he lived in Paris during the school year, and once arriving here he could enjoy the carefree life playing all over the property. Of course, his strict grandmother wouldn't allow him to have complete idle time, and she hired a tutor who was a seminary student, to attend to the children's studies. The boys, he said, usually became bored with their studies, and would invariably suggest going for long bike rides, as they loved to leave the seminarian far behind. My husband was probably more than thirteen at the time, but years' worth of laughs have come from some of his stories." She smiled and got up to remove the plates, her own plate untouched. Setting the plates on the sideboard, she turned to refill the wine glasses.

"Did your husband spend time here only in the summer months?" Josiane asked.

"No, his family came here for many holidays throughout the year. In winter, they would go hunting on the grounds with his grandfather. They would always bring back rabbits, deer, or wild boar because the family forests, like I said, were extensive and filled with wild game. Probably still are." She winked.

Madame quickly excused herself to go to the kitchen,

where she retrieved the next course. Bowls of hot aromatic soup were placed before us with another basket of bread. Large chunks of carrots, onion slices, and celery were nudged aside by chunks of meat, which Madame said was chicken but with a more distinctive gamey flavor—much like rabbit.

"So," I said to continue the earlier conversation, "did you say your husband's grandmother had always lived here in this house?"

"No, but when she married, she moved here as a young wife."

"Was her life different than what you have experienced living here?"

"Oh my, yes!" she blurted out, laughing. "His grandmother was quite the grand dame of this old house. She experienced this chateau when it still had some prestige, money, and influence. My husband remembers at least ten servants in attendance to his grandmother—a majordomo; at least one chef and his wife, who would assist; Old Antoine, the butler; plus, a chauffeur, gardener, hunting guard, and of course, the farmers. In fact, in the small houses surrounding the chateau, up to fifty people lived to attend solely to this family. They oversaw the farm animals, vegetable gardens, and hunting, along with the care and upkeep of the chateau and the family.

"His grandmother ruled with a very strict hand and, I guess, even though she is long gone, we still uphold some of her household rules. They would always dress for dinner, with a dinner jacket, and were served by a *maitre d'hotel*, precisely at 7:30 pm. I still insist on at least dinner beginning at 7:30. My husband tried to have our children do as he had been forced to do under his grandmother's iron hand, and that was for the children to eat only in the children's dining room until they reached the age of twelve. But I hadn't been raised that way and insisted that we all eat right here together. He finally gave in to that."

"You said your husband came from Paris—is that right?" Josiane asked.

"Yes. Both my husband and I were born and raised in Paris."

"Ah," I said, "can you tell me if you were there during the beginnings of World War II?"

"But of course." She seemed surprised at the change in topic but leaned closer to the table awaiting the next question.

"I have been wondering how people survived the . . . well, the Exodus. I have heard several stories about that. Could you tell me something about your experience?" I looked over at Gretchen, suddenly remembering that her family may have been on the other side of the war.

"Are you alright with this subject?" I asked her.

"Yes. I'm curious about it, too, as much of my family was from France." She leaned forward to hear Madame's answers.

"I was born in 1944, so what I remember is only what was told to me. But during the war, my father was a stockbroker at the stock exchange in Paris. When the Exodus came for us Parisians, he stayed in Paris and the rest of our family fled. I think he hoped to hold on to our house and our valuables if he stayed. Our family went west of Paris to other family members' homes. They found those homes open to them, as those family members had fled farther to the west. As I was told, the families stayed out of Paris for a few months, but when it was safe to return, they did so. But once they returned, they found it very difficult to get food. What I mostly remember my family talking about was that we, in our family, nearly starved. My father was able to continue working, but it was difficult as the Germans were in charge."

"That's very similar to what your mother told us, Josiane," I said.

"Yes," Josiane replied. "She was forced to leave my older brother behind—he was only four years old—to flee from Paris to Bordeaux to help establish a new Citroën factory. She was a single mother, so it was up to her to provide for her son. By the time the Citroën employees arrived in Bordeaux—which was no easy feat, as they had to walk—Marshal Pétain had surrendered France to the Germans, so there was no need for building the plant elsewhere. My mother returned to her son in Paris and to work in the Citroën plant—this time, for the Germans."

"Do you have a hatred of Germans?" Gretchen asked Josiane.

"No. In fact, once I graduated from school, I worked in Germany for a time. That was very upsetting to my father, who never forgave the Germans for what he felt were the atrocities of war. But I was rebelling against him, I suppose." She grinned, spooned up the last mouthful of soup, and laid her soup spoon to the side.

"I suppose I should find out more about what my family did during the war, but they never wanted to talk about it. So, I never pressed them," Gretchen said.

"That must be typical, and we often don't think to ask those important questions until we are much older. Older than you are, for sure," I said to her.

Madame de Bonneval stood up again and carried the dishes to the adjoining kitchen. After a slight delay, she returned with two large platters: one with roasted rabbit in a mustard sauce, another with small roasted vegetables—potatoes, mushrooms, peppers, and zucchinis. The succulent yet pungent aromas from the rabbit were irresistible. We plunged into the food as Madame poured a nice Sancerre wine to accompany the feast. The food was superb!

"What about your husband's family, Madame? Were they also caught up in the war?" I asked.

"Oh, yes. My husband's father, Gaston de Bonneval, was in the French Army. In fact, he was caught by the Germans, and when he came back home from the war, they say he weighed only forty-five kilos."

"How much is that, Josiane?" I whispered to her.

"Less than a hundred pounds. That's very lean, indeed," she said.

"Yes," Madame continued. "I guess it was quite dramatic for the family. But because of my father-in-law's experience, he taught my husband to always look after others, so my husband became a doctor. He has recently been elected as a Mayor and a Consul General in our local politics.

"But after the war, my father-in-law became the aide-de-camp to Charles De Gaulle for over twenty years—until 1964, after De Gaulle came back into power."

"Wow! That's impressive," I said. "I imagine he had plenty of tales to tell."

"It is so interesting," Josiane said, "how war impacts people's lives. It is so horrendous that somehow we determine to become better people because of it, and it sounds like your father-in-law did just that."

"One reason I've been asking about the war," I said, "is because we have been traveling all around the upper regions of France asking people about family traditions and foods, and somehow we always end up hearing about people's experience of war. Without fail, I have found that people who suffered so extraordinarily during the war, first, hold family as sacrosanct, and second, hold fast to the traditions that bind their families together. And that is usually over food!" I waved my fork in the air as if it was a magic wand, as there we were sharing food and traditions in that chateau.

"Do you still have family gatherings here?" Josiane asked Madame.

"Oh my, yes. We have carried on many traditions from both sides of our families. In my family, there were gatherings every year in September, just before the school year began. We still celebrate in this way with a big dinner party.

"My brothers and sisters all came together recently. Just my siblings—no children, grandchildren, or spouses. There were seven of us, but our ages are so spread apart that our childhoods were quite different. My parents had children from 1929 to 1950. So, we all had wonderful stories to share with each other. We had such a grand time." Her blue eyes sparkled as she pushed an errant blonde curl off her forehead and into place.

"And you and your children? Do you get together often?" I asked.

"My, yes. We get together three or four times per year. We are together for Easter and Christmas, plus any other reasons to congregate. It is quite marvelous."

"Do you have favorite foods you like to prepare for different holidays or events?" I asked, returning to my usual script.

"We just had Easter, so that's easy to remember. First, we begin with *le mimosa*. She smiled broadly. "And then, one of the family favorites is hard-boiled eggs, cut and slathered with mayonnaise."

"Do you call those Deviled Eggs?" I asked.

"Yes, Carole," Josiane said.

"And we almost always have a chocolate cake for family birthdays. And for Christmas we always have turkey. Always. Engagement dinners are always very special, with one of my specialties called *Canard avec Pêches*. After roasting the duck, you make a sauce with sautéed peaches. It is quite delicious."

"What would you say is your secret to cooking success?" I asked. Anyone who can take on a family, and an immense family home the way she has, is a success in my book.

Madame thought for a minute, then said in an animated whisper, "When you want to cook, you have to be in the kitchen!" She threw her head back and laughed at her own joke, with the rest of us joining in.

"I would imagine that this is quite an extraordinary undertaking," Gretchen said, waving her arms about to include the whole chateau.

"*Mais oui.* Sometimes the children come down here just to help us out. It has at times been difficult to keep this old place going. When my husband was first given this property to take care of, he was so pleased. We knew much work needed to be done on the chateau, and still does, but we had no idea what a large undertaking of time and money it would require."

She again sat back in her chair, as if the very words had rendered her exhausted. "Yes, he was the only family member who would even take this house on, and it has almost done us in." She sighed but smiled.

"We thought when we first moved here, that we had a solution to maintain the property by opening a bed-and-breakfast. But because of the custom of splitting the inheritance of this property, the chateau did not come with the surrounding lands that had, over the years, provided the income necessary to maintain this house. There are only the remaining 247 acres. We found that to open for business, we had to add thirteen new bathrooms to the existing four and repair over forty leaks in the roof." She shrugged her shoulders and shook her head from side to side.

"I guess I'm condemned to live my life with only toil and sacrifice." She let out a Gallic puff, a wave of her hand, and laughed at her own joke.

"Have you thought of selling your house?" I asked.

"Every day. But this house has been in my husband's family for more than three hundred years. It would be difficult to let go of—and it would be difficult to sell."

"I imagine that you have felt a bit confined in this house," Josiane said kindly.

"Oh my, yes. Even though my husband has become a mayor to our local village—following in the footsteps of his father—there are few, if any, other cultural things we can attend. And certainly, no travel. Ah, but that's enough about me. How about your travels?" she said, changing the subject with a cheerful lilt.

Once our evening repast had come to an end, Josiane and I made our way up the three—count them—three lengthy flights of stairs to our room. And, as I shuffled along, I chastised myself to Josiane for how critical I had felt earlier when I first had entered this house. Of course, I had had no idea what the history had been or what it would have taken to maintain or run a domicile such as this. But this evening, I had found a renewed respect for Mme. de Bonneval and all she had undertaken. She was making the best of a difficult situation, and we had been accorded the luxury of enjoying a lovely conversation and a night in a 'real' chateau. I was, indeed, grateful.

As I recall, I slept well that night, except for awaking often to the sounds of what I assumed was the hallway cuckoo clock. Not every hour, mind you, but every few minutes. I must have said something aloud, as eventually Josiane rolled over to enlightened me.

"That's no cuckoo clock; what you are hearing is a 'real' cuckoo outside in the nearby forest. Simply put a pillow over your head and ignore the bird," she mumbled drowsily.

Well, I had never seen a cuckoo, so I burst out of my cocoon of covers to race across the cold floor to the window in hopes of catching sight of this elusive bird. But, alas, the darkness kept her hidden. Sigh! Back to bed.

Auvergne

CHAPTER FIFTEEN

Coming Home to the Farm

"There is only one happiness in life, to love and be loved."
—George Sand

*A*fter a light but cheerful breakfast with Mme. de Bonneval, Josiane and I wrangled our bags back down the umpteen steps to the first floor, out the door, and across the gravel parking lot before heaving them once again into the back of Josiane's station wagon.

"You'd think I would get good at this, Josiane," I said.

"Well, lucky for you, you won't have many more days of dragging your bags about," she said with a sad smile. She knew our days of travel were almost at an end.

"Ah, *c'est vrai*," I said. "It seems I'm rushing off in the middle of our tour, but I think I need to sit with all that I have learned and try to digest it, so to speak." I had been on the road with Josiane for well over three weeks and had traveled through Italy for two weeks prior to this on another food tour. My bones needed to get home to my own bed.

"At least we've gotten a good start, don't you think?" Josiane responded, more cheerfully.

"How about you, Josiane? Have you gotten the answers you came for? About your mother, that is?"

"I'm hoping to have even more answers after we meet with Christian tomorrow."

Once we hit the main road, we drove north to the village of Nohant, in the region of Berry. Having just left the six-hundred-year-old Chateau de Thibault, I was getting used to visiting these lovely old aristocratic homes. In a few miles, we pulled up to the outside gates of a fortified manor house built of sandstone.

"This is lovely!" I said. "Where are we?"

Josiane handed me a brochure. "We are at the museum and home of my favorite female author, George Sand. Have you heard of her? She is quite famous, but I don't know if her writings are translated into English."

I had heard of her but couldn't recall a single book title to save my soul. But there we were, at a particularly lovely house which, according to the brochure, had been reconstructed in the 1450s. The date of the original house was not given. I quickly perused the brochure: "From 1837 until her death in 1876, Sand spent long summers, usually from May until November, at this house, where she entertained many of the most famous artists of the time, including composer Franz Liszt, writers Honoré de Balzac and Gustave Flaubert, and painter Eugène Delacroix. From 1839 until 1847, Frédéric Chopin lived with her in the house, writing his Fantasie in F Minor, the Sonata Funebre, the two *Nocturnes*, Op. 37, and the four Mazurkas, Op. 41."

As we got ready to climb out of the car, Josiane told me more. "Many of George Sand's most famous novels, including *Consuelo, La Mare au Diable (The Devil's Pool)*, and *Le Meunier d'Angibault (The Miller of Angibault)* were written in this house, and most of her novels are set right here in the Berry countryside and villages around Nohant. I think that is why I find visiting her home so fascinating."

I understood the draw, as I had sought out the homes of some of my own favorite authors in France, England, Italy, and the U.S. It's like visiting a touchstone—a connection with the author, with their characters and the story.

We spent the better half of the morning and into the early afternoon on a tour through the three-story manor house. Each room had been beautifully appointed or restored into the fashion George Sand had known and loved. Her portrait was prominent throughout, and her love of creativity was evident. Chopin's portrait and his music were also on display. The enormous kitchen was lined with copper pots and pans. One of the unique sections of the house, and there were many, was the room for a puppet theatre. And rooms were filled with costumes. It was easy to imagine that an artist, composer, or author could find comfort in this house, as well as discover the ability to coax the creative juices to flow.

We wandered through the beautiful and extensive gardens, then returned to the house and crossed the road to a lovely tea shop that served a light lunch.

After leaving Sand's childhood home near the village of Nohant, we each slipped into our own separate thoughts as we began our drive south. The flat plains of the Loire River Valley gave way to soft, undulating hills, which yielded to mountains that rose up to great heights and cascaded into steep knife-edged valleys. We were entering the gates of the very center of France: the mountainous region of the Massif Central.

I found myself reflecting on what a strong woman George Sand must have been to have commanded such a meritorious life—to have accomplished so much while living in such an unconventional way. Born into wealth with a lineage to royalty, she chose to establish her own way and provide for her own financial needs after eight years of an unhappy marriage. In the 1830s, when divorce was almost nonexistent, she moved her children to Paris, obtained a divorce and, under a masculine *nom de plume*, began her writing career, which included eighty novels. Her early novels were romantic, possibly reflecting her own numerous liaisons, which were notorious. Her later novels expressed her serious concern with social reform, especially for women to find the type of freedom in their lives that was a matter of course for the men of her day.

Freedom, as a matter of course. Now that would have been helpful for Marcelle. My mind always came back to Josiane's stalwart mother. Marcelle had captured my soul. As an unmarried mother at eighteen, she had made her way into Paris from her hometown of Vannes to find work to provide for her son, Martial. The Citroën factory work had been a saving grace. Then, struggling and alone in the City with World War II looming, she fell in love for the first time, conceived, and gave birth to her second son, Gérard. How had she managed? How had she been able to save her children with war filling every moment of the day and night? Freedom was what she sought for her family.

I looked out at the passing countryside and tried to imagine what it had been like for Marcelle when she passed through this region for the first time, on her long train ride from Paris. It was probably 1943, and she was fleeing from German-occupied territory in Paris, to the safety and comfort of the hills of the Auvergne area—the Free Zone—and with the hopes of creating a home for her two sons. Martial, six years old by then, had preceded her, as all school-age children had been sent from Paris in order to protect them. The Allies had been expected to begin bombing, and the French seemed it was the most humane thing to do. And as soon as her baby, Gérard, was a year old, she chose to leave behind the man she loved in order to save her baby from the nightly bombings which had begun in earnest. She had boarded a train south, with the promise that her love would follow, and she prayed for the best. Little did she know he would not be coming.

Josiane and I were driving through this land she had traveled by train. I opened my eyes more fully to gain clarity, as if this would help me understand Marcelle and her past. War has created many, many women like Marcelle over the millennia, who were forced to care for their children alone, with no family to turn to, and no reliable income to make ends meet. Yet, somehow, they manage. But, how?

The extensive fields that blanketed the Loire Valley had given way to small plots of ground enclosed by meter-high rock walls. Within the enclosures, bright green shoots of wheat waved gracefully as the wind lifted and rose through the landscape. Sprinkled alongside the rock walls and the roadways were springtime wildflowers that raged in rich pinks, purples, and blues. All seemed to grow in abundance and to dance to the tune of the wind—dipping and rising in unison.

Breaking the silence, I asked, "What time of year did your mother first come to the Auvergne, Josiane? Was it in the springtime? Like now?"

She furrowed her brow, then looked around her, as if seeing outside the car for the first time that afternoon.

"I think it was in April or May." She rubbed her eyes a couple of times. "I would imagine what she first saw looked much like this. Probably exactly like this. Not much has changed here in many, many years."

We rounded a curve on the narrow road and caught a glimpse of a woman herding cows as she walked up and over a knoll. Her red checkered head scarf bobbed along the hillside until it disappeared from our sight. High on a ridge above us we could see children riding their bicycles, as a small herd of goats skittered down the hill out of the children's way. Josiane slowed and rolled down her window, and the children's laughter cascaded down the hill toward us. She waved at the children and laughed as if joining in on their game.

"You're probably right," I said, smiling. "These rutted old roads may have been worn with time, but life has definitely not moved to the new millennium. I would like to believe we are seeing the land like your mother first saw it in 1943."

I watched with fascination as the children climbed higher and higher on the ridge until they, too, disappeared from view.

Josiane rolled up her window and speeded up the car, winding down the hill and through a small village that held a smattering of dilapidated stone houses. She pointed at an abandoned *lavoir* next to a small scum-coated pond as she slowed in the village. Images of women from centuries past, busy scrubbing their families' clothes, flitted through my mind. I would never see a *lavoir* again without thinking of Marcelle.

Although the village seemed uninhabited, chickens and ducks made their way across the road and waddled into a roadside garden. Without hesitation, they busied themselves rummaging through the rows of spring peas for a late-afternoon snack.

"We are finally in the region known as the Auvergne," Josiane said, as a formal introduction to the area. "It is, as I've told you, the very center of France and is known as the heart of France. Once you've met my brother and the people of Auvergne, you will understand that this is true. They are all heart!"

"Very pastoral. Immensely beautiful," I said. "Is it mostly farming country?"

"Yes. Farming is still how most people survive. A farmer today can barely eke out his living, but it is such a part of who he is that he can't leave the farm to live elsewhere . . . except maybe to work as a mason. Perhaps my brother will tell you some of that history. But I must tell you, the people here are quite shy—not used to strangers—and you'll find them reluctant to open up. Don't be hurt by that. They have good minds, but do not wish to display intellect as a means of discourse."

With those words, and after traveling for several more hours, we continued through Montluçon, down through Evaux-les-Bain, and then along the winding mountain ridges on a narrow two-lane roadway.

Finally, around six o'clock we arrived at Martial's farm. The old gray stone farmhouse looked forlorn in the soft purple light as the late afternoon glow dipped behind the house and dropped from sight. Josiane honked the horn wildly signaling her arrival, but only the geese acknowledged her presence by flapping their wings and resounding with an equally obnoxious racket. She laughed out loud, turned off the car, and jumped out. The kitchen door swung open and out stepped Jeannine, Martial's wife. A shy grin crept across her lips, as her roughened hands brushed blonde straggles of hair back from her brow. Josiane, always the most demonstrative of her family, grabbed her in a hug and kissed both cheeks in greeting.

"How are you, dear sister?" she asked. "And where is my brother?" She peered over her sister-in-law's shoulder and into the house, waiting for her big brute of a brother to come barreling out the door.

"He's gone into Fontanières for a few moments. He thought he would be back before you arrived. I guess he's having one too many cups of coffee at the *café*. But not to worry. Come in, come in."

Fontanières. That was the village Marcelle had lived in. We were almost at her home. I walked to Josiane's side as I was introduced to Jeannine, first in French, then in English. "Carole, this is my dear sister, Jeannine. She is the best person who ever came into my brother's life. The very best. Maybe she will tell you all about it." She translated for Jeannine's benefit. Jeannine's broad face lit from within. She blushed.

"I'm happy to meet you," I said, extending my hand. Jeannine reached out to shake hands, but instead embraced me, then stood back, a bit embarrassed. She turned quickly, led us into the house, down a small hallway and directly into the kitchen. The redolence of cinnamon in freshly baked pastry, which had embraced us the moment we stepped from the car, now hit us full force. Both Josiane and I grabbed our stomachs as we inhaled with delight.

Again, that shy smile appeared on Jeannine's face, as she went directly to the coffee pot and began filling it with well water, measuring out coffee grounds, and bantering with Josiane. They conversed easily, catching up on each other's activities and family tales, while I, still unused to this awkward moment of first arrival and never understanding what was being said, wandered around the room trying to imagine what life was like in this kitchen. In this home. I remembered Josiane telling me something about this house and farm being passed down through generations in Jeannine's family. As I tried to judge the age of the house, my eyes scanned the stucco-coated walls and up and over the cracks that etched themselves across the ceiling. The floorboards were timeworn and uneven, but the room was clean, albeit filled with typical odds and ends of clutter. A plastic table covering, once bright with light blue and yellow flowers, now scrubbed almost completely white, extended the full length of the kitchen table, and a small bouquet of forget-me-nots sat prominently in a pale green canning jar in the center. Josiane pulled out a chair and invited me to take off my coat and sit down. Once the coffee finished perking, Jeannine set steaming mugs of coffee before us, along with cinnamon twists, and joined us at the table.

Is there a more wonderful aroma in the world than coffee with fresh cinnamon twists?

"Since Martial isn't back, Carole, would you like to ask Jeannine some questions about her life on the farm? Would you be comfortable with that, Jeannine?" Josiane asked.

Jeannine hesitated for a moment. She looked cautiously at me, then at Josiane. But because Josiane had prepared her with the reasons for my visit, she gave in to her reserve and replied, "Well, I, uh—of course. I don't know why you would want to know about this old place, but I can tell you what I know."

"Well, to begin with, where were you born?" I asked, as I swung out the tape recorder and a pad and paper from my trusty bag.

"Right here. I was born in 1947 and grew up in this house, on this very farm."

"She was probably born on this very table," Josiane said. "Well, maybe not *this* very table . . ." She began to giggle, then signaled me to continue. She had told me previously that she herself had been born on a kitchen table, during World War II.

"What village is closest to you? Is it Fontanières?"

"No, we're nearest the village of Gênet, just to the south of us. Like I said, there's not much to tell, as life here has changed little over the course of my life." She shrugged her shoulders and took a bite of her cinnamon twist.

"Are most people into farming, like you and Martial?"

"Yes. This has always been a very poor area of the country, and certainly remains so today, so farming was the one way to survive. This farm was the family home of my great-grandfather, their last name being Bougerrolle. My father and grandfather had only sons—until I was born. So, I, too, worked here on the farm with my family, and walked three miles every day to school. In the winter months, it was very difficult because we didn't have many clothes, and very few warm clothes. And none for special occasions."

"Since you mention special occasions, did you celebrate any holidays?"

"During holidays, we didn't have much in the way of specialty foods, as we were very poor, as I said. And things have not changed much," she said with a shrug, "but at least living on the farm we always had food. Especially eggs. Many, many eggs. And we had chickens, rabbits, and our own milk cows for making milk, butter, and cheese. We still live off our own vegetable garden year-round, because we preserve and can many fruits and vegetables. The potato crop usually yields around 500 kilos of potatoes, and that amount will last us through the winter months. It is very important to have a good crop of potatoes, and this only comes if we have rain and good weather. And where we live the weather is not always good, plus the land has always been poor quality."

"Jeannine, tell Carole about the *Fête du Cochon*," Josiane encouraged. "We just heard about that the other day from a tour guide near Chateauroux."

"That has always been a fun time of year. The *Fête du Cochon*, or Festival of the Pig, is when each farmer who raises a pig, invites all the neighbors to assist when it is time for the pig to be butchered. It is usually a lot of work, but the workload is shared by all the neighbors, as everyone enjoys helping each other."

"What happens at this festival?"

"First of all, someone would come with a gun to shoot the pig, and if they had no gun, we would slit the throat of the pig. After the pig was dead, we would clean the pig to remove the bristles from the skin. The blood is collected, and blood sausage is made. Every piece of the animal is used—nothing is ever wasted. The innards are used and made clean and beautiful, and that is what we call *tripe*. The pig is then placed into a salt solution called *saumure*. This is to cure the pork, especially for hams. Hams are also smoked along with sausages and *pâté*. *Pâté* is canned and preserved for the winter months. During the *Fête*, the families not only work together throughout the day, but they also eat together. This is one of the rare times that we would share a meal with another family, so it was always very, very special for me."

"It sounds delightful, but certainly a lot of work," I said.

Jeannine shrugged her shoulders. "It was simply one more part of farm life. I can't imagine being on the farm without having to work long, hard hours. But it's an existence that is all I know—and love."

We heard the front door open and slam shut and the thudding steps of Josiane's brother as he lumbered through the house. "Especially sharing it with Martial." Jeannine beamed as her husband burst into the kitchen.

"Martial! Martial!" Josiane leapt up from the table and wrapped her arms around her brother. His arms folded her fast to his chest and he stood holding her for a long moment.

"Martial," Josiane said, finally separating from her brother's embrace, "I want you to meet my dear friend Carole."

I stood up and walked around the table to shake his hand. He, too, pulled me to him and kissed both my cheeks. I'm sure a surprised look swept my face, and now I was the embarrassed one. I mumbled a self-conscious *bonjour* and returned to my seat opposite Jeannine, but my eyes stayed on Martial. Here was the man, who as a small boy had been left behind by his mother, Marcelle, when she was forced to evacuate from Paris during the Exodus. After her return to Paris and to him, he had been sent out of the City with all the other school children due to the fear of bombing by the Allies. He had been sent to Fontanières, which was her destination on that long train ride from Paris, so that she could be with him again. All because of the war. I knew so much about him—maybe too much—but this was part of the story Marcelle had shared with me. I squirmed uncomfortably in my seat. I held an unfair advantage that I did not wish to betray.

Martial was just as Josiane had described: his face was weathered with a deep tan, even though it was spring. He was stocky, his shoulders somewhat stooped. And just like she had said, when he sat down and rested his elbows on the table, only his hands moved as he talked—just his hands in small turns and swirls. As he doffed his hat, I could see that the dark, thick hair Josiane had raved about had given way to a gray-streaked crown. But it was his eyes that caught my attention. They were the same color as Marcelle's, and as he looked at his sister, a twinkle appeared at the edges of his eyes, and I could have sworn I saw a reflection of his mother in his smile.

"Come join us, Martial," Jeannine said, standing to grab another cup and filling it with coffee. "Carole is asking us questions about life on this farm."

Martial stripped off his heavily padded canvas coat and pulled up the chair next to his wife and across from Josiane. Josiane reached across the table and took his hands into her own. She murmured a few words in French, and he smiled broadly, relaxed into his seat, and took up his cup.

"I was just asking your wife a few questions about farm life," I said as an opening. "Or times of celebration." He waved his hand for us to continue, and he picked up a cinnamon twist and inhaled it.

"I remember at the end of the school year," Jeannine said, "and the beginning of summer vacation, our school would hold a celebration. We kids would get up in front of the audience to sing a few songs we had learned during the year, and sometimes we would perform a short play. The kids who had been successful during the year would receive their prizes for academic achievements. That was a time of celebration and we had such fun with all the families gathered together at our school."

"Did you participate in the school plays, Jeannine?" I asked.

A wild rush of color flooded her cheeks. She stared down at her cup and murmured, *"Oui."*

"Good for you, Jeannine," Josiane said. "Now, what were your summer months like?"

"During the summer months, for special occasions we

would prepare fruit pies. We always had plums from the orchard, strawberries from our patch, and apples. Always so many apples."

"Tell Carole how you made the pies," Josiane said.

"The pies were very, very simple with a dough made with a little bit of flour and butter, plus the fruit, of course, a bit of sugar, and then we popped them into the oven. Nothing fancy."

"Jeannine," I said, "I remember, too, helping my mother and grandmother bake pies and cakes, but I can't imagine anything as wonderful as having your own apple or plum trees. We had our own small vegetable gardens, but we never had fresh chicken eggs or our own butter. That sounds like a life of wealth to me."

Jeannine listened to Josiane's translation and again reddened. Her head nodded up and down as she peered down at her cup. Noticing the rest of her pastry, she popped it into her mouth.

"I remember another one that I loved. On the first Monday of every month, it was always a special time for our family to attend the farmers market. Our entire family would walk many kilometers into town—seven to be exact. This was the time to sell a cow, pig, horse, or an ox for the money our family greatly needed. And the market was where my father could buy things for the farm, such as bales of hay, twine, and gas for the tractor. It was also where we could sell things, so we could make payments on the farm loans.

"There was also a weekly farmers market. We would sell chickens, eggs, and cheeses we had made. My parents could purchase food, supplies, clothing, and most things we now normally buy at regular stores."

"Are these events still taking place?" I asked.

"Well, we don't walk into town anymore," laughed Martial. "If we relied on that mode of transportation, we wouldn't get much else accomplished."

"And there was the annual wheat harvest," Jeannine said. "As a child, this was another neighborly activity my family enjoyed. One battery of people would travel from one farm to another. The men would work together, and the women would prepare the food for the harvesters. The children from the town families sometimes came out to help with harvesting, because they thought it was a fun thing to do. I suppose it seemed like fun if you lived in town, but all the same it was always a lively time. Usually there was music that was played, and we would have dances right in the farmyard." She cast a smile at her husband.

"Isn't that how you two met?" Josiane asked, catching the look and laughing.

Jeannine blushed. "Yes, but that's a story for later."

So far, all I have heard is of hard work and harder work for this family. Surely, there was some fun to be shared.

Martial broke in. "I started working in the fields from the age of twelve on. And I started dancing at age fifteen—I still love to dance. I used to ride my bicycle many miles to get to the dances. Sometimes I would come back from the dance at five or seven o'clock the following morning." He pulled his hand through his hair and a slow grin enveloped his face.

"Tell Carole about the time of the big storm, Martial," Josiane prompted.

"Please do," I encouraged. "What happened?"

"Well," he chuckled and tipped back on his chair, "as I recall, it was the summer of my fifteenth birthday, and the day of one of our biggest summer festivals in the region. Everyone from kilometers around had been excited for weeks anticipating this dance. There was to be an exceptionally good band performing that night. At a previous dance, I had attracted the eye of a good-looking gal, who I hoped would be in attendance, so I was especially looking forward to it." Again, his eyes lovingly found his wife's, and Jeannine blushed once again.

"Carole," Josiane interrupted, "Martial was not always good with his words when he was younger, but I have been told that he could sweep the women off their feet with his elegance on the dance floor, especially in the waltz. Right, Jeannine?" She smiled at Jeannine.

Martial licked the cinnamon glaze off his fingers. "After I got off work that afternoon, I went down to the pond, pulled off my work clothes and boots, then scrubbed myself raw. Then I put on my best dancing clothes and best shoes—well, my only shoes—and headed out. I got on my bike, my only mode of transportation, and rode those dusty, dry roads 35 km. to the dance. Oh, I flew down those roads as I could hardly wait.

"By the time I arrived, the barnyard was already filled with pick-up trucks and cars and people were everywhere! Lighted lanterns swung from the trees and tables were loaded with more food than I had ever seen. Laughter rang out and everyone was talking, eating, drinking and having a great time. I quickly put my bike into the barn for safe-keeping and walked out to join the crowd. I headed for the food; I was so hungry. I hadn't eaten all day and I could just taste . . . . But, before I could down a drink or grab a snack, the band began to play—as if they had been awaiting my arrival." He winked at Jeannine.

"Well," said Martial, with a bit of bluster, "when the band began to play, they played some popular songs from the 50s, along with some waltzes. I had mastered the waltz. Don't ask me where or how I learned, but I had." Question marks formed on three sets of eyebrows, but he plowed on.

"I could see that lovely young lady—Jeannine—across the farmyard who I was hoping to impress and I was making the rounds with some of the other gals, dancing with this one and then that one, all in order to work up my courage to finally ask Jeannine. I was biding my time as the evening was young and I had the entire evening to make my move. I had thought it all out ahead of time while riding over on my bicycle." Martial turned in his chair, smiled at his wife and reached over to take her hand.

"After a few sets of dances, the owner of the farm and his hands began to set off a string of fireworks. I looked around for Jeannine but couldn't see her except as a silhouette in the glow of the red, blue and gold flashes of light. As I was working my way around the edge of the crowd, a bolt of lightning suddenly joined in with the fireworks and the sky lit up, as if electrified. At first, all were in awe, but then panic struck, as everyone dashed to the barn for cover. Even before I was able to get inside, the sky opened up and rain and hail came down in torrents. The wind ripped at the trees, and the lanterns, which had been so festive a few moments before, were shredded in front of our eyes. The food table went flying and the band grabbed their instruments and they, too, raced to the barn to get out of the rain.

"When the storm was finally over, most people were soaked and rushed to their cars and trucks to leave. I went in search of my bicycle. It was then I found it had been trampled in everyone's rush for the barn." His fingers played a little tattoo with his spoon as he talked. "The front wheel was bent at right angles. Mangled! After attempting to straighten it, all

I found I could do was drag it all the way home--35 km. back home." He sighed. "And, all for the love of dancing . . . and my dear Jeannine." He looked up, his eyes filling with mirth. "And, to top it off, after walking all those miles, I also lost the heel of my shoe. My best good shoe."

"Your only good shoes," Jeannine corrected.

Martial grinned at me. "It was weeks before I had money to replace my shoes," he said as his body rocked back and forth as he laughed silently. He closed his eyes tightly and tittered until a light chuckle broke loose. Surprisingly, tears began to flow down his cheeks as he held his sides with laughter. Now, loud chortles erupted from Josiane and Jeannine, and I found myself caught up in the contagion.

"And after all that," Josiane guffawed, "you didn't even get a dance with your true love."

"What a marvelous story," I said. The whole scene had come to life in living color and a light-hearted side of Martial was suddenly revealed. I relaxed back again into my chair.

"Alright, back to the subject, back to the subject," Josiane cajoled, but I could tell she was delighted her brother had shared this part of his history.

"Okay, okay," Jeannine continued, as if there had been no pause. "In the winter, we had a tradition called *Ma Veillée* in the next town over. This was a gathering of people from the same neighborhood. During those cold months, the evenings were long and lonely, so we would get together and drink a little wine at one of the homes and play cards to keep ourselves entertained. We wouldn't bring a lot of food to these gatherings, as we did not have a lot to spare, so we would eat at home and then go to town. We gathered to talk about everything that was going on in the neighborhood—everything from gossip to politics."

"Yes, politics," Josiane intoned. "We French always talk politics."

Not wanting to get distracted, I asked, "You celebrated Christmas, right?"

"Oh my, yes. Christmas was probably the only time my folks would get out of their work clothes and celebrate. We would prepare a turkey and had a special *Gateaux de Savoie* cake."

My ears perked up. "*Gateaux de Savoie* cake?"

"This is a cake prepared with *crème de patisserie* and the fruits which we canned from the summer. *Gateau de Savoie* is a large brioche-type cake—like a sponge cake, which includes eggs, sugar, flour, and corn starch."

"I remember that to make extra money in the winter months, my parents purchased a knitting machine, and we would add to our income by making socks and mittens. We would make socks for the Army and for others. Many of the farmers and their wives, like us, would spend the long winter months working on moneymaking projects in our homes because none of us could work in the fields at the time. Also, the men learned how to weave baskets and taught their children how to weave baskets . . ."

Josiane broke in. "My own father taught me how to weave baskets, and I still have a basket that he made, and one that I made." She beamed.

"I remember you mentioning that when we were visiting Veronique in the Nord-Pas-de-Calais."

"*Ah, oui!* I did," she exclaimed.

Jeannine nodded and proceeded undeterred. "The women, during the winter months here, did a lot of sewing and mending of clothes. They would 'turn the collars' on their husband's and sons' shirts so they could be used for another season. They would cut sheets in half and sew them back together so that the worn areas of the sheets would now be on the outside edges and not worn out in the middle. That way they could be used for one more year."

"That makes practical sense," I said.

"And once a week, we women would go to the *lavoir* in the center of town to complete the washing of our clothes."

"Whoo, boy, Jeannine, you have struck a chord with Carole. She loves to hear about the *lavoir*. We'll probably have to make a pilgrimage there in the morning." Josiane giggled.

"I'm sorry to ask so many questions, but I really do find this interesting."

"Well, Carole, in the winter months, many times we would have to break the ice in the *lavoir* before we could access the water, so, of course, it was extremely cold. Each village had at least one *lavoir* and some had several, but never was it comfortable in the winter."

"Yes," Josiane added. "In my mother's village of Vannes, there were three *lavoirs*. One about every five hundred yards or so along the Marle River."

"We just visited Vannes and I got to see one of those *lavoirs*," I chirped.

"What I remember," Jeannine said, "is that the women would come together to rinse out the clothes in a final rinse, as they would have washed the clothes at home. We hauled the wet clothes to the *lavoir,* rinsed them again, and with the help of others, squeezed the water out of the clothes before hauling them back home to hang on the lines."

"What a difficult and heavy affair," I said. "And now?"

"Now we have marvelous machines that do most of the work for us. I only wish my mother had lived long enough to enjoy such inventions. But we still hang the clothes outside to dry."

"Yes," Martial chimed in. "It used to be that farmers helped each other, but now, almost all of us have our own machines and equipment. When I served in the Army in Algeria, I worked alongside the Algerians to help them improve their farming methods. But I noticed they had more modern equipment than we, the French, had ever seen. I thought that couldn't happen, but obviously it did. Progress does not go backward, but it's not always efficient."

"I know from the pictures you have scattered around the rooms, that you have children. Is that right?"

"Yes, our first child is Christian, who you will meet tomorrow. Our second child came a year and a half later. That was our daughter, Martine. And then later—thirteen years later—we had our dear Patricia."

"That's little Patou, as we call her," Josiane said, as a point of information for me.

"We had planned on having only two children, but my mother and father continually scolded me for only having two. They wanted us to have a larger family to help with the farm. Some families had as many as seven or nine children, but we felt we couldn't afford more than a few. As it was, we were still living with my parents here in this house and our farm was too small to support all of us."

"Martial, you spoke of going to the Algerian War," I said, changing the subject again. "I was wondering if any of your family experienced an impact from that war." Martial pushed away from the table and poured himself another cup of coffee.

"Hmm," Jeannine said. "No, nothing in my family as far as the Algerian conflict. Just my Martial." She looked over her shoulder at him.

Martial had come back to his chair, but after sitting

down, had dropped his head near to his coffee cup. Light streaks of gray crossed back and forth through his deep brown hair. I decided not to push the topic.

"Martial, once you decided to marry Jeannine, how did you approach her? This was after your Algerian experience, right?" I asked.

"Yes, it was after I returned from Algeria. And how did I approach her father? Very carefully." He laughed. "My father-in-law was definitely against us getting married, as he was hoping Jeannine would find a man who had some land or money to add to the family—and I had none. I was just a common farm laborer, but I convinced him that I was a hard worker and that I could help them out on the farm."

"Yes," Josiane said, "I'll never forget that he came home one summer and worked long and hard in Piennes to make money to prove to Jeannine's family that he could support her."

"And he did just that," Jeannine said, touching her husband's shoulder.

"Oh yes, Carole. Our mother had to come and convince Jeannine's mother and father to allow her son—Martial—to have Jeannine's hand in marriage. Obviously, it worked out beautifully, didn't it?" Josiane murmured.

As an aside to me in English, she said, "Martial also felt a lot of pride in his accomplishments. He felt compelled to prove that he was a hard worker and that he deserved the trust first from his father-in-law and mother-in-law. He succeeded in that, for sure. Later, they were very proud of Martial." She beamed at him.

"Josiane, I remember you told me a story about men in this area who worked as traveling stone masons. Is that right?"

"Yes, they were called *maçon creusois*, or stone cutters

from the Creuse Department. They would leave home in the winter to travel to big cities to work as masons and make money, while their fields lay fallow. I believe there is a book written by Jean Giono about them."

"When we men returned," Martial continued the story, "we would have money to help our families and to help plant crops for the summer. We did this because the crops that were grown would not be enough to feed our whole family and provide income for the year. I worked as a stone mason from 1968 to 1973, but I did not travel away from home to do that." He looked over at Jeannine.

"I wouldn't allow him to leave me," Jeannine said.

"It was a very hard life," he muttered. "I much preferred farming to working as a stone mason. And I had no desire to leave my family." A look of love floated between the two.

"Jeannine, do you have any recipes you would like to share with Carole before we take you two out for dinner?" Josiane asked.

"Give her my favorite one," Martial said, getting up from the table. The *Pâté de Pomme de Terre*. Speaking of dinner, I better go and wash up."

In moments, we heard him shuffling up the staircase to the bedrooms above. And then a bellow came from the stairwell. "And give her the *Terrine de Lapin (Rabbit Terrine)*. She'll like that one, too!"

Auvergne

CHAPTER SIXTEEN
Martial Looks Back

*T*he following morning, I awakened to the rooster crowing outside the window and the early morning sun giving off enough light to read the clock. It was shortly after 6 a.m. and the sun splashed a rosy cast onto the blankets and crept up the walls. I had slept well during the night, despite a few little skittering sounds. I guess I hadn't been completely mad, as there on my pillow lay a few mouse droppings. Ah, life on a farm!

Just then, I heard a clatter from the kitchen near my room and smelled coffee wafting under the closed door. A soft murmur of French ebbed into my consciousness and I listened for Josiane's voice. No. Too early, even for her. I rolled over and went back to sleep.

Later, after a breakfast of fresh baked bread, butter, fried bacon, eggs, and *saucissons* (sausages), Martial led Josiane and me out the back door and into his garden. With great pride he showed us a plot of land bounded on the edges with sunflowers and enclosed with heavy mesh fencing. He pointed out where he had just planted fresh sweet peas and asparagus and showed me where he planned to place lettuce, radishes, squash, potatoes, and corn. He proudly showed us where his tomato plants would go once the weather warmed. In addition to the vegetables and flowers, he had made a little bower with his flowering bushes.

"Future raspberries and blackberries will grow here, along with some table grapes," he promised.

I stepped out of the gated enclosure where birds fought for our attention in the almost bare cherry trees and hens pecked near our feet for a succulent worm or two.

"Let me show you where I'm going to build my house," Josiane called to me. She grinned at Martial and walked defiantly to the edge of the property. She turned around and waited for the two of us. The point where she stood had an unobstructed view from the top of a long hillside that dropped into a beautiful sea of light green and yellow in the valley below.

"When Martial gives me permission, I'm going to buy this parcel of land and build right over there—so I can always have this view. Isn't it beautiful?" she beamed. Martial looked at her with chagrin.

"Josiane, you know I can't divide this property. It's not mine to sell, and Jeannine won't divide the . . ."

"Oooooh, Martial," Josiane cooed, "you know I am only teasing. But you know how much I love being near you. And of course, this view."

He nodded. "Instead, let me show you our rabbits." Martial steered me toward a pen where he gathered up a floppy-eared rabbit from the hutch.

"This one has been a family pet for years. He's most fortunate, as we will never eat him. But his brothers? That's another story," he laughed.

We walked around the farmhouse, out to the barns to look at the equipment, and back into one of the outbuildings, as Martial proudly told me the history of the property.

"Because the farm has been deeded to Jeannine from her side of the family—she is known as the *cultivateur* (farmer)—I will never receive income from the farm. But I am comfortable with this position and very grateful to her. It's not as if it's a large farm—only ten hectares—not enough to provide income for even one family anymore—but I've had a good life here." He paused and relaxed into a comfortable stance. Just then a horn honked in the farmyard and he stuck his head out the door to catch Jeannine waving goodbye as she pulled out of the driveway to head into town. "An errand to finish before Christian arrives today," she called out.

Eventually the three of us wandered back into the warmth of the kitchen, where we found a fresh pot of coffee waiting. While Josiane poured the coffee, Martial and I sank down at the table as if having put in a hard day's work. Only the sound of the ticking clock resounded throughout the kitchen, as I reflected on some of the stories I had been told about Martial. I remembered Josiane stating, "Let me say that we were never encouraged to share our feelings openly, or to give voice to our feelings. I would imagine that most of Martial's thoughts wrap around things like, would the chickens give eggs, will we have enough feed for the cattle in the winter . . . thoughts prone toward basic survival. Nothing more."

I had been curious about Martial memories of his mother, Marcelle. But, before I could broach any question at all, Josiane shocked me by asking a question of her own: "What do you remember of the Exodus of Paris, Martial? Do you remember that time at all?"

It was asked with gentleness and sincerity, but it was such a bold question—so out of the blue, even though Josiane and I had been wondering about this for months.

Martial sat stark still, staring at his fingernails, giving thought to the question. His head bent forward and a glint in his hair reflected light from a kitchen lamp. His dark blue work shirt, which had seen years of wear, stretched across his shoulders. I held my breath. This felt like such an invasion of this private man. Surely Josiane knew what she was doing. She loved and adored her brother.

I turned toward Josiane, who was speaking softly in French to her brother. She reached across the table. His reddened hands did not yield to her touch but remained tightly folded on the tablecloth before him.

Josiane whispered again. Not understanding what was being said, I worried. Like moving from one prayer bead of thought to another, my thoughts churned. As did my stomach. Martial picked up his coffee bowl, then set it down once again. Minutes passed. Sixty-two years had come and gone since the Exodus, and yet I feared the ripe emotions of his memories might break free as if it had happened yesterday. Were we prepared?

He mumbled something, then glanced at me and back at his hands. He took a handkerchief from his pocket and blew his nose long and loud.

"Josiane, do you want me to leave the room?"

Josiane whispered to him again and he tucked his handkerchief back into his pocket, sniffed loudly, and spoke. "Yes, I remember the Exodus, Josie. But mostly I remember the bombing that went on before the Exodus—before Maman was forced to leave for Bordeaux with the Citroën workers. But the bombing stopped once the Germans arrived."

"What do you remember? I'm trying to understand what you and Maman experienced during that time. She told us some of her story, but so many parts of it were left to be filled in. And now, of course, she is gone."

"As you probably know, I was staying at the nurses' home —the home for the children of the Citroën employees—and the only home I knew as a young child. As I was told later, it was in the suburbs of Paris, far from where Maman was living or working." He pulled his cup forward and took a sip of coffee. "What I do remember was how much I loved it when Maman would come on the weekends to spend time with me. That was what I . . . well, all of us at that home, looked forward to. Seeing our parents. But then the bombing began.

"I'll never forget the shrill scream of the bombs as they hit the ground, and everyone was shocked and scared. At first, my friends and I thought it was funny. I would watch the older ones peek out of the blackened window shades of our room when we heard the roar of the planes. They played a game of trying to dive under our beds before the explosion. I was still too little to understand. But after the first few attacks, when we heard the sirens our nurses would rush us children across the street into the Métro underground. I remember calling for Maman, as I feared I would never see her again."

"You were so young, Martial. Only four at the time, and you had every reason to be frightened," Josiane said.

"Yes, I suppose so. As it was, I was only able to spend weekends with her, but after the bombing raids began, that came to a stop, too."

Martial was speaking more calmly. I shifted back in my seat at the table and tried to relax.

"And when Maman came and told me she was being sent to Bordeaux with her job, we all knew what to expect. My friends and I were all told by our mothers to remain where we were, until they could send for us. So, I don't recall that our lives changed much during that time. Actually, I don't remember.

"But at the time of the Exodus," he said, once again wiping his nose, "the Germans had begun marching in from the north while everyone else, including Maman, evacuated to the west and to the south. Even our French government fled!" He fairly spit out the words, even though he would have been too young to understand what that had meant at the time. His words carried the venom of second-hand knowledge.

"It was at this time the Germans began their occupation of Paris, so the bombing raids stopped. We felt safer after that. And we simply did as we had always done—play in the playroom and wait for visits from our mothers."

"Do you remember if you had enough to eat during that time?" I asked.

Martial paused to think. His fingers circled round and round the handle of his cup. "I don't think I was aware of being hungry. I guess I was just aware of having so much more to eat once I moved south—here to the Auvergne."

"In 1943, the bombing started up again, right?" Josiane prompted.

"Yes," he said, "but this time it was the Allies bombing Paris." He hesitated, looked at me, then lifted his chin up.

"I became terrified of those raids, too. Again, fearful of losing my mother. But this time I was older—I was at least seven by then—and I would get up on the edge of my bed with the other boys to peer out of the little holes made in the blackout sheets like we had done before. We were able to see if the planes were coming . . . see them before we had to go to the shelters. That was the only power we had in our lives.

To know when they were coming . . . But, oh, there were so many nightmares.

"I guess it was around that time that all the children of Paris of a certain age—I was eight by then—were put on trains bound for the Free Zone."

"But that was better, right? Safer?" Josiane asked.

He shrugged. "I remember leaving Maman behind, and I was more frightened of losing her than I was of the bombing raids. It was the first time I had been on a train without her. We had taken the train on occasion to go to the countryside on vegetable runs. You know, to get fresh vegetables for dinner during the war years. Each train was named after a different vegetable. Anyway, when I got on the train by myself, I didn't know if I would ever see Maman again. I was with one of the nurses and some of my friends, but none of us knew where we were going."

"Do you remember Maman putting you on the train?"

"I remember Maman crying so hard, and I was crying . . ." He wiped his eyes with his handkerchief, then took a swallow from his tepid coffee.

"To this day, when I smell the acrid stench of coal smoke, it almost buckles my knees."

"Coal smoke? From the train?" I asked.

"*Oui.* From the train." Martial looked at me as if he was suddenly aware I was still sitting there.

"What do you remember about your train ride?" Josiane asked.

"Very little, other than that smell. It was horrible, and the train ride was very long and there were lots of Germans on board with us, which scared us. I suppose in the end I was so relieved to get off the train that . . . that I've never left!" he said with a final note of triumph. "Just a few sorties to Algeria and Piennes, but other than that I've rarely left my home here."

Just then we heard the crunch of car tires on the gravel. Jeannine drove into the farmyard, and Martial jumped up to help with her packages.

I sat, allowing Martial's last words linger. He had told us so much, but was it worth the price? I reached over and placed my hand on Josiane's arm, as she sat staring into space.

"Are you all right, Josiane?"

"Of course, Carole. I was just trying to imagine what my brother's life must have been like. What sorrow he has experienced. He is such a tender soul. Never any hard feelings that he speaks of."

Just then, Jeannine and Martial entered the kitchen carrying packages of cheese and bottles of local wine.

"We can provide only so much from our own farm," Jeannine laughed. "Have you heard anything from Christian? Has he called to tell us when he'll arrive?"

"No," Martial said, "so I imagine he's not far away. We'll be seeing him soon."

He put the wine bottles on the counter and unwrapped the cheeses and placed them into containers in the refrigerator.

"Can we help, Jeannine?" Josiane asked.

"Not right away. I just need to get a few things done before Christian comes, so if you two need time to yourselves, now is probably the time."

Josiane and I put on our jackets and headed out the back door. The wind had picked up a little, but the sun was warmer than when we had been out earlier. Two old chairs sat on the knoll overlooking the valley Josiane so loved. She sat down in one and I pulled up the other. The valley was a canvas of light and dark greens undulating with the cascading winds. We sat silently, processing the conversation Martial had shared. I reflected on how the talk of war collapses time: people return in their minds to the very moment when an event has occurred, even though six or seven decades have passed. I had not expected that response but came to realize this was key to my understanding of what life was like living in a war zone. And I had so much more to learn.

CHAPTER SEVENTEEN

Mysteries Solved, or Are They?

*C*hristian, I'm so happy to see you," Josiane said as she welcomed him into his father's kitchen. "And I appreciate you meeting us here."

"No problem," Christian said, as he kissed his Aunt Josiane, then his mother, and hugged his father. Tall and in his thirties, with light brown hair and a slight build, he was a masculine version of his mother, but with his father's dark eyes. He walked over to me as Josiane introduced us, in English. Christian had been working with Josiane over the past several months to help resolve the mystery of Marcelle's father's identity.

The story told about Marcelle's father was that he had died during the war, but no evidence had been found to confirm that belief. And because Marcelle carried a different surname than her mother, she wondered if she was an illegitimate child. Had she been born out of wedlock? There had been a code of silence surrounding those uncomfortable family details, and this was one of the questions that had never been answered. The search for identity is a haunting, but human desire. No, it could be more than human desire; it could be a crushing of the soul as well as the human spirit. So

Christian was only too happy to help his grandmother even after her death.

I had not met Christian on the first part of our tour. We had spent time with his wife, Sophie, and daughters near Rennes in Brittany, but Christian had been out of town on business. His smile was warm but reserved, yet I felt like an interloper.

As he turned to the stove to pour himself a bowl of coffee, he asked me, "Want to join us for coffee?"

I did, of course, but instead said, "Maybe I'll sit outside in the sunshine and read while the four of you catch up. I'm sure you have some important things to share with your family, Christian. And you don't need the bother of translating every word." I refilled my coffee bowl for the umpteenth time that morning.

Josiane nodded to me. "I'll call you in shortly," she said, as I picked up my book and disappeared out the back door. She and I had traveled many miles to find answers to Marcelle's final request, but now was not the time to interfere.

Josiane told me later that the secrets were revealed as follows: Josiane had sat down across the table from Christian, and next to Martial.

"All right, Christian, what did you find out?"

Christian riffled through a sheaf of papers, straightened them, and said, "To begin with, Papa, I asked Grand-mère to look into some of her history." He nodded toward his father, who immediately dropped his head and averted his eyes.

"I think she would have been surprised—and pleased—at how much information I was able to gather, just off the internet." Martial remained silent.

"Yes, Christian," Josiane said, "You told me a number of facts while Carole and I were out on the road. Thank you for that help."

"What are you two talking about?" Martial asked. "Cut to the chase." Cords on his neck had tensed.

"Please be patient, Père. I've worked hard to find this information and could not have done it without Grand-mère's and Tante Josiane's help. Once Grand-mère was able to find some important dates and names, I was able to find out some information about our family."

Jeannine refilled the coffee bowls, and as she passed Martial, tenderly touched his shoulder.

"Grand-mère asked me to look up the name of her father—or see if I could find it. I located the documents, as did Josiane, which included one Raymond Pourrez."

He spread several photocopied pages across the tablecloth, facing his father. At the top of the first page, in bold print, was *Ascendance Pourrez, Marcelle* (Ancestry of Marcelle Pourrez).

And just below were not only dates, but thumbprint-sized black and white photos of their ancestors. Some names the family was aware of, but others they had never known:

POURREZ, RAYMOND

BORN – 12/27/1892 – PARIS

DIED – 9/30/1970 – PARIS

There it was! Marcelle's father's last name was Pourrez! The man who had eluded Marcelle all her years now stared up at them from a miniature photograph. A black and white image only three centimeters (about one inch) square showed a handsome young man with dark hair and a well-trimmed mustache, wearing a World War I uniform and staring over his left shoulder.

"And here is our grandmother's name," Josiane said.

Tetiau, Honorine
Born – 7/27/1898 – Vannes
Died – 8/14/1936 – Cherbourg

The dates loomed as they calculated the ages for the two names. Honorine, Marcelle's mother, had died young. But these were the facts: she died at age thirty-eight, so Marcelle would have been eighteen. Calculating the age for Raymond, their grandfather (or great-grandfather, for Christian), they were stunned. He had lived and died in Paris and was age seventy-eight at his death.

"So why did our mother never know who he was?" Martial asked. "She carried his last name all those years, and never knew the truth. But wasn't her mother always known by her maiden name—Tetiau? Why didn't he contact Maman, especially when she was living in Paris? Or with me? I was born there, too."

Pain stole into Martial's voice and it cracked as he tried to control his emotions. Tears began to slide down his cheeks. He shoved back from the table, but his son convinced him to stay.

"There's more, Papa. There are more details here, which might explain some of your questions."

He turned the page, and there they saw in bold, black ink:

The wedding date of Honorine and Raymond
Pourrez: 5/9/1916 – Vannes, Brittany

"1916? Is that what it says?" Josiane stood and turned the pages around so she could see for herself. She gasped and sat down hard on her chair. Stunned silence enveloped the room as each of the four family members tried to make sense of this news.

"Here is the evidence, for certain—our mother was born legitimately. She was born two years after her parents were married," Josiane declared. A note of sadness filled her voice, "*Mon Dieu!* In all our mother's life, she never knew who her real father was—and only a few months after her death, we find proof of his identity. She was a legitimate child." She laid her head on her arms on the kitchen table and silently wept.

Martial stood up and shoved his chair back so it slapped the floor with a bang. Unable to sit still any longer, he strode out the back door and into the garden. Jeannine followed silently.

When I saw Martial and Jeannine enter the garden, I smiled, but noticed Martial's grim expression. I walked back into the kitchen and saw Josiane slumped at the table. "Are you all right?" I asked. "What news have you found?"

"Oh, Carole, Christian has presented us with our first maternal family tree." She slid the pages toward me. I leaned down to peek.

"Oh my," I said, "look at this beauty!" I pointed to the small image of Honorine. Her lovely young face was cradled in a black fur wrap, and dark bobbed hair circled her face in soft wisps and tails. Her full mouth was sculpted into the hint of a smile as she looked shyly at the camera.

"She looks so much like you, Josiane. This sweet coquette—she looks just like you."

Christian, who understood my English, leaned over and took another look at the picture.

"She's right. That is you, Tante Josiane."

Josiane swiped her tears from her face and looked at the

photo once again. A glimpse of recognition flashed through her eyes.

"Well, maybe in days past . . ." she said with a slow smile rising to the surface. She took out a handkerchief and began dabbing at her tears.

Jeannine and Martial walked back into the kitchen, she with a freshly killed chicken, he with a fist full of potatoes and home-canned beans from the larder. I didn't know what had transpired between them, but Martial seemed in better stead. I walked over to help Jeannine prepare the food, while Christian, Josiane, and Martial wandered back out into the farmyard. I have found that cooking is a language all its own and can be easily mastered without words or translation. I stood at the sink, appreciating Jeannine's quiet company. A few French words eked out; a few English. We laughed and gestured to each other to get the work done.

By the time Jeannine called the others in for lunch, I could tell Josiane had worked her magic on Martial. He was in good spirits, and Christian appeared to have had a massive load lifted from his shoulders. Learning our identity is elemental and critical to understanding ourselves. And there is something all-powerful about finally learning a defining truth about our biological roots. The knowledge itself gives us power to accept or reject the information received, as we now own it. It is ours. It was so sad that Marcelle had missed out on that powerful experience.

After a delicious *déjeuner* of roasted chicken, potatoes, and green beans with *lardons,* accompanied by a scrumptious pear tart Jeannine had baked earlier that morning, Josiane and I helped clean up the kitchen. Then it was time for a walk.

"You know, Josiane," I said, as we walked along. "My family had a similar story. My great-grandmother, Iva, was a proud old bird if ever there was one." I held up my left hand where my gold wedding band caught the sunlight.

"This wedding ring was handed down to me from her. I'm told she traveled from Kentucky, all the way out to the Kansas Territory after the Civil War in search of her father. He had left his family of ten, maybe twelve, children not long after their mother died in childbirth. My great-grandmother was told that he had headed west in search of a better life for his family. Supposedly he would send for them. Several years passed as all the children were parceled off to relatives or sent to state-run schools. At the age of seventeen, my great-grandmother boarded a train by herself, then a stagecoach, in hopes of finding a trace of her father. She never found him. Her search left her alone and in the barren western plains of Kansas.

"She became the first schoolteacher in that desolate area. Eventually she found a husband, had five children, and had a good life. Forty years later, when one of her brothers came for a visit, he confessed that he believed their father had never left Kentucky. My great-aunt—her young daughter at the time—witnessed this confession and remembered how her uncle had thrown his head back and guffawed. 'Isn't it interesting,' he had laughed, 'that a family living in the very next county has the same angular jawbone, same facial structure, and the same last name as us?'

"My great-aunt told me my great-grandmother became 'angrier than a wet hen' and went screaming into the house, slammed the door, and never allowed anyone to mention that story—or her father's name—again."

"Hmm. That does have a familiar ring," Josiane said.

"Sometimes I think our lives are nothing more than the tapestry of family myths we carry around with us. Where is the truth? How much has been left out? I'm sure there is an incredible story behind the marriage of Marcelle's parents."

"Probably. But those who would know that story are long gone," Josiane said with a shrug.

We walked past the old barn, the barking dogs, the squawking chickens, and on down the country road until it became a lane and ended at a pond. Next to the pond was a dilapidated, old building with ducks taking turns paddling into the building and out again.

"Carole," Josiane exclaimed, "there's the village *lavoir.* Your favorite building in all of France. A bit run-down, but *c'est la!* There it is!"

"The village *lavoir?*" My head swiveled in every direction. "What village would that be?" The landscape was covered in hardscrabble—a land that had returned to nature many years after having been overworked.

"The village of Gênet. Although you can't tell it now, this used to be a bustling little place." She looked around. "Now it's nothing more than a few run-down farms. Time has made its mark."

"And as the building continues its slide into oblivion, the land retakes its natural wonder. It is beautiful here, isn't it? No wonder your brother chose to stay here and fell in love with Jeannine and the land.

"Do you think you could show me your mother's house before I fly home?" I asked. "I would love to know where she spent her last years."

"Sure. We could drive over there now, if you would like. It would give Christian and his parents some time together."

We walked back to the car and headed south down the D996. It wasn't long before we reached the quiet village of Fontanières. It was mid-afternoon and all appeared to be napping. Only a few shops lined the main street; only a few cars were in view. And there, tucked off on a side street—on a street facing the main road—was Marcelle's house. It was an older building—a narrow, three-story beige stucco house— tucked comfortably between two buildings that might have been garages or barns or blacksmith shops. The window trim, gate, and front door were a burnished redwood color, and the windows and door were outlined in red brick. Vanilla-toned shutters enclosed the windows. A small delicate fetish of dentil trim dangled from the roof and the uppermost dormer window, giving the place a gingerbread-house touch.

Josiane took out the key Martial had given her before we left the farm and inserted it into the lock. With a loud squeak, the door swung open. We entered a small sitting room in the front of the house.

"My mother enjoyed spending most of her time in this room. She could sit near the window and peer out through the lacy curtains to the many bird feeders and birdhouses in the front yard. She especially enjoyed their sounds and pranks in the winter months when she lived here by herself."

I thought back to the first time I had invited Marcelle and Josiane to my home for coffee and conversation. Marcelle had sat in one of my kitchen chairs, her toes not quite able to touch the floor, and her feet swinging back and forth under the chair, until one shoe had dropped off her foot with a thump. She had been looking out the window, watching the birds in my backyard noisily feasting at a feeder. I remembered how her dark eyes sparkled and her smile lifted with joy. That was the start of this journey. The very beginning of getting to know this incredibly lovely, complex, and strong woman—Marcelle.

We walked from the sitting room to the back of the

house and into the kitchen, passing by the staircase that led to the bedrooms upstairs. The kitchen, I could see, accommodated her most essential needs. It was a compact space with a small sink below a back window that looked out onto a narrow backyard; a small refrigerator and stove; cupboards; and a modicum of counter space. A table for two was ensconced into the space, but I could imagine it had accommodated many more than that in years past. Space, in French homes, never seems to be an issue when drawing in the family for gatherings.

Upstairs there were two bedrooms, and above that an additional space that housed many of Marcelle's worldly goods, papers, and letters. That was where Josiane had discovered her mother's letters and found many of the clues that led to the answers about her past. They had been here, all along. The pieces simply hadn't included the essential dates to pull the truth forward—until now.

"Say, do you want to meet one of my mother's oldest and dearest friends? She knew her when Maman first moved here during World War II."

"I would love too. Does she live nearby?"

CHAPTER EIGHTEEN
The Earliest of Memories

A couple of days later, Josiane and I found ourselves sitting comfortably in Marie Plouffe's living room. She had invited us for *déjeuner,* and after an hour of conversation, she led us into her kitchen for a meal of *Tourte de Viande,* a pork and veal meat pie topped with puff pastry. The rich aromas that had whetted our appetites over the past hour were exchanged for the savory flavors that filled our mouths with delight. Glasses of dark red local wine, poured earlier and waiting at each place setting, made a lovely accompaniment to the *Tourte.*

"Marie, this is divine!" Josiane blurted. "I remember my mother preparing this excellent dish many times when we were children, but I doubt I've had it since. Did you teach her this recipe? This is so good! Don't you just love it, Carole?" She took a sip of wine, then plowed on without waiting for a response.

"Sometimes we didn't have the specified meat for this dish, so Maman would use leftover *lard maigre,* which is lean duck grease, Carole. My father loved it, but I didn't. Too much fat, but like I said, this is excellent. Puff pastry and all."

"Yes, Marie, this is delicious," I agreed. "Hopefully you

will share your recipe with us. There is something distinctive about the herbs you've used, too. What are they?"

Marie had been sitting quietly, her plate half-filled with meat pie. She seemed exhausted, but also happy to spend time with Josiane. Both sorely missed Marcelle. Mention had been made earlier of her poor health, and she must have worked all night to prepare this feast.

"The herbs?" Marie answered. "Just a fluff of fine herbs I have growing wild around my garden—perhaps a bit of tarragon, chervil, parsley. Maybe I threw in a bit of fennel. I don't remember and I can't seem to taste flavors the way I used too."

"Whatever you added, this is marvelous," I said. "Josiane has introduced me to so many new flavors in French traditional foods, but this is exceptional."

"Speaking of traditions, did Josiane teach you about this tradition, Carole?" Marie leaned up to the table. "When coal or wood stoves were not so common, the *potée* I usually cook was prepared in a cast iron cauldron which would hang on a pot hook or pot hanger placed over the fire in the fireplace. The name of the pot hook in French is *la crémaillère.*"

"Oh, Carole, this is why I brought you here," Josiane said. "Marie, I remember them being used in my paternal grandfather's home. It used to be a tradition that when people moved into new homes, long, long ago, the first thing they would do is to hang the pot hook in the fireplace."

"*Mais oui,*" Marie said. "It was called *pendre la crémaillère.*"

Josiane wiped her mouth with her napkin and explained. "*Pendre la crémaillère* in English means housewarming. It was considered a special housewarming gift for a young couple. Don't you just love that?"

"Didn't we see one of those at that museum the other day?" I asked. "The Museum of . . ."

"The Musée d'Arts et Traditions Paysannes. We saw one of those hooks, but I had forgotten about the tradition until now." She turned to Marie to describe what the two of us had seen in the museum a few days before. Marie nodded in understanding. Then Josiane changed topics.

"You know, Marie, in all the years of growing up with my father, he rarely talked about what he did in the *Maquis* during World War II. As kids, we were afraid to ask him about his past, but can you explain to Carole and me how the French Résistance was different from the *Maquis?*" She patted her napkin again against her mouth and waited. This was not the most prominent question she had in mind—she wanted to know more about her mother during the war and knew that the war had brought Marie and her mother together. But it was a good question to begin with.

Marie sipped her wine as she collected her thoughts. "*Certainement.* I can understand your confusion, as the French Résistance was difficult to define, even for those of us involved. Have you told Carole about the war? Does she know any of these details?"

"Yes, she knows many things and is very interested. In fact, it was Maman who told her some things before she died."

I nodded my head and wrote as fast as I could. The tape recorder was on the fritz.

"I guess it made a difference where you were in France and what job you were given," Marie said, as she stood and uncovered a platter laden with local cheeses. Before she set the platter on the table, Josiane jumped up and took our plates from the table and grabbed a basket of sliced baguettes and the bottle of wine. She poured more wine into my glass and her own. Marie waved her off. They both sat back down.

"Some of the freedom fighters concentrated their efforts on politics," Marie said as she sliced wedges from each of the cheeses. "Some of the fighters concentrated on propaganda, while others helped the Allies as they dropped supplies or troops. But there was a considerable number, known as the *Maquis*, who devoted their energies to sabotage and fighting. Your father, Josiane, along with the rest of us, was attached to the latter. I think we were probably considered a ragtag bunch by military standards, but believe me, we felt our efforts helped to win the war. We were responsible for letting the Allies know if the forests were clear of German mines, if the bridges were safe to cross, and if the Germans had been evacuated from the villages. We would ring the church bells to indicate all was safe, and then we would watch carefully as the Allied soldiers passed through." Her back straightened as she sat forward in her chair. She appeared taller than moments before.

"All guerrillas, insurgents, or 'terrorists' as the Germans called them, were members of the FFI (*Forces Françaises de l'Interieur*) and came to be known as the *Maquis.*"

"What does *Maquis* mean in English?" I asked Josiane.

"*Maquis* is a Corsican word that means 'bush' and refers to groups of people who take refuge together while living and working in the wilderness."

"Oh, like living in the bush."

"Exactly," Marie said. "I remember when the hills near our home were suddenly filled with *Maquis* in the spring of '43. This must have been due to the forced German labor requirements when they could no longer get French volunteers."

"That makes sense," Josiane said. "My father said something about running away from Piennes in the Lorraine to avoid being taken to the German forced labor camps. He told me the Germans had taken over the local iron mines in Piennes where he, his brothers, and his father worked. The Germans, I guess, needed iron ore to continue to feed their war machine. I think my father said the Germans were afraid the local miners would sabotage the mines." She piled a layer of *bleu* cheese onto a slice of bread and sipped her wine.

"Of course, they were correct," she mumbled with her mouth full, "as they imported Russian workers to take my father's family's jobs, while some of his brothers were shipped off to work at camps near the Russian border. My father and his brother, Robert, simply escaped and reappeared down here. Right?"

"I believe so. I don't know how simple their escape was, but both appeared around here. Let me think, as it's been a long time," Marie said. "I'm having a bit of difficulty with my memory, so bear with me."

"You know, Marie," Josiane said, as she ran her finger along the dull edge of her knife, "I remember my favorite uncle, Raymond, was sent to the Russian Front. I wondered why he was never bitter about that. He was so unlike my father in that he had a ready smile and loved to laugh. I would ask him what it was like during the war and he would say, 'You know, Josiane, it was so cold, we had to use a saw to open our wine.'" She tittered at the memory.

"*Oui.* That was a common response to a very difficult time," Marie said. "And it was important to keep our sense of humor." Josiane and I nodded in understanding. We'd heard that same joke from friends in the Alsace.

Marie was quiet for a moment, then looked up at Josiane. "I don't know if I'm out of line here, Josiane, but I felt your father was somewhat bitter *before* the War. He seemed to carry his anger and bitterness with him like a badge." She looked cautiously at Josiane, then at me.

"It's all right, Marie. You can say anything you want in front of Carole. She's helping me sort out some of my family's story, and she's thinking of writing Maman's story."

Marie looked a little surprised but nodded as if it all made sense. She continued, "There were some young men who did not expect to return home after the war. I believe your father was one of these . . . until he met your mother, anyway."

Josiane broke off another bit of bread and started to nibble it. "Could you answer the question I asked a few months ago, after my mother's funeral? Do you think that my father loved my mother?"

A long hesitation followed, then Marie answered. "If not, he certainly made a good show of it. I think they both were very much taken with each other. Of course, with the war raging at that time, every moment was considered precious. Time and life are precious. Never underestimate how powerful that can be for two people alone in the world during a time of war."

"I know what you're saying, Marie," I said. "My mother experienced a similar dilemma after World War II. She used to call it the Silent War."

"The silent war?" echoed Josiane.

"Yes. She said this was the time after war ended, when war brides were faced with getting to know their husbands, sometimes for the first time. A great many couples had rushed into marriage just as men were being shipped overseas. They may have known each other only days or hours before they left. But having someone waiting back home gave each a reason or purpose, which kept them going. Unfortunately, once reunited, many couples found they had little in common. Divorce was unacceptable, so they each faced marriage in a war of silence."

"Makes sense. Now that you mention it," Josiane said, "on rare occasions my father *would* talk about some of his activities. He seemed proud of being part of the sabotage he was party to. Were you involved with that too, Marie?"

"My husband, Jacques, was. But because we owned one of the few radios in the area, my role was to keep one ear on the radio and the other listening for the approach of troops. I picked up the codes given on particular nights from broadcasts out of England. I didn't know the finer details, but the *Maquis* took action against the railroads in particular. We would receive word whenever a train of German soldiers was to pass through here, and my husband would head out into the night. The *Maquis'* jobs were to also destroy power lines, bridges of all sorts, hydroelectric plants, and communication lines . . ." Her voice drifted off for a moment.

"You must have been terrified all the time, Marie," I said. "I can't imagine living under that kind of threat, day in, day out."

Marie laughed. "Now that I think of it, I can't either. I guess we were too young and naïve to know any better." She paused. "But we had been robbed of our hopes and dreams. Our futures had been placed on hold. Just like your mother described to you, Carole. We *had* to make a better life for our children, for ourselves. Anything less was unimaginable!

"So, we were very grateful to men like my husband and your father, Josiane. Without the *Maquis* or the Résistance . . . or without the Allies, our lives would no longer have been French. I know it is difficult for you to understand what that meant at that time, but for us, it was an absolute. Maybe the *Maquis* didn't prevent the enemy from controlling our country, but they certainly caused serious problems for them at every turn. And they did form a network of communications that worked in tandem with General De Gaulle."

"De Gaulle? Really?" I asked. "I thought he was stationed in England during that time."

"He was, but the instructions I received on the radio were directly from him. He felt the Allies could not be successful without the activities of the *Maquis*. Years later I remember reading that your General Eisenhower also gave us credit. He mentioned 'the ceaseless harassing activities of the Résistance eventually eroded the Germans' confidence.' In other words, we helped to shorten the war."

"Whoa! I'm sorry I didn't take an interest before," Josiane said, "but like I said, every topic in our home had the potential to cause an explosion."

"Sounds like wartime was dangerous for everyone," I said.

"Believe me, it was," Marie said. "Of course, the *Maquis* living in our midst made it difficult or unsafe for all the peasants and farmers around us, because the Germans were often coming to the farms to search for them. At times, we didn't know who we could trust. But by 1943, most were like us, simply wanting our country back and willing to take the risks necessary to get the job done."

Josiane walked to the stove and picked up the tea kettle. She began to fill it with water. "Tea, Marie? May I prepare you some tea?"

"Yes, *cherie*, that would be lovely. Do you want dessert now?"

"Perhaps in a few minutes. Thank you."

"So," I said, "during this time, Josiane, your mother met and fell in love with your father and the two were married. Right?" Marie looked up at Josiane.

"Right," Josiane said, as she plunked the teapot back on

the stove. She had heard this part of her parents' story many times, but for affirmation she was especially interested in Marie's version.

"Yes, I remember your mother saying that it seemed a frivolous thing to have a wedding under such circumstances," said Marie, "not knowing from one day to the next if we would live or die. But that is how it was."

She laughed out loud again, shaking her head. White ringlets bobbed about on her head as if they had a life of their own, and the tension that had built up in her face relaxed.

"I remember that once they had announced getting married, a smile spread across your mother's face, which wasn't erased until long after they moved from here. Your mother's greatest dream was to be married and have a family. I believe she really did love your father, so they were married on 6 January 1944. It was the eve of Epiphany, or Twelfth Night, and because we were all used to celebrating this special night of the Three Kings, I baked a version of the *Gâteau des Rois,* which also served as their wedding cake. Do you still celebrate Twelfth Night, Josiane?"

Just then, the teapot surprised us with an exceedingly loud whistle. We all jumped, and Josiane burst into nervous laughter. She must have been afraid to hear some of Marie's questions or answers.

"Oh my, yes," Josiane said, as she tried to contain herself. She fiddled in the cupboards for the tea. "Tea? Where will I find your tea?" Marie waved her finger in the direction of a canister near the stove.

"As you may or may not know, Carole," Marie said, "the *galette,* which comes from the northern regions of France, is made of *feuilletée,* or a flaky type of dough, while the *Gâteau,* which I always prepared, is only made south of the Loire. It is made like a *brioche* in the shape of a puffy crown. Josiane, you are probably used to the *galette, n'est-ce pas?*"

"That's right, Marie. Did you get that, Carole? I didn't realize the difference between the cakes, Marie, but I do remember what fun we had during the celebration. In fact, my niece Corrine, who has two little boys, loves the tradition of children hiding under the table and choosing who next receives slices of cake. They squeal with glee when someone finds the special *fave,* or favor, in the cake and is crowned 'king. Somehow, they all end up with crowns and march around the table.'"

"I remember Corrine and her delightful little boys," I said. "How sweet! Sounds like a fun tradition. Is this the same as Epiphany?"

"Right," Josiane said, "that's what we call it in the States. Now that I think of it, Marie, I don't remember my folks making anything of their anniversary, but we regularly celebrated Twelfth Night together. So, what else do you remember about the day of their wedding?"

Josiane handed Marie and me cups of tea and started picking up the rest of the plates as she headed back to the sink. It seemed she needed to busy herself in Marie's kitchen. I could feel anxiety radiating off her as she passed behind me. Perhaps she was afraid of hearing uncomfortable details. It was only yesterday that she had learned the identity of her grandfather, and the fact that her mother had died not knowing of her legitimate birth. Maybe the conversation with Marie was too much. Marie was looking a little weary, as she started to stand to join Josiane. I got up, placed my hands on her shoulders, and guided her back down into place.

"It's my turn to help, Marie," I said, and made my way to Josiane's side.

Marie relaxed back into her chair, took a deep breath, and began again.

"Their wedding . . . I believe I was about as excited as they were, but it was a quiet little affair that we held at our farm. Of course, they had none of their families in attendance. You know, I can't remember if your father's brother, Robert, also a *Maquis*, was there. He traveled around the area quite liberally while your father, Jules, stayed in our region. Of course, your brothers, Martial and Gérard, were there, along with our son, Fréderic, my husband, Jacques, and his mother, Henriette. Plus, me. Oh, and the Ambert family. They are the family who took your brother Martial in when he was first sent from Paris, remember?"

Josiane had turned from the sink and was leaning against the counter, her cup of tea cradled in her hands. She nodded and Marie continued.

"We tried to keep it very low key, no outward celebration, and just a quick and secret trip to the church. Now that I think of it, I remember the little boys hiding under the table and playing at choosing the king. Of course, it was set up that your parents became royalty for the evening, but I can still remember those little guys taking turns marching around with paper crowns jauntily affixed to their heads."

"Shortly after that I came into the world," Josiane proclaimed. "Exactly nine months, minus two days. I was born in the Ambert's farmhouse near the village of Mainsat."

Josiane had regaled me with this part of her story before, so I turned on the hot water in the sink to begin washing the dishes.

"Well, not exactly, Josiane," Marie said slowly. Josiane started in place.

"Go sit back down, Josiane," I urged her. "This is your

own story, and this may be the last time you get to hear it."

Josiane carried her teacup to the table and slid back into her chair. Her eyes were wide with surprise.

"Dear Josiane, you were born in an abandoned farmhouse in a remote hideaway called La Croix. It was only five kilometers from our farm, so it was nothing for us to walk that route several times a day. And we did what we could to help supply your family with staples for their place—beds, bedding, a chair or two, a table . . . some old mismatched dishes . . ."

"I probably got the mismatched dishes," Josiane giggled nervously, "but that's so strange that my mother never mentioned that. How did that take place? Why did they move from the Amberts?"

"Once your parents were married, they felt they needed their own place, their own privacy. And it was at that time that Mme. Ambert insisted Martial stay with their family longer so your parents could settle in. I think she wanted Martial as her own son and took that opportunity to push her will in that direction. It made sense at the time, because your mother was still nursing Gérard, and there wasn't much room in that old shack for many, that's for sure. And, remember, they were in hiding."

"Would you like your tea warmed up, Marie?" I asked.

"That would be nice," she said, "but let's adjourn to the living room, my dears. My living room chairs are much more comfortable on my tired old bones."

While I replenished the teacups with fresh tea and placed them on a tray, Josiane and Marie walked arm-in-arm into the living room. Easing Marie into her chair, Josiane kindly lifted Marie's tired feet onto the ottoman.

"Ah, this is so lovely," Marie said, as I placed her tea

within reach. "What a special treat it is to have you both here, *mes cheries.*"

"Thank you. It is for us, too," I said as I placed Josiane's cup on the coffee table before her and sat down next to her on the sofa.

"You know, Marie," Josiane said as if the conversation had not stopped, "I remember my mother telling me about how dangerous the times were back then. She talked about how frightened she had been for everyone—for Martial, Gérard, my father. And then she would say, and I can repeat it like a mantra, 'And there I was, once again, pregnant. Your father was attending to the needs of the war and I never knew if he would return to us. Then, one fine September day, the day was so beautiful, the sky so blue, the sun so warm, yet I was filled with trepidation. Your Papa had just left on a mission and shortly thereafter, I was certain my time had come to give birth. I had become so very close to Marie . . . to Josiane-Marie . . .'"

Josiane stopped suddenly. Her head snapped back as if she had been slapped. She said, "Marie, I believe that was the first time I remember hearing your name. It was when Maman was telling me about my birth. All those years ago," she wailed, "I knew your name. But only as Josiane-Marie. I hadn't connected your name with my mother's dear friend, Marie . . . you. Not until now. I have been so self-absorbed. I am so ashamed. I'm only now, at this late date, putting together the people my mother cherished most in her life." She put her head into her hands and began to moan. I reached over and placed my arm around her shoulders.

"Now, now, *ma fille pauvre* (my poor girl). Don't you fret," Marie said. "It's not that our friendship was secret. It's just that you got married and moved away from France before your father retired and your parents returned to Fontanières. I suppose we all simply connected in different circles. But during the war, your mother and I shared a most intimate friendship that continued throughout the years in our letters. And once your parents returned, we again became close, but we never talked about the past. Not until long after both our husbands had died. Neither of them was fond of talking about the war. Your father especially."

"Josiane, what do you remember your mother telling you about your birth?" I asked.

"Maybe I better ask Marie. What do you remember about that time?"

"Well, *ma cherie*, I remember arriving at La Croix on that beautiful day your mother described and seeing her in incredible pain. She was in labor with you and having difficulty, so a midwife was out of the question. I immediately rushed out to find someone to carry a message to the doctor. At that time, any movement, whether day or night, was considered suspect, and your parents were hidden away for a reason. Your father had opened that tiny little hovel of a place for any *Maquis* in the area. So, of course, that made your home even more dangerous. I don't know how she did it, as there was so little to work with, but she wanted Jules—your father—to be proud of her." She took a deep breath and let it out.

"Like I said, I knew there were still a few freedom fighters in the area, so I had them send word to the doctor. Oh my. He was one courageous man. He came despite having to walk many kilometers, around the German soldiers and along hidden footpaths to avoid the main roads. And at that same time, our area was being threatened with bombs from the Allies. Josiane, you picked a fine time to arrive." She laughed out loud. Josiane looked up with a sheepish smile.

"I remember returning to the kitchen where your mother was crouching down on the floor, writhing with pain. I'll never forget the horrified look upon your brother Gérard's face. Anyway, I pretended that your mother was playing a game with them until the doctor came. It took hours, but when he finally arrived, a place was made for your mother—right on the kitchen table. Guns, ammunition . . . all were swept from the table onto the floor and, in no time at all, there you were. You came kicking and screaming into the world. Yes, you were bright red, squalling up a storm, but oh so beautiful. A prettier baby I never saw." A loving smile softened the lines in her face, as she looked upon Josiane.

"The birth of a baby is always a miraculous event . . . no matter the timing," I said quietly.

Josiane reached over and squeezed my hand. "My mother told me later that night some of the *Maquis* went out to find my father to let him know I was born. She told me they all celebrated with great joy, quietly, but they celebrated, none-theless. I suppose that's why I don't do anything quietly now. Everything with me is a wonderful celebration." She tipped her head back and chortled.

"Do you remember, Carole, when I first told you the story of my birth? It was because you wanted to know the impor-tance of the family table in a French family's life. And, as I told you, in my case, it was where I was born!" She laughed heartily at the tale and nestled back into the sofa, pulling an afghan over her legs. A sense of relief seemed to lift from her. At least part of the story she knew from her mother matched the story Marie had just shared. I settled back into the sofa beside her. Marie took a slow, easy sip of her tea, eyes smil-ing, as she looked upon her guests.

"What can you tell me about my father back then?"

Josiane asked her. She couldn't seem to leave this subject alone.

"Well," Marie said, measuring her words, as she set her cup back down, "he was very intense. Like I said before, he always seemed angry. I thought it was because of the war, as did your mother. But later she told me that his anger never subsided and was a large part of his past. Something about the early death of his mother. But I suppose because of his disposition, he made an excellent freedom fighter. He hated the Germans . . ."

"Boy, did he ever! If I remember anything about my father, it was his pure loathing of them. Long after the war and I was grown and gone from home, I took a job in Germany. Oh, Marie, Carole, I thought he would disown me." She laughed. "I guess you had to be there at the time, but it eventually became a family joke of sorts."

"Like I said," Marie continued, "his hatred of Germans prompted him to be one of the first to volunteer for the most dangerous of missions. The *Maquis* could usually get hold of hand grenades to blow up trains, and your father seemed to enjoy the most dangerous type of activity. I also remember the men used to carry automatic weapons, but we rarely had ammunition. That didn't stop your father from carrying a gun every day. At the very least, he loved to change the road signs so the enemy would be confused. Anything he could do to make their lives miserable he would do it. As I've mentioned a few times, he was also good at relaying information. It was nothing for him to walk forty or fifty kilometers through the back woods, night or day."

"Did you say that the codes were transmitted through radios?" Josiane asked.

"*Mais oui.* Like I mentioned before that job fell to me

most of the time. The BBC was the only broadcast we could trust. No French station could broadcast anything other than German rhetoric and propaganda. But the BBC could give us news, and on certain nights of the week they would give us secret messages and codes. Did I tell you this already?" Josiane and I shook our heads.

"Anyway, whenever I received a message of an incoming flight, I would get a notice off to the men who would race into the night to rendezvous at the delivery spot. They were to carry lanterns or some form of beacon to signal the planes, but they had to be so careful. The Germans were also listening for planes and would be on the prowl to catch the men in the act. When I think about it now, I can't believe how cavalier we became, but then we were all so young. And I'm not certain we had another choice. Fortunately, now, it all seems like a bad dream."

Marie stopped and thought for a moment. "As I recall now, when I would listen to the BBC, I would listen for four specific beats. That was the signal for the French edition of their broadcast. These were the same notes as the opening of Beethoven's Fifth Symphony. It was also the same rhythm used in the Morse code for the letter V, which stood for *Victoire*. I can remember feeling connected to the whole world during those quiet, yet suspenseful moments in our house. It was very empowering, I must say." She let out her breath.

"I can imagine, Marie." I gasped, as if I, too, had been holding my breath.

"Speaking of the Fifth Symphony," Josiane said, "do you remember the music of . . . either Rimsky-Korsakov or was it Aram Khachaturian's *Saber Dance*?"

"Why yes, Josiane, I remember we used to listen to that

piece on the radio repeatedly . . . years ago. I believe it was composed just after World War II broke out. Why do you ask?"

"While listening to your stories just now, it came to me that, perhaps, that was one of my first memories. That very music. The *Saber Dance*. I'm wondering if it was at your house that I first heard it. Is that possible?" She leaned forward and looked at Marie with a questioning glance.

"What is it you remember, Josiane?" I asked.

"I remember it was a fine spring day. My parents, along with Gérard and me, decided to take a walk through the woods, over a stream and up a long hill to visit friends. I'm thinking now it must have been to your farm, Les Genêts. Anyway, I remember as we were approaching the farm, a wild thunderstorm rose up and lightning crackled all about us. We were about to cross a stone bridge—for some reason I remember it stretched across a very lively stream—when suddenly lightning split an old chestnut tree in the woods nearby and killed a cow that we had just passed. I remember squealing, and my parents must have panicked. My mother was carrying me, and I remember her fingers gripped my fat little legs too tightly. Anyway, our parents immediately hid us from the rain under the bridge hoping the stream would not rise too high, as the rain had become torrential. I remember our parents holding us up, up, as their feet were getting soaked. Once the storm was over, the sun came back out and we started walking up a long hill. It was at that time I heard music for the very first time. And it was coming from a radio. It was quite dramatic, much like a musical recurrence of the storm we had just experienced. I've never forgotten it. Years later my mother told me the music I heard was called the *Sabre Dance*. And then we continued up the hill . . ."

"To our house," Marie exclaimed. Tears welled in her eyes as she struggled to get up from her chair. "I don't know how you remember that, but you are right. You came to our house." She slid down on the other side of Josiane and encircled her with her thin arms. She drew Josiane to her and held her close.

"I, too, remember that time," Marie said, "but you couldn't have been more than eighteen months old. *Ma cherie*, your memories bring me great joy!"

"War is a beastly business, it is true, but one proof we are human is our ability to learn, even from it, how better to exist."

—M.F.K. Fisher

EPILOGUE

Farewell to Marcelle

*T*his way, Carole," Josiane said, as she waded through puddle after puddle along the pathway. "She's over here."

We wended our way through the cemetery in search of Marcelle's grave. A spate of rain had delayed us that final morning, en route from Martial's farm to the airport in Lyon. I would fly home later that day, as our tour was ending. Not that I didn't want it to continue, and Josiane had so much more she wanted to show me. But I knew it was time to go home, regroup, and think about all I had learned.

Maybe it's my Scandinavian heritage, or a Midwestern attitude, but once I reach a certain point of being away from home, I feel too much of a good thing is just that—too much. I need to go home.

The rain had stopped and only a few remaining drops fell from the trees as we continued along the path. Josiane had walked ahead of me, and in the shadow of some lingering clouds, I could see she had reached our final destination: Marcelle's resting place. Before I could catch up, she had slipped a large blue ceramic coffee cup—her mom's coffee bowl—out of a white plastic bag she was carrying. She took a handkerchief from her side pocket, wiped rain off the top of her mother's gravestone, and placed the cup on top.

"There you are, Maman. Now you can rest in peace. Savor your coffee now for all eternity." She stepped back and smiled.

My whole body went slack at the sweetness of her gesture. I was in awe. "Is this a family tradition, Josiane?" I asked, as my eyes swept over the multitude of nearby tombstones. I hadn't taken notice before, but a smattering of other stones were also crowned with coffee bowls.

"What does this mean, Josiane? Is this more than a family tradition?"

"Oh, Carole," Josiane beamed, "this is one of my favorite traditions. You see, my mother will now have her favorite cup with her—forever. She would love that. I couldn't deliver the cup before, because I had promised I would help find her father. But now, it is *fini.* It is complete." She beamed with pride.

We stepped back and stared reverentially at the black obelisk before us; our journey was truly at an end. A long moment of silent prayer sallied between us, and then, as if a last gasp of air had been forced from a communal balloon, we exhaled in tandem.

"You know, this is where it all began for me, Carole. This tour we've just completed. It all began right here."

Her comment surprised me. I had thought we were on this culinary tour in order to honor her mother. If not, then what had we been doing?

"Look at the marker," she said as she stepped forward again. Her index finger traced the words on the stone. "This says *Famille Pourrez* (The Pourrez Family). Pourrez! Don't you understand?"

I blinked to focus more clearly as I stared at the tombstone. Nothing was forthcoming. I was clueless. In all our weeks of traveling together, I thought we had managed to get along well—as long as she translated my questions into

French and the answers into English. But on this last day, when I felt I had finally come to a better understanding of Josiane, her family, and the French, I was thrown for a loop. What was she saying? I knew it was of utmost importance.

"Let me explain myself," she began again. "This tombstone, which marks the lives of my family and ancestors, is labeled with the surname Pourrez. A name whose origins were, until now, unknown. Even my own father, who is buried here, does not have his own surname of Zabé engraved here!"

She walked over to a small wrought-iron bench and used her now-dampened handkerchief to wipe the seat dry. She motioned for me to join her. I sat down on the cold, still wet bench and we both stared at the grave.

"Shortly before my mother passed away, she asked Christian and me to find out who her father was. And then weeks later, when I stood facing this tombstone at her funeral, I knew I had to find some answers. For myself. For my mother. For my brothers. And to do that we—you and I—needed to take this trip of hers."

"Oh," I said, sitting forward. "I get it. You had another goal, in addition to the promise we made to honor your mother's wishes of touring together."

"Exactly right. Despite feeling sad that Maman never knew that she was legitimate, I feel good that my brothers, who also carry the Pourrez name, now know more about their roots. At least their grandparents' roots. As do I."

"Do you think we should also investigate why your grandfather never returned?" I asked.

"*Non!* For now, I am satisfied with what we know. And through prayer, I am happy to relay the good news to my mother. In time, we may pick up some of the unanswered questions and follow those further. But, for now . . ."

"Like they said in the movie *City Slickers,* 'We'll jump off that bridge when we come to it!' Right?"

Josiane collapsed in a fit of giggles. "Right," she said, as she tried to catch her breath. She wadded up her handkerchief and stuffed it into her purse. She hesitated. "I suppose I will always have questions, but by resolving some of the mysteries around my mother's life—the Pourrez identity, for instance—I feel more at peace. I feel that Christian and I accomplished something very special for Maman."

"And, therefore, for all your family," I said. "At least you now know the connection to the name Pourrez." Josiane looked up and beamed at the coffee bowl perched on the top of the granite gravestone.

"So, Carole, did you find the answers you came to find in France?"

I nodded. "I think so. Before I came, I thought I wanted to know about *haute cuisine,* but by visiting with all the families in their homes, I have found the significant importance of *cuisine pauvre*—the peasant cooking style that everyone uses. I also learned the importance of migration and immigration due to wars, which brought the feast of cultural and culinary riches to the French.

"I also believed I knew what held French families together: their favorite foods, their holidays, their cultural or religious traditions. But what most opened my eyes came from their responses when I asked what it had been like living with war. I'll never forget when I asked your mother what special recipes, she, as a young wife, cooked for her family. She answered, 'Well, my dear, we never had to diet.'"

Josiane exploded with laughter. "Yes, she certainly made that clear."

"Then she clarified by stating, 'It was during World War

II; we were in hiding; and we were lucky to have a potato or two for our family. Recipes? That was something we could only dream about.'

"That simple statement—about living with war on one's doorstep—changed my life, Josiane. I knew at that moment I needed to understand your mother's story better, and most importantly I needed to understand how families survived under such difficult circumstances. Of course, our conversations before your mother's death helped a great deal, but I could never have done any of this without you and all the many interviews you arranged for me across France. You have been a great friend and a real blessing."

"My pleasure, Carole," Josiane said. "I wanted you to learn my mother's story as well, since you were helping me discover not only who she was but who I was. I, too, am grateful." She wrapped her arms around me and hugged me to her. *I loved her like a sister.*

"It has been a wonderful time, hasn't it?" I said. "So much to take in. So much to digest."

"And so many great recipes to take home and test. Right, Carole?"

"And for you to translate into English," I said, with a grin.

"Oh, I'll have to get Marie's recipe for *Tourte de Viande.* My, oh my, I sure learned a lot about my mother, father, and myself yesterday, didn't I?" She giggled. *It had been a bit overwhelming, I was sure.*

"Yes," I said, "Marie's explanations were vivid and greatly helped in my understanding of what it was like living with war. And I have a better appreciation and understanding of why the French hold family so dear—too much deprivation, loss, and tragedy in their past. I imagine that is one reason the EU was formed, don't you?"

Before she had a chance to answer, I continued, "But, on another note, since we are here visiting your mother, I have something for you."

I reached in my purse and pulled out a poem I had copied for Josiane. It was one that had helped me after I had lost my mother a few years before. I don't know where I found it, but I presented it to Josiane. She stood and walked closer to her mother's grave. She quietly read the stanzas, as tears flowed freely down her face.

> *Your Mother is always with you. She's the whisper of the leaves as you walk down the street, she's the smell of certain foods you remember, flowers you pick and perfume that she wore, she's the cool hand on your brow when you're not feeling well, she's your breath in the air on a cold winter's day. She is the sound of the rain that lulls you to sleep, the colors of a rainbow, she is Christmas morning.*
>
> *Your Mother lives inside your laughter. And she's crystallized in every tear drop. A mother shows every emotion . . .happiness, sadness, fear, jealousy, love, hate, anger, helplessness, excitement, joy, sorrow . . .and all the while, hoping and praying you will only know the good feelings in life. She's the place you came from, your first home, and she's the map you follow with every step you take. She's your first love, your first friend, even your first enemy, but nothing on earth can separate you. Not time, not space . . .not even death!*
>
> —*Anonymous*

She pressed the poem against her heart and turned toward me.

"Thank you, *ma cherie*! I will cherish this always. I will cherish you always. Thank you."

No more words were needed. We turned and headed back to the car, but before long we were planning our next adventure.

FINI

RECIPES *from* *the* CHAPTERS

Nord-Pas-de-Calais

CHAPTER ONE
Potjevlesh
(Meat Pot)

"Now to begin with, Carole, this Flemish specialty, called *Potche-Vletche* or *Potjevlesh* in Flemish," Veronique said, "means 'meat pot.' As you can see, my mother has prepared it as a terrine of three meats which have been roasted together with the bones. In years past, this usually was leftover meat from other meals put all together—it could be rabbit, chicken, and pork; or veal and bacon—all roasted with a lot of herbs like parsley, lovage, onions, shallots, garlic, a splash of white wine . . . What, Maman?"

"Never with beer. We cook a great many things with beer, but not this recipe," Madame Pund said, emphatically. She paused and took a sip from her beer.

Ingredients

4 chicken legs
4 rabbit backs
8 pieces of veal neck
8 slices of fresh bacon
2 cups of onions, cut into 1/4" rings

3 sprigs of thyme

3 bay leaves

1 tablespoon juniper berries

8 cloves

salt and ground black pepper taste

4 cups of dry white wine

1 1/2 cups red wine vinegar

2 cups meat stock

1/2 oz. powdered gelatin

Directions

Debone the chicken legs and cut the meat in half. Cut the rabbit backs into two pieces each. Alternate all the layers of meat into a terrine. Add rings of onion over the top. Add the spices, salt, and, pepper and spread over the whole. Pour in the white wine and 1 cup of the red wine vinegar.

Preheat the oven to 300°F and bake the terrine covered for three hours. Then, add the remaining vinegar and more salt and pepper to taste. Dissolve the gelatin in the meat stock in a double boiler over hot water on the stove. Pour the mixture over the terrine and return the terrine to the oven for 15 more minutes. Remove from oven and cool to room temperature, then refrigerate. To serve: Invert terrine on a cutting board and cut into slices. Serve cold as a starter with pickled gherkins, pearl onions and toasted rye bread—or baguettes slices. Serve with a good strong fermented Flemish or Belgian beer. [Adapted from *Recipes for Redemption: A Companion Cookbook to A Cup of Redemption*]

CHAPTER TWO

Soupe à l'Oignon Gratinée
(French Onion Soup)

"A fabulously authentic, easy and traditional recipe for French onion soup, or *soupe a l'oignon gratinée*, as the French call it. This recipe was given to me by an old French lady who has been making it for her family for more than 70 years and they never tire of it—it's so delicious!

Did you know that onions were—in ancient times—considered an aphrodisiac? In France in the old days it was customary for newlyweds to be served onion soup on the morning after their wedding night." Or, in Brittany, 'milk soup' was served with plenty of garlic. Could that have been the same tradition?

Enough for 4 very hungry or 6 hungry-ish people

Ingredients

1/4 cup butter
1 1/2 cup onions (any type will do but chop them finely)
1 large clove of garlic, chopped (or more if you like it a lot!)
1/3 cup all-purpose flour
8 cups rich beef stock
1 cup white or red wine
1 bay leaf
2 sprigs thyme
Stale baguette or toasted rustic croutons
3/4 cup grated *Gruyère* cheese
Salt and pepper to taste

Directions

Melt the butter in a large pot and add the onions, stir occasionally over a low heat for about 20 minutes until they are a deep golden color and starting to caramelize. Add the garlic and flour to the onions and stir constantly for 2 minutes.

Gradually add the stock and wine, stirring constantly, and then bring to a boil. Generously, season to taste and add the herbs, cover the saucepan and simmer for around 20 minutes.

Slice the stale baguette and toast them lightly—then break into small pieces about an inch or so across. You can leave the slices whole if you prefer.

Serve the soup into dishes, whack the bread on top, sprinkle with the grated cheese, and broil until the cheese is bubbling and you can't wait any longer to dig in!

Bon appétit!

P.S. if you want to freeze leftover soup, leave out the bread and cheese and it'll last in the freezer for a couple of months.

[*Janine Marsh – The Good Life France*]

```
┌─────────────────────────────┐
│          Normandy           │
└─────────────────────────────┘
```

CHAPTER THREE

Sea Scallops Baked in a Shell with Mushrooms and Bechamel Sauce

My grandmother, from Le Havre, taught me a trick. When you cook sea scallops they usually shrink. She learned during the war that if you put scallops in a bit of boiling milk to cover for just a minute or two, they will absorb the milk, puff up, and not shrink. You then take them out of the milk, place them on a paper towel to extract the milk, then sauté them in plenty of butter, garlic, parsley."

Serves 4

Ingredients

1 lb. sea scallops, sliced in two (prepare with trick above)
4 large St Jacques scallop shells, cleaned
3 large button mushrooms, thinly sliced
1/4 cup, butter
1/4 cup, olive oil, divided
1 shallot, chopped
1 onion, chopped
1 clove of garlic, minced
2 teaspoons Knorr powdered fish stock
1/2 cup dry white wine

Bechamel Sauce

1 1/4 cup milk, warmed
2 tablespoons butter
2 tablespoons flour

salt and pepper to taste

1/3 cup Gruyére cheese, grated

Directions

Preheat oven at 400°F.

Begin by preparing the scallops, as above (to avoid shrinkage).

After patting dry, lightly sauté the scallops in butter. Set aside. Keep the cooking juices. In a separate frying pan, sauté the mushrooms in olive oil. Remove the mushrooms and set aside.

In the same pan, prepare white wine sauce by adding 4 more tablespoons of olive oil, the chopped onion, shallot and garlic clove and brown for about 5 minutes. Then add in the white wine mixed with the fish stock powder and simmer. Blend both preparations together, then set aside. Prepare the Béchamel Sauce.

Béchamel Sauce

Melt the butter and quickly add flour by sprinkling over the butter. Whisk the two together. Then add in the scallop juice and incorporate. Next, add the white wine sauce. Add warm milk and stir over low heat until a thick sauce is obtained. Season to taste with salt and pepper. Reserve.

Next, divide the scallops, mushrooms, and onion/shallot/garlic mixture into the four empty shells. Top with béchamel sauce. Add grated Gruyere cheese or breadcrumbs (optional)

Bake for 10 minutes in the oven until the top *'gratinates'* or becomes lightly browned.

Serve hot.

—*Karyn Foucher*

··

CHAPTER FOUR
Harira
(Moroccan Chicken Soup)

Makes 10–12 cups

Ingredients

2 cups onion, diced
2 tablespoons olive oil
3 large carrots, peeled and cut into ½" cubes
2 tablespoons minced fresh ginger
1 tablespoon minced garlic
1 box couscous
zest of one lemon

Ras El Hanout
(The name is given to a type of regional spice mixture used throughout the Northern Algerian and Middle Eastern countries and consists of the following or is a regional mixture):

1 teaspoon *each* smoked paprika and ground
  coriander
1/2 teaspoon *each* ground cumin, cinnamon, and
  cardamom

1/4 teaspoon *each* ground turmeric, nutmeg and red
  pepper flakes
1/2 cup dry white wine – (If you can't use alcohol for
  religious reasons, use 1/4 cup lemon juice + 1/4 cup
  water)
4–5 cups chicken broth

3/4 lb. cooked chicken, chopped (or half store-
  roasted chicken)
1 can chickpeas, drained and rinsed (15 oz.)
1 can diced tomatoes in juice (14.5 oz.)
1 can artichoke hearts, drained, quartered (13.75 oz.)
1/3 cup kalamata olives, pitted and quartered (I just
  dumped them in whole)
salt & pepper to taste
1 cup each minced fresh cilantro and parsley

Directions

Sauté onion and carrots in oil in large pot over
medium heat until onion is soft, 5 minutes. Add
ginger, garlic, and all the spices and cook 1 minute.

Deglaze pot with wine, reduce until nearly evaporated,
then stir in broth, chicken, chickpeas, tomatoes,
artichokes, and olives. Bring soup to a boil, reduce
heat to medium-low, and simmer 10 minutes or put
the soup into a crock pot on low for several hours.
Season soup with salt and pepper, if desired.

Prepare the couscous. I used one box and followed
those directions. You can also zest a lemon into the
mix, if desired.

When serving, add a mound of couscous into a bowl, then ladle in the soup and sprinkle with chopped cilantro and parsley. Enjoy!!

[*Adaptation from Cuisine at Home recipes*]

CHAPTER FIVE

Poisson Soupe

(Fish Soup)

Ingredients

3 cups of chopped onion, divided

1 cup dry white wine

30 medium mussels, scrubbed and debearded

6 Italian parsley sprigs, divided

2 tablespoons butter

2 1/2 cups fennel bulb, finely chopped

2 cups leeks, finely chopped

4 cups boiling water

2 extra-large Knorr fish-flavored bouillon cubes

3 thyme sprigs

1 bay leaf

1/2 cup half-and-half

1/4 cup crème fraiche

2 large egg yolks

1 3/4 lb. cod or other firm white fish, cut into 1-inch pieces

12 oz. sea scallops, cut into 1-inch pieces

1/4 cup chopped fresh Italian parsley

1 tablespoon 1" julienne-cut lemon rind

1/2 teaspoon sea salt
1/4 teaspoon black pepper
croutons

Directions

Combine 1 1/2 cups onion, wine, mussels, and 3 parsley sprigs in a Dutch oven; bring to a boil over medium-high heat. Cover and cook two minutes or until mussels open; discard any unopened shells. Remove mussels with a slotted spoon; set aside. Strain cooking liquid through a sieve into a bowl, reserving liquid and discard solids. Remove meat from mussels and discard shells.

Place Dutch oven over medium heat; melt butter. Add 1 1/2 cups onion, fennel, and leeks; cook ten minutes or until tender, stirring occasionally. Combine water and bouillon, stirring until bouillon cubes dissolve. Add bouillon mixture and reserved cooking liquid to onion mixture, stirring to combine.

Prepare a bouquet garni with the remaining three parsley sprigs, thyme, and bay leaf on a double layer of cheesecloth. Gather the edges of the cheesecloth together, and tie securely with cooking twine. Combine the bouquet garni and broth mixture; bring to a boil. Reduce heat, and simmer ten minutes. Remove bag and discard.

Combine the half-and-half, *crème fraîche*, and egg yolks in a medium bowl, stirring well with a whisk. Gradually add 1 1/2 cups hot broth mixture to egg mixture, stirring constantly with a whisk. Return egg mixture to pan. Cook five minutes or until soup thickens slightly (do not boil), stirring constantly. Add fish and scallops; cook five minutes or until fish is done, stirring frequently. Stir in mussels, 1/4 cup chopped parsley, and lemon rind; cook one minute until thoroughly heated. Stir in salt and pepper. Ladle into individual soup bowls and add croutons.

[*Adapted from a Susan Hermann Loomis recipe, April 2004*]

....

CHAPTER SIX
Tarte Tatin with Calvados

Serves 6

Ingredients

1/4–1/2 cups all-purpose flour
1 lb. puff pastry
4 cups of medium apples, a mix of types
1/2 cup of baker's sugar
4 oz. calvados
1 vanilla pod, halved lengthways, seeds scraped out,
   or 1 tablespoon vanilla
2 oz. butter, cubed

Directions

Preheat oven to 375°F. Prepare a flat, clean surface for rolling out the puff pastry. Sprinkle with a light film of flour, then roll out to a circle at just about one and a half to two inches thick. The diameter of the circle must equal the diameter of the oven-proof frying pan you will be using, plus two inches as an overlap. Put the pastry aside. Prepare the apples by peeling, coring and slicing in halves.

Place the frying pan over a medium heat and add the sugar, calvados, vanilla seeds and pod. Let the sugar dissolve and cook until the mixture forms a light caramel. (Do not touch hot caramel.) Add the apples, and carefully stir in the pan and cook for about 5 minutes until the apples start to soften. Add the cubed butter, then carefully lay the pastry over the top. Quickly tuck the pastry down inside the edges of the pan. Use a wooden spoon, so as not to burn yourself on the caramel.

Bake the Tarte Tatin for about 25 to 30 minutes, until golden, with crispy caramel bubbling up from underneath the edges. Take it out of the oven. To serve the tarte, you will need to carefully flip the frying pan onto a serving platter. Hold the platter up to the pan with an oven glove, then quickly turn it out. Put it to one side for a few minutes to cool slightly, then serve with ice cream or crème fraîche. Enjoy!

[Adapted from recipes from Chef Jamie Oliver]

Teurgoule
(Five Generations of Rice Pudding)

The history behind this special dessert goes back to the 18th century and was supposedly due to a gift given by the French king to the people of Normandy who had lost their wheat crop. He managed to find and deliver rice to the starving Normans. And, as an extra-special gift, a recipe was also handed down from the king's royal kitchens.

The following recipe came from Patrick Foisnard, whose recipe came from his great-great grandmother's recipe and was also mentioned by Karyn Foucher.

Serves 6 to 8

Ingredients

1/3 cup short-grained round Arborio rice
1/4 cup powdered sugar plus 2 tablespoons (made up of brown sugar, vanilla-flavored sugar, and vanilla bean)

1 teaspoon vanilla-flavored sugar/vanilla bean or
  1 tsp cinnamon
1/4 teaspoon sea salt
4 cups whole milk

Directions

First, you need round rice. You let it soak in a saucepan with a little bit of water and let it swell, then drain it, but do not rinse, in order to keep the starch. Then, in a separate pan, bring whole milk to a boil, with brown sugar, vanilla-flavored sugar, and vanilla bean. Add the rice and cook for one hour at low heat. Remove vanilla bean. Then put the mixture in a terra cotta plate or terrine.

Bake at 300 F° for two hours. Never stir when it is in the oven! You can stir a little bit when it's in the saucepan, if you want, but not in the oven. During the baking process, the surface of the mixture will be covered by a dark film. The rice will remain at the bottom of the dish, and the cream will come to the top. *Voilà! Teurgoule!* [*Sous Chef, Patrick Foisnard*]

Andouille de Vire
(Andouille Sausage from Normandy with Mashed Potatoes and Apple Cider Sauce)

Serves 4

Ingredients

1 lb. andouille sausage, cut into thick slices
  (count about ¼ lb. of *andouille* per person)
1/4 cup water
2 lbs. potatoes, peeled and cut into two-inch chunks
2 tablespoons butter
1–2 sprigs each of chives and chervil, chopped
2 cups *cidre fermier,* or cider from the farm
2 apples, chopped
1/4 cup heavy cream

Directions

Begin by placing the andouille sausage slices into a large frying pan with a 1/4 cup of water. Cover and simmer on low heat for about twenty minutes.

Next, place the potatoes into a large pot covered with water and bring to a boil. While the potatoes are boiling, pour the *cidre fermier* or 'cider from the farm,' into a saucepan. Add two chopped apples to the cider, reduce over medium heat, and mix. Once it is mixed or stirred, add the heavy cream or whipping cream, season to taste, and again reduce. Add the andouille to the sauce to commingle the flavors.

Mash the potatoes and add butter, chives and chervil. Mound potatoes onto a wide platter and place the sausage around the edges with the cider sauce poured lavishly overall.

Brittany

CHAPTER SEVEN

Pork Tenderloin with Apples and Calvados

Serves 4

Ingredients

2 lbs. pork tenderloin
salt and ground pepper
1 tablespoon canola oil

2 oz. butter, divided
1 lb. small new potatoes, peeled
3/4 cup water
1 lb. Golden Delicious apples
2 tablespoons calvados
1 cup applesauce
1/4 cup heavy cream
A couple of sprigs of thyme

Directions

Season the pork tenderloin with plenty of salt and ground pepper. Heat the oil in a heavy pot which will hold the meat. Add 1 oz. butter and brown the meat on all sides. Remove the meat and add the potatoes to the drippings and sauté until golden, about four minutes. Return the meat to the pot, add the water, cover and simmer on low for one hour. Check often and turn the meat and potatoes regularly, so as not to stick.

Twenty minutes before the end of cooking the meat, peel, core and quarter the apples. Cut each quarter into three slices. Melt the remaining 1 oz. butter in a small sauté pan and add the apples along with 2 tablespoons calvados. Stir in the applesauce and heavy cream. Warm through.

Serve the pork tenderloin on a platter surrounded with the potatoes. Mound the apples over the pork. Sprinkle the thyme over the top. Enjoy!

[*Adapted from France the Beautiful Cookbook*]

CHAPTER EIGHT

Sweet and Savory Crêpes

Makes ten 6" crêpes

Ingredients

1 cup all-purpose flour
1/4 teaspoon. salt
1/2 cup milk
2 large eggs
1/2 cup water
2 tablespoons clarified butter, melted, plus more for pan

Directions

In a medium bowl, sift together the flour and salt. Make a well in the center. Whisk together the milk and eggs in another medium bowl. Pour the milk mixture into the center of the well, slowly whisking in the flour from the sides of the well. Add 2 tablespoons clarified butter and whisk to combine. Strain the mixture through a fine-mesh sieve into a mixing bowl. Cover with plastic wrap, and chill in the refrigerator for 30 minutes.

Remove the batter from the refrigerator. Heat a 6-inch crêpe pan or nonstick frying pan over medium-high heat. Brush with clarified butter, and heat until very hot. Add a couple of tablespoons of batter, turning and swirling the batter in the pan to completely coat the bottom.

Cook until brown on the bottom, 1 to 2 minutes.

Flip the crêpe with a spatula, and cook golden-brown on the other side, about 1 minute. Repeat with remaining batter. As you continue, you will need to use less butter in the crêpe pan.

These crêpes can be used with either sweet or savory fillings. Savory galettes can be filled with everything, from a fried egg to ham and cheese to sautéed vegetables. Sweet galettes/crêpes are lightly sweetened with warmed jam or sprinkled with powdered sugar and served as dessert or as an after-school snack.

[From *Recipes for Redemption: A Companion Cookbook to A Cup of Redemption*]

Moûles avec Cidre et Crême
(Mussels with Cider and Cream)

Serves 4

Ingredients

4 lbs. mussels
1 clove of garlic, finely chopped
2 shallots, finely chopped
2 tablespoons butter
1 sprig each of parsley, bay leaves and thyme
  (*bouquet garni*)
4 oz. white wine or cider
4 oz. cream (thick and salted, if available)
1/4 cup of freshly chopped parsley

Directions

Rinse the mussels under plenty of cold, running water. Discard any open ones that won't close when lightly squeezed.

Remove the fibrous beards protruding from between the tightly closed shells and then scrub the shells with a stiff vegetable brush. Give the mussels another quick rinse to remove any little pieces of shell or sand.

Sauté the garlic and shallots in butter with the bouquet garni, in a pan big enough to take all the mussels—it should only be half full.

Add the mussels and wine or cider, turn up the heat, then cover and steam them open in their own juices for 3 to 4 minutes. Give the pan a good shake every now and then.

Remove the *bouquet garni* and discard any unopened mussels. Add the cream and chopped parsley. Then after one minute, remove from the heat.

Spoon into four large warmed bowls and serve with lots of crusty bread.

[From *Recipes for Redemption: A Companion Cookbook from A Cup of Redemption*]

CHAPTER NINE

Pintade au Cidre
(Guinea Hen in Cider)

Serves 4 to 5

Ingredients

3 1/2 lb. Guinea Hen (similar to chicken in size but
  has a more gamey taste, like pheasant)
salt and pepper to taste
1 cube butter, cut into eight pieces
1 1/2 cups of dry hard cider

Directions

Preheat the oven to 425°F Sprinkle the hen inside
and out with salt and pepper. Place in a roasting pan
and sprinkle with butter. Pour the cider around the
bird and place in the oven. Baste every 10–15
minutes, for about 50–60 minutes. Check the bird for
doneness with either a meat thermometer or when
the juices run clear.

Rest the bird on a carving board covered with foil.
Place the roasting pan on the burner and place on
medium-high. Simmer the juices and season to taste.
Carve the hen and arrange on a warm platter. Serve
the heated juices with the bird, as well as with
mashed potatoes. *[Adapted from Joie de Vivre.]*

CHAPTER TEN

Kouign Amann
(Breton Butter Cake)

Serves 4 to 5

Ingredients

1 1/2 cups of unsifted flour, less 1 tablespoon
1 tablespoon cornstarch
zest from 1/2 to 1 orange or 1/2 teaspoon of orange
  flower water
1/2 envelope of dried yeast
1/2 cup lukewarm water, plus 1 tablespoon
10 tablespoons lightly salted butter
1/2 cup granulated sugar
1 egg yolk, slightly beaten
pinch of salt

Directions

Put the flour and cornstarch into a bowl; add the orange flower water and the salt. In a separate bowl, combine yeast and lukewarm water to activate the yeast, then add to dry ingredients. Work into a soft dough and flatten into a round, ½ inch thick by 6 inches in diameter, cake. Set on a slightly buttered plate. Cover with plastic wrap and let rise until double in bulk, approximately 2 hours.

Knead the butter with your thumb or fingers to make sure that it is soft and pliable. Then, shape into a 4-inch by 1/2-inch thick slab on a piece of parchment paper. Refrigerate until dough is ready.

Have the sugar ready. Lightly flour the work surface, flatten the cake of dough into a small 6-inch square. Put the butter into the center, shaped as a square 4 inches by 1/2-inch thick. Enclose the butter inside the dough by folding corners over butter. Let stand for 5 minutes. Roll the dough into a 12-inch-long flat band, keeping it 4 inches wide. Sprinkle with 1/3 of the sugar. Pass the rolling pin over the sugar to press it into the dough. Fold the bottom of the dough toward the center, then the top to cover the bottom. Turn the dough by 90 degrees, so that it will now look like a book ready to open. Cover with plastic wrap once again and store in the crisper of the refrigerator for at least 30 minutes.

Take the dough out of the refrigerator and give it a second turn. Before closing the dough, sprinkle with the second 1/3 of the sugar. Fold and give a third turn. Before the third folding, sprinkle the last third of the sugar onto the dough, less 1 teaspoon. Wrap and refrigerate another half hour. Give a last turn and with the rolling pin, tease the dough into the shape of a round cake as close as possible to an 8-inch or 9-inch cake pan. Transfer the dough to the cake pan which has been slathered with butter. Dock (slash) the top of the cake into a crisscross pattern, cutting at least 1/4 inch deep into the dough.

Keep the cake at room temperature and let the dough rise within ¼ inch of the edge of the cake pan. Brush the top of the cake with the egg yolk, sprinkle with the last teaspoon of sugar, and bake in a preheated oven at 375° F for 25 minutes. The top of the cake should be nice and golden, and its bottom should be a lovely buttered caramel layer. Serve warm with crème fraîche and/or a bowl of *café*.

[*Recipes for Redemption: A Companion Cookbook to A Cup of Redemption*]

....

CHAPTER ELEVEN

Cotriade

(Fish Stew)

Like Bouillabaisse in the south of France or Cioppino here in our own country, the *Cotriade* can be as diverse a stew as the fishing villages and ports the fishermen sail into along the Coast of Brittany. This is a stew concocted of whatever seafood is available at the time.

Serves 6

Ingredients

4 lbs. of mixed fish (gutted, scaled, and the heads
    removed)
2 lbs. red potatoes, cut into chunks
1/3 cup of saindoux or lard, or 1/3 cup canola oil
1 cup of sliced white onions
salt and pepper to taste
a splash of white vinegar or white wine

Directions

Melt the saindoux, lard, or canola oil in a large (6 qt) pot and cook the onions until golden, about 5 minutes. Stir with a wooden spoon. Stir in the potatoes and salt and pepper. Then add enough water to cover all ingredients and simmer for about 15 minutes.

Add the fish to the simmering liquid beginning with the firmest of fish and working down to the least firm. Let the liquid return to simmering after each addition. Season with salt and pepper and simmer for 15 more minutes.

Remove the fish and potatoes with a slotted spoon and place into warmed bowls. Add a ladle full of broth and serve with dark bread. A dash of vinegar or a little white wine into the soup will lift the flavors. Enjoy!

[Adapted from Micheline or Mimi and used in *Recipes for Redemption: A Companion Cookbook to A Cup of Redemption.*]

Milk Soup – Wedding Tradition

"I believe the milk soup is prepared with milk, plus some garlic and spices. Originally, it was served to the young married couple at the beginning of the wedding reception. It was to represent a marriage—which has its smooth days and spicy days. But, on the last of these many days of the wedding celebration, the soup is served again to the married couple just as they go to bed. It is prepared very spicy, indeed. It was meant to tease and make great fun with the newly married couple. I've heard it can get quite raucous, at times. I don't know, as I wasn't married here in Brittany. I'm glad I wasn't." She covered her mouth with her hand and giggled.

[Mimi recounts this tradition in Chapter Eleven and ideas from *The Horse of Pride* by Pierre-Jakez Hélias]

Loire Valley

CHAPTER TWELVE

Truffle-Infused Scrambled Eggs

"I imagine you slice them thinly, correct?" I asked. "By the way, how do you cook with truffles?"

"*Mais, oui.* You must slice them paper-thin. People who have never used truffles before should use them for the first time with eggs. It is the easiest way." She placed her teacup down and began to demonstrate with her hands.

"You put one truffle in a box of twelve eggs, which have not yet been cooked, and seal a plastic bag around them. We keep the eggs and truffle in a bag for four to five days. The flavor of the truffle goes directly into the eggs. Then you can cook the eggs, soft boiled or any other way. You can prepare scrambled eggs with thin slivers of truffle. You can even crush fresh truffles and mix them with butter and spread the truffle-butter on a piece of bread that you dip into the soft-boiled egg. It is *délicieuse!*" [Madame Garlandau, from the Truffle Farm]

Soup with Mushrooms, Foie Gras, Crême Fraîche, and Truffles

"Oh," Madame Garlandau said with a Gallic puff, "you can prepare potage with mushrooms, *foie gras*, crème fraiche, and truffles. Prepare a cream of mushroom mixture, to which you add slivers of truffles. Then add the cream. In serving, use individual terrines or earthenware, preheated; add the uncooked *foie gras* cut in small pieces. Pour the potage on top of the *foie gras* in the terrine and serve."

Potage Valery Giscard d'Estaing (V.G.E.)

This is Potage Valery Giscard d'Estaing, named after a former French *President de la République*. The president's chef, Bocuse, invented the recipe and it was so superior, he won the Legion of Honor award. The soup is made with chicken stock, shredded carrot, a little piece of celery stalk, and chicken breasts cut in small pieces and sautéed. Cook these ingredients. Then cut small cubes of *foie gras*, one truffle per dish cut in two pieces. Be sure to brush the truffles under cold water to clean them. Then put all the ingredients in individual terrines, one truffle per terrine; wrap the terrine in puff pastry dough to completely seal it. Once the dough is baked, serve the terrine. As you break through the dough with your fork, all the flavors are released. Yummy."

[*Madame Garlandau, from the truffle farm*]

Mashed Potatoes, Robuchon-Style

"This recipe is for potatoes mashed with butter, more butter, and much more butter."

—Josiane Selvage

"It is easy to think of potatoes, and fortunately for men who have not much money it is easy to think of them with a certain safety. Potatoes are one of the last things to disappear, in times of war, which is probably why they should not be forgotten in times of peace."

—M.F.K Fisher

CHAPTER THIRTEEN

Escargots in Garlic Butter for Escargot Festival

"What do you call a group of snails? An *escargatoire* of snails!"

2 to 3 dozen snails from cans plus same number of snail shells

Ingredients for Escargot Butter

1 1/4 cube unsalted butter
2 tablespoons parsley, finely chopped
1/4 cup garlic, crushed, finely chopped
salt and crushed black pepper

Directions

Soften the butter; add the finely chopped parsley and crushed garlic. Mix thoroughly; add salt and crushed pepper. Traditionally the snail's shells were used to serve the escargots. They had to be cleaned, which was an enormous task. It is now a day much easier to use dishes specially designed for the presentation of escargots. One escargot was placed in one shell (or whole in the dish), and generously covered with the butter garlic mix. The oven was preheated to 350°F and escargots cooked until the butter was bubbly. And this "enchanting delicacy" had to be served immediately, with an excellent Riesling wine.

[Adapted from *Recipes for Redemption: A Companion Cookbook to A Cup of Redemption*]

Salade au Chèvre Chaud
(Warm Goat Cheese Salad)

Serves 8
Ingredients for Salad

1 log of goat cheese, sliced into eighths (1/2" thick)
8 slices French Sweet baguette
2–3 cups of your salad greens – arugula, spinach, mâché
toasted walnuts

Ingredients for Dressing

1/4 cup white wine or champagne vinegar

1 teaspoon shallot, minced

1 teaspoon garlic, minced

1/2–1 teaspoon Dijon mustard

1/2 teaspoon sea salt

1/8 teaspoon freshly ground black pepper

1/4 cup extra virgin olive oil

Directions

In a small bowl, whisk together vinegar, shallot, garlic, mustard, salt and pepper. While whisking, slowly add the olive oil to emulsify.

Slice the baguette into slices of about ½ inch wide and toast the bread on one side in oven at 375°F. Turn the bread over and place the goat cheese slice on the bread and broil until lightly browned.

Place the salad greens into a bowl and toss with the vinaigrette. Sprinkle with toasted walnuts. Serve the salad onto separate salad plates and place a couple of cheese toasts alongside. Enjoy!

CHAPTER FOURTEEN

Lapin à la Moutarde
(Roasted Rabbit in Mustard Sauce)

Serves 4

Ingredients

1 rabbit, cut into pieces

salt and pepper to taste

1 tablespoon canola oil
4 tablespoon Dijon mustard or strong mustard
1 sprig thyme
2 tablespoon butter, cut into slivers
6 tablespoon white wine
2/3 cup heavy cream

Directions

Set oven to 425°F. Rinse the rabbit and use paper toweling to dry. Sprinkle the rabbit head to foot with salt and pepper. Oil a roasting pan and place the rabbit into the pan. Spread the rabbit thoroughly with the mustard and tear the leaves from the sprig of thyme, sprinkling it over the body. Dot the rabbit with the slivers of butter and pour the wine in beside the rabbit. Place in the oven for 50 minutes, basting regularly with the juices. Once roasted, take rabbit out of the pan and place on a warmed platter and cover with foil. Place roasting pan on the top burner and turn on to simmer. Add the cream and stir with a wooden spoon to loosen the *fond*, or the bits. Cook for a couple of minutes and pour sauce into a gravy boat. Serve the rabbit with mashed potatoes and the gravy.

[Adapted from *France The Beautiful Cookbook*]

Canard aux Pêches
(Duck with Peaches)

Serves 4

Ingredients:

4 lb. whole duck, or 8 whole duck legs
2 tablespoons sugar
1 tablespoon potato starch or flour
2 tablespoons brandy
29 oz. Del Monte cling peach halves, in heavy syrup
1 *bouquet garni*
2 celery stalks, sliced 1/4"
2 white onions, sliced 1/4"
2 carrots, peeled and sliced 1/4"
salt and pepper to taste
2 tablespoons white flour
1/2 cup butter
1 tablespoon white vinegar

Directions:

Set oven to 400°F. Truss the duck. Work two tablespoons butter into the flour to create a smooth paste. Season the duck with salt and pepper, then coat it with the butter/flour paste. Put the vegetables in the bottom of a roasting pan with the *bouquet garni*. Place a metal rack over the top of vegetables and place the duck on the rack. Roast for one hour.

Remove duck from pan and keep warm, covered with foil. Remove vegetables to separate platter, then strain liquid from roasting pan into saucepan. Skim fat from the top, add the peaches and 6 tablespoons of the peach syrup. Cook for five to six minutes, turning the peach halves halfway through.

Quarter the duck and place on a warmed platter. Reserve the carving juices. Arrange the peaches around the duck and keep hot.

Pour carving juices into the saucepan. Mix brandy with the potato starch and add to the pan. Bring to a boil, stirring and adjust the seasoning.

Meanwhile, dissolve sugar in the vinegar in a small saucepan over medium heat. Once it obtains a caramel color, blend it into the sauce. Finally, whisk in the remaining butter and serve the sauce in a gravy boat with the duck.

[*Adapted from Madame de Bonneval and Joie de Vivre*]

Auvergne

CHAPTER FIFTEEN
Paté de Pomme de Terre
(Potato-Meat Pie)

"To me, life without veal stock, pork fat, sausage, organ meat, demi-glace, or even stinky cheese is a life not worth living."

—Anthony Bourdain

First, in this case a pâte is a pastry, so this is a basic potato-meat pie. For the pastry dough, Marcelle used a lard pastry dough—or *pâté au saindoux* (her very favorite). It became a favorite for Martial, as well.

Serves 4 to 5

Ingredients for Pastry (pâte)

2 1/2 cups of sifted all-purpose flour
1/2 lb. of warm melted lard (or saindoux)
2 whole eggs
1/2 cup warm water
2 tablespoons salt

Directions

Prepare as you would a regular type of pie dough. This provides a top and bottom crust. Roll out the bottom crust and place in a pie pan.

Ingredients for Filling

1/2 cup of chopped semi-salty *lardons* (thick bacon)
1 lb. Yukon gold potatoes, peeled and sliced into thin
  rounds
1/2 cup of chopped onion
5 garlic cloves, finely chopped
1 tablespoon chopped parsley
salt and pepper to taste
1 egg yolk beaten with 1tablespoon water

Directions

Blanch the lardons (bacon) in boiling water for three minutes to diminish the saltiness. Then, place them in a *sauteuse* (or frying pan) to render the fat. Add the potatoes, onion, garlic, then salt and pepper to taste. When the filling is slightly golden, layer them into the bottom crust, sprinkle with the chopped parsley, place the top crust on and crimped the edges. Glaze the pâte with the egg yolk mixture using a pastry brush. Bake in a pre-heated oven set at 350° F. for one hour. Serve with a green salad. Voilà!!

[From *Recipes for Redemption Companion Cookbook*]

....

CHAPTER SEVENTEEN
Capon
(Roasted Chicken)

Serves 4

Ingredients

1/4 lb. butter
5 lb. capon, the fresher the better and in this case, it
   was straight from the farmyard—fresh, cut into 6
   pieces: 2 from breasts, and 4 from the thigh and legs
salt and pepper to taste
2 tablespoons white flour
1/2 cup dry white wine
1 cup chicken broth
bouquet garni (parsley, bay leaf, thyme, and celery tied
   together)
1 cup heavy cream
4 egg yolks
1 tablespoon lemon juice

Directions

Melt the butter in a large skillet. When it is foaming, sauté the capon pieces, turning often so they will not brown, but will turn golden. Sprinkle with salt and pepper and cook over medium heat for 25 minutes. Sprinkle with flour and cook, covered, 10 minutes.

Stir in the wine and broth, add the bouquet garni, cover and cook slowly 25 more minutes until tender. Place the capon in a serving dish. Blend the cream and egg yolks well. Stir slowly into cooking pan, off heat to avoid curdling. Stir in the lemon juice, then strain the sauce through a fine sieve. Bring this sauce almost to a boil. Remove from heat, stir well. It should be just thick enough to coat the capon. Spoon the sauce over the pieces of bird and serve with boiled new potatoes.

[Adapted from Antoine Gilly's *Feast of France* and *Recipes for Redemption: A Companion Cookbook to A Cup of Redemption*]

CHAPTER EIGHTEEN

Tourte de Viande Auvergne

(Meat Pie)

This is a traditional yet elaborate meat pie with *pâté brissée* (pie dough) base and a puff pastry top which is baked. Ten minutes before the end of the baking period, a savory egg-and-cream custard is poured through a hole (chimney) in the pie crust and returned to the oven to set.

Serves 4 to 6

Ingredients

4 oz. puff pastry
4 oz. pie dough
4 oz. veal, medium diced
4 oz. fresh pork, medium diced
1 cup Riesling
2 shallots, minced
1 onion, minced
2 garlic cloves, minced
2 bay leaves
2 sprigs thyme
4 cloves
salt and pepper to taste
Quatre Épices (4 spices) **
parsley, chopped
1/2 cup heavy cream
2 eggs (1 yolk + 1 whole egg)
nutmeg

Directions

Day One: Marinate the meat, cut into medium dice in the Riesling, salt, pepper, Quatre Épices (4 spices), shallots, garlic, and onion, along with the chopped parsley, bay leaves, thyme and cloves, overnight. Longer, if you have time.

Day Two: Preheat the oven to 400°F. After preparing the pie dough, press it into a buttered and floured pie pan lined with parchment paper. Place the meat on the pie dough leaving a narrow border all around the edge.

Roll out the puff pastry into a round to more than cover the pie. Cut a small round hole in the middle of the dough, before placing it onto the pie. Brush the surface with beaten egg yolk. If you want, make a small chimney in the middle hole (you may use a tube of cardboard covered with foil). Cover the meat pie with the puff pastry taking care to moisten with a little water to glue the edges together. Remember, the top will shrink a little. Bake in a hot oven for 45 min.

While the *tourte* is baking, beat the egg and yolk with the cream. Season with grated nutmeg, salt and pepper.

Remove the pie from the oven and with the help of a funnel pour the cream mixture through the chimney. This operation is a bit delicate. One needs to add a little at a time and then tilt the pan to disperse the liquid throughout the pie. Return the *tourte* to the oven for 10 more minutes.

[Adapted from a recipe from *The Cookbook: Cuisine of France and Recipes for Redemption Companion Cookbook*]

**Quatre Épices*: Literally meaning "four spices," this is a spice mix used mainly in the French kitchen, but also found in some Middle Eastern kitchens. The spice mix contains ground pepper (white, black, or both), cloves, nutmeg, and ginger. Some variations of the mix use allspice instead of pepper or cinnamon in place of ginger.

The blend of spices will typically use a larger proportion of pepper (usually white pepper) than the other spices, but some recipes suggest using roughly equal parts of each spice.

In French cooking, it is typically used in soup, ragout and pot-cooked dishes, vegetable preparations and charcuterie, such as pâté, sausage and terrine, including this *tourte de viande*.

Gateau des Rois
(The King's Cake – Epiphany)

"The *Gâteau des Rois* was also served as your parents' wedding cake, Josiane," Marie explained. "And, as you may or may not know, Carole," Marie continued, "the *galette,* which comes from the northern regions of France, is made of *feuilletée,* or a flaky type of dough, while the *Gâteau,* which I used to prepare, is only made south of the Loire. It is made like a *brioche* in the shape of a puffy crown. Josiane, since you were raised in the Lorraine, you are probably used to the *galette, n'est-ce pas?*"

"*C'est vrai*, Marie," Josiane said. "Carole, this is a special cake filled with almond cream and/or frangipane. It is quite delectable!"

"So, do you have a recipe for that cake?" I prompted, my appetite now in full tilt.

"Oh, my heavens, no!" responded Josiane. "That's what patisseries are for! We certainly wouldn't want to put them out of business."

ACKNOWLEDGMENTS

My deepest thanks go to my dear friend, Josiane Selvage, who led me on this and many other unforgettable French journeys. And for her willingness and ability to translate every bit of French on the spot during each and every interview, to painstakingly transcribe all the audio tapes along with the many French recipes for these books, and for her unwavering encouragement to allow me to search for answers to her mother, Marcelle's story, which culminated in my historical novel, *A Cup of Redemption* and also *Recipes for Redemption: A Companion Cookbook to A Cup of Redemption*.

And to Josiane's French family and friends, as well as my own, who welcomed me into their homes, who taught me their traditional French family recipes, served me incredible homemade meals, taught me the history of their region, and shared their family's stories, cultural traditions, favorite recipes. A gift of a lifetime! My thanks go out specifically to Veronique Gindre (Dunkirk), Karyn Foucher (Le Havre), Louisette (Rouen), M. Barreaux and Patrick Foisnard (Manoir de la Roche Torin), Sophie Pourrez (Rennes), Micheline Thionet (Damgan), Madame Garlandau (Truffle Farm-Richelieu), Patrice Morcel and Sylvie Pretseille (The 30s Restaurant, Chinon), Madame de Bonneval (Chateau de Thalmiers), Jeannine and Martial Pourrez, Christian Pourrez and Marie Plouffe.

I also want to thank my team of 'experts' who helped keep me on track and task through editing, critiquing, and encouraging me: my writing group of twelve years, Lucy Murray, Cheryl Ray, Mary Ellen Hill, and my personal editor, Darlene Frank. Also, I want to thank Mike Morgenfeld, my cartographer extraordinaire; Jonathan Farrell, my Bay Area publicist; Steve Higgs, corporate chef and culinary supporter; Geoffroy Raby, avid supporter and owner of the French bistro, Cuisinett, San Carlos, CA; Abigail Crayne, director of Draeger's Cooking School and lead for the Literary Lunch series; and Robin Bantz, supporter and good friend. You all have made my writing come alive and have added great joy to the whole literary experience.

And those skilled and always helpful women at She Writes Press: Brooke Warner, Lauren Wise, Mimi Bark, Cait Levin, Stacey Aaronson, and Leah Lococo, with whom none of these books could be possible. And, to the team of Caitlin Hamilton Marketing & Publicity, my thanks for a job very well done. I appreciate you connecting me to so many new venues—and people and countries who embraced my work. Thank you.

And last, but not least, timing is everything! In my case, it became a blessing. As I was preparing to test these traditional French recipes for Book Two of the *Savoring the Olde Ways Series*, a literal "shut-down" due to the pandemic arrived on my doorstep. The ability to go freely about shopping for ingredients at my favorite markets came to a halt, and I was faced with the prospect of an unmet deadline. Attempting not to panic, I wrote an SOS in my newsletter enlisting help from others who were sequestered at home: "Would you like to join me in my 'virtual test kitchen'?" I did not know if anyone would respond, but respond, they did. Within less than a week, I had heard from over forty people, and sent out more than eighty copies of the nineteen traditional French recipes needed to be tested. Over the course of two months, I received notes, edits, and photos of completed recipes from as far away as England and France, and across the entire US.

All, like me, were under quarantine. And all, like me, had difficulty finding ingredients. Substitutions, suddenly, became a creative force. But, traditional French recipes, better known as *cuisine pauvre,* or peasant dishes, were originally prepared from simple ingredients and with what was available. That was the norm. As this simple correlation dawned on me, I realized this experience was a blessing—it brought a better understanding and resonance for the very themes I hold dear in my culinary travel series: family favorites, traditional in nature.

For those of you who took the challenge, I cannot thank you enough—for your time, your consideration, and your perseverance. I could not have completed these tests nor met my deadline without you. Thank you so very much! I salute you! My team of "virtual test kitchen chefs" all participated with at least one recipe: Barbara Stark-Nemon, Sandy Turner, Pauline Jones, Linda Ryan, Penny and John Dancer, Sue Lockwood, Adam and Sandi Kahn, LuAnne Graves, Dildar Pisani, Leslie and David Nack, Patty Corcoran, Sandy Hardaker, Lisa Meltzer Penn, Tina Heffernan, Barbara Artson, Peggy Cohen, Geri Rypkema, Arthur Wood, Paula Cuneo, Bonnie Schmidt, Carol and Tim Petersen, Carolynn Ziance, Karyn Foucher, Liz Allison, Ingrid Pugh, Geri Spieler, Janice and Steve Bell, Megan McDonald, Evelyn La Torre, Robin and Paul Bantz, Pam Copeland, Judy Donohue, Andrew Smith, Shannon Amerman and Tod Klinger.

Travel isn't always pretty. It isn't always comfortable. Sometimes it hurts, it even breaks your heart. But that's OK. The journey changes you; it should change you. It leaves marks on your memory, on your consciousness, on your heart, and on your body. You take something with you. Hopefully, you leave something good behind.

—Anthony Bourdain

ABOUT THE AUTHOR

photo credit: Chris Loomis

CAROLE BUMPUS began writing about food and travel when she stumbled upon the amazing stories of women and war in France. Her historical novel, *A Cup of Redemption*, was published in October 2014, and her unique companion cookbook, *Recipes for Redemption: A Companion Cookbook to A Cup of Redemption*, was released in August 2015. Book one of her *Savoring the Olde Ways Series, Searching for Family and Traditions at the French Table*, was published in August 2019 and received a 2020 IPPY Award for European Regional Memoir. Her second of this series is due to be published in August 2020, and the third book, *A September to Remember: Searching for Culinary Pleasures at the Italian Table*, is due to be released in April 2021. She has also had three short stories published in the Fault Zone anthologies: *Words from the Edge*, *Stepping up to the Edge*, and *Over the Edge*. A retired family therapist, Bumpus lives in the San Francisco Bay Area.

Visit her website at www.carolebumpus.com.

Look for the Next Book in the Series, April, 2021

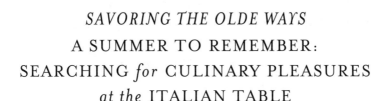

SAVORING THE OLDE WAYS
A SUMMER TO REMEMBER:
SEARCHING *for* CULINARY PLEASURES
at the ITALIAN TABLE

Opening the Door to Italy:
Entering the Land of Sensuality and Sumptuous Flavors

CHAPTER ONE
When in Mi-lano, Buy Mi-lanese

*T*he plane bucked and shuddered over the tops of the French Alps before sweeping down over the snow-filled valleys of northern Italy. Foreboding clouds swirled about the plane obscuring our only view of Milan before we dropped like a rock into our descent. On the ground, we were rushed into a queue which stretched across the tarmac as rain began to fall.

This was the first day of our month-long dream vacation to Italy. It had been a crisp September morning in '98 when my husband, Win, and I left San Francisco, but after hours in flight and hours of delays in Frankfurt, we finally were allowed to board this small plane for Milan. Sleepily, we forced ourselves to quicken our steps as we were herded like a gaggle of geese into the terminal.

Knowing little Italian, we realized our disadvantage as we craned our necks forward in order to catch the sharply delivered announcement in *Italiano*. We had no clue what was said. Too exhausted and bleary-eyed to focus, I figured I would deal with this language thing later—or so I thought.

Standing in the baggage terminal, which must have stretched for miles, we scanned the carousels for our bags. As we lumbered along, I noticed a river of luggage—I mean it—a river of dust-covered luggage, which was cordoned off from the rest of the crowd. Dates were scrawled across their surfaces from weeks before. Questions softly pricked at my semi-conscious mind, but it didn't dawn on me then, that I, too, would be forced into an imaginary boat to cross this River Styx in order to find my bag. Yes, my bag! The big bag which held every last piece of clothing I had packed for our month-long journey.

Once it was clear my suitcase had not made the flight, I nonchalantly waved my hand and said to my husband, "*Allora! Non problema!*" (These were the only Italian words I knew at the time.) They'll find it and deliver it to our hotel!" Confidently, I strode into the office to file my claim, in triplicate and without a word of English, where I realized it *was* a big *problema*. The immensity of the office, which was composed of five open counters and long lines at each, gave rise to a newly discovered anxiety. My bag was only one of perhaps thousands—no millions—of lost bags this office handled annually. My heart sank. No matter. The officials were cordial, seemed efficient, and were very encouraging. Plus, we were exhausted. After one more hour of standing on one foot and then the other, we finally made our way through another queue to find a taxi.

I would like to say I remember *seeing* the city of Milan on our drive to the hotel, but the truth is, I only *heard* the city of Milan. The heavens opened with a vengeance and rain began beating a deafening tattoo on the roof of the car obscuring our view. All the while, the taxi driver happily bellowed at top volume to compensate for the techno-music blaring from his radio. He expertly navigated the stream-swollen boulevards and we arrived at our hotel only somewhat scathed.

The hotel room was lovely, with a wide balcony overlooking the city. Upon pulling back the draperies the sun, for a brief moment, broke through the clouds. We caught our first glimpse of the magnificent spires of the crown jewel of Milano, the *Duomo*—one of the most beautiful gothic cathedrals in all of Europe. Yes, we would visit her the following day.

After a long shower, I stepped out of the tub. It was at that moment it truly hit me: I had nothing clean to put on. My husband, being the accommodating sort (and it was easy for him, as he had all his suitcases), offered me a pair of his briefs. I hesitated, but finally succumbed. I had no choice. (And, ladies, I must admit I found his underwear quite comfortable.) I strutted about in front of him, modeling his black cotton *unders* as they caressed my bum.

Win, ever the one to take command, said, with a flick of his hand and a swagger to his step, "When in Milano, buy Italian!"

It sounded good to me, so even though I hated to pull my sweat-soaked slacks and sweater back on, I was confident that at least I was wearing clean underwear. (My mother would have been proud.) We headed out.

SELECTED TITLES FROM SHE WRITES PRESS

She Writes Press is an independent publishing company
founded to serve women writers everywhere.
Visit us at www.shewritespress.com.

Searching for Family and Traditions at the French Table, Book One by
Carole Bumpus. $16.95, 978-1-63152-896-5. Part culinary memoir
and part travelogue, this compilation of intimate interviews,
conversations, stories, and traditional family recipes (*cuisine pauvre*)
in the kitchens of French families, gathered by Carole Bumpus as
she traveled throughout France's countryside, is about people
savoring the life they have been given.

Recipes for Redemption: A Companion Cookbook to A Cup of Redemption
by Carole Bumpus. $19.95, 978-1-63152-824-8. A uniquely
character-centered cookbook that offers delicious recipes—and
savory stories—straight from the pages of *A Cup of Redemption.*

*Away from the Kitchen: Untold Stories, Private Menus, Guarded Recipes,
and Insider Tips* by Dawn Blume Hawkes. $24.95,
978-1-938314-36-0. A food book for those who want it all: the
menus, the recipes, *and* the behind-the-scenes scoop on some of
America's favorite chefs.

*Seasons Among the Vines: Life Lessons from the California Wine Country
and Paris* by Paula Moulton. $16.95, 978-1-938314-16-2. New
advice on wine making, tasting, and food pairing—along with a
spirited account of the author's experiences in Le Cordon Bleu's
pilot wine program—make this second edition even better than the
first.

Tasting Home: Coming of Age in the Kitchen by Judith Newton.
$16.95, 978-1-938314-03-2. An extraordinary journey through the
cuisines, cultures, and politics of the 1940s through 2011, complete
with recipes.